SCOTTISH QUEENS
1034–1714

SCOTTISH QUEENS 1034 1714

ROSALIND K. MARSHALL

BIRLINN

This edition published in 2019 by
Birlinn Ltd
West Newington House
10 Newington Road
Edinburgh EH9 1QS
www.birlinn.co.uk

First published in 2003 by Tuckwell Press

ISBN 13: 978 1 780275 97 0

British Library Cataloguing in Publication Data

A catalogue record for this book is available on request
from the British Library

Printed and bound by Clays Ltd, Elcograf S.p.A

for my friend Dana Bentley-Cranch

LIST OF CONTENTS

LIST OF ILLUSTRATIONS

Early Scottish Queens 1034–1305

Macbeth=Gruoch (c. 1005–after 1035)

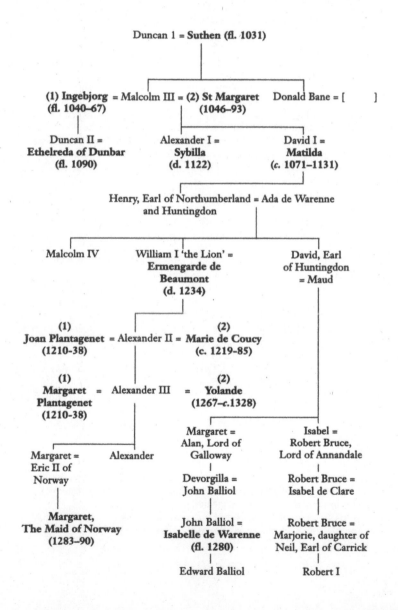

Duncan 1 = **Suthen (fl. 1031)**

(1) Ingebjorg = Malcolm III = **(2) St Margaret**   Donald Bane = [   ]
(fl. 1040–67)   **(1046–93)**

Duncan II =   Alexander I =   David I =
Ethelreda of Dunbar   **Sybilla**   **Matilda**
(fl. 1090)   **(d. 1122)**   **(c. 1071–1131)**

Henry, Earl of Northumberland = Ada de Warenne
and Huntingdon

Malcolm IV   William I 'the Lion' =   David, Earl
                    Ermengarde de   of Huntingdon
                    Beaumont   = Maud
                    (d. 1234)

(1)   **(2)**
Joan Plantagenet = Alexander II = **Marie de Coucy**
(1210–38)   **(c. 1219–85)**

(1)   **(2)**
Margaret = Alexander III = **Yolande**
Plantagenet   **(1267–c.1328)**
(1210–38)

                                    Margaret =   Isabel =
                                    Alan, Lord of   Robert Bruce,
Margaret =   Alexander   Galloway   Lord of Annandale
Eric II of | |
Norway   Devorgilla =   Robert Bruce =
  | John Balliol   Isabel de Clare
Margaret, | |
The Maid of Norway   John Balliol =   Robert Bruce =
(1283–90)   **Isabelle de Warenne**   Marjorie, daughter of
                                  (fl. 1280)   Neil, Earl of Carrick
                                    | |
                                  Edward Balliol   Robert I

Bruce and Stewart Queens 1306–1587

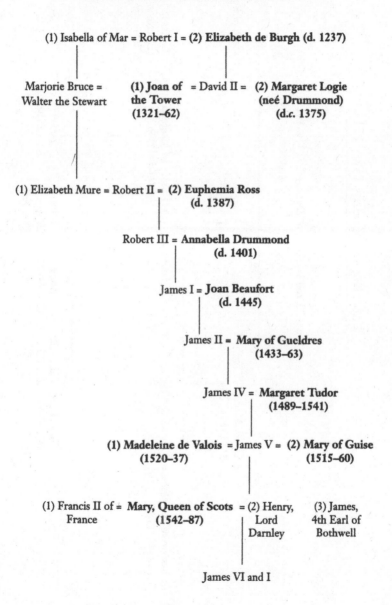

(1) Isabella of Mar = Robert I = (2) **Elizabeth de Burgh (d. 1237)**

Marjorie Bruce =
Walter the Stewart

(1) Joan of = David II = **(2) Margaret Logie**
the Tower   **(neé Drummond)**
(1321–62)   **(d.c. 1375)**

(1) Elizabeth Mure = Robert II = **(2) Euphemia Ross**
                          (d. 1387)

Robert III = **Annabella Drummond**
              (d. 1401)

James I = **Joan Beaufort**
          (d. 1445)

James II = **Mary of Gueldres**
            (1433–63)

James IV = **Margaret Tudor**
            (1489–1541)

(1) Madeleine de Valois = James V = **(2) Mary of Guise**
      (1520–37)   **(1515–60)**

(1) Francis II of = **Mary, Queen of Scots** = (2) Henry,   (3) James,
     France   **(1542–87)**   Lord   4th Earl of
                                     Darnley   Bothwell

James VI and I

Later Stewart Queens 1589–1714

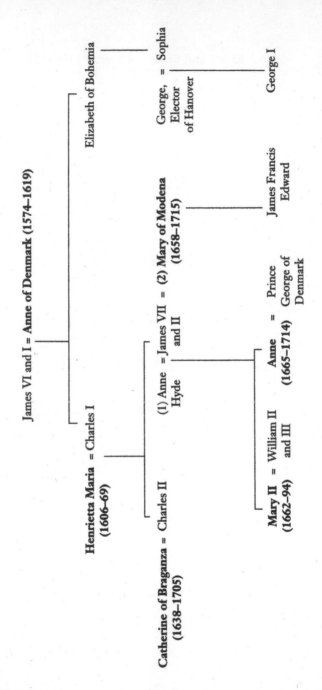

PREFACE

Leaving aside the wives of Duncan I and Lulach, neither of whom was necessarily alive when her husband reigned, there were thirty-one Scottish queens from the accession of Duncan I in 1034 until the death of Queen Anne in 1714. Four were queens in their own right, and the other twenty-seven were consorts. This is obviously a very small, extremely élite group and in theory its members should be much better documented than any other women of the past. In practice, however, they are almost equally elusive. Our knowledge of the wives of kings before the early sixteenth century is fragmentary, and even the later consorts are overshadowed in the records by their husbands. However, when the surviving details of their careers are gathered together, we have not only an entertaining procession of vivid personalities. We may also gain a better understanding of what queenship meant in Scotland.

When Tuckwell Press invited me to write this book, I had to decide how many queens to discuss. Coming up to the present day within the allotted number of words would have meant condensing the earlier chapters to the point where I lost much valuable information. I could have stopped when Anne of Denmark disappeared over the Border in 1603, but I had two reasons for continuing beyond that point. I thought it worth emphasising that exotic consorts such as Henrietta Maria and Catherine of Braganza were Queens of Scots, and I wanted to remind people of the frequently forgotten fact that both Mary of Modena and Queen Anne spent some months in Scotland, albeit before they became respectively Queen Consort and

Queen Regnant. I therefore decided that Anne, the last Stewart monarch, was the appropriate subject for my final chapter. Subsequent queens did not come north until Victoria developed her passionate love of the Highlands, after which queens consort and regnant alike had a relationship with Scotland which was in part formal, carrying out official engagements here as in the south, and in part personal, relaxing at Balmoral and enjoying some measure of private life.

Throughout the text I have modernised spelling, translating into English where necessary. After due consideration, I decided to use the names by which the various queens and others seem to be best known, hence the apparent inconsistency of 'Marie de Coucy' and 'Mary of Guise'. Anglicising 'Don Carlos' into 'Prince Charles', for instance, could have conjured up the wrong mental image in the reader's mind, and so he retains his Spanish title. Names of publications abbreviated in the notes are to be found in full in the Bibliography, which does not list those sources cited only once.

Finally, but most importantly, I am sincerely grateful to Professor Geoffrey Barrow for looking at my early chapters and to Dr Athol Murray for his comments on the entire text. I would also thank Dr Rosemary Mander, Dr Ruth MacQuillan and Susan Groag Bell. Finally, my thanks to the owners of the copyright of the illustrations. Their names will be found in the captions.

RKM
Edinburgh, 1 July 2002

CHAPTER ONE

LADY MACBETH TO ST MARGARET

The first Scottish queen whose name is known to us appears to be none other than Lady Macbeth, that byword for evil, ruthlessness and the worst excesses of ambition. There is one other possible candidate. In an early list of Scottish kings someone, probably the compiler, has inserted beside his mention of Malcolm III the words 'his mother was called Suthen'. Suthen would have been the wife of King Duncan I who ruled Scotland from 1034 until 1040. She is not named in any other source, but the fourteenth-century chronicler, John of Fordun, says that Duncan's wife was a relative, possibly a sister, of Siward, Earl of Northumbria. It is generally taken that Malcolm was born about 1031, so his mother was obviously alive then, but the problem is that we do not know whether she survived until her husband came to the throne in 1034. For the first named consort, we must therefore wait for Lady Macbeth.[1]

Lady Macbeth's reputation derives from Shakespeare's famous tragedy, called after her husband. This powerful drama recounts how Macbeth, urged on by his adoring wife, murders King Duncan I as he lies asleep in their castle and seizes the throne for himself. Shakespeare does not indicate Duncan's age, but the King is usually played as a frail old man to add poignancy to his plight. After Macbeth has dispatched their victim, Lady Macbeth smears the royal attendants with the dead man's blood so that they will be blamed for the crime. This done, she is overwhelmed by guilt and sleepwalks, endlessly trying to wash away the blood from her hands. Shortly afterwards she dies. The manner of her death is not specified, but the implication is that she has committed suicide. Macbeth is then killed by Duncan's vengeful son, Malcolm.

Such is the account given in the celebrated 'Scottish play'. No one, of course, would expect Shakespeare to give a strictly factual catalogue of events. His genius lay in creating powerful works of dramatic imagination, and directors and producers of his plays add their own interpretation. In reality Duncan, for instance, was not an aged and infirm man when he died. He was thirty-nine. He had ruled for six years when Macbeth rebelled against him and either killed him in a skirmish near Elgin or had him assassinated. There is nothing to suggest that Duncan was a guest in his house at the time. So did Shakespeare also alter Lady Macbeth beyond all recognition, transforming a perfectly innocuous woman into the villain of the piece?

If we look at the various sources used by Shakespeare, we will find that he was not the first to cast Lady Macbeth in the role of her husband's evil genius. The dramatist almost certainly knew Hector Boece's history of Scotland which had been published in Paris in 1526, and he was probably familiar with William Stewart's *The Buik of the Croniclis of Scotland*, a verse adaptation of Boece, apparently written in 1535. Shakespeare would also have read Raphael Holinshed's *History of Scotland to 1571*. Little is said about Lady Macbeth in Boece's text, but Stewart's adaptation claims that Macbeth's wife taunted her faint-hearted husband with cowardice in her efforts to persuade him to commit the murder. Holinshed echoes this theme, commenting that Lady Macbeth 'lay sore' upon Macbeth to get him to murder Duncan, for she was 'very ambitious, burning in unquenchable desire to bear the name of a queen'. Shakespeare's interpretation is rather different, of course. He does not portray Lady Macbeth as someone anxious for her own advancement. She is passionately in love with her husband, and her only desire is to see an increase in his prestige. All her thoughts are for him.[2]

Just as we should not look to Shakespeare's *Macbeth* for historical accuracy, neither can we accept his sources unquestioningly on the assumption that because they were written more than four centuries ago, they are probably correct in what they say. On the contrary, we have to remember that although they may seem to us to be hallowed by antiquity, the writings of Boece, Stewart and Holinshed were composed almost five hundred years after the events they describe. So when did Lady Macbeth first assume a sinister character? Where did Stewart come by his interpretation of her? Did she feature in oral tradition, perhaps, have the details of her own life been wrongly remembered, or has she been confused with someone else altogether? It is impossible to say, for the facts are few and far between.

We know neither the year nor the place of Lady Macbeth's birth, but it seems that she bore the Gaelic first name of Gruoch. It used to be said, with some confidence, that she was the granddaughter of King Kenneth II, who was murdered in 995, but more recent historians have identified her as the grandchild of Kenneth III, daughter of his son, Boite. She would have been born about 1005. At some point, presumably when she was in her early or mid teens, she was married to Gillecomgain, a nephew of Finlay, Mormaer of Moray. A mormaer was the high steward of one of the ancient Celtic provinces of Scotland. The word is Gaelic, like Gruoch's own name, and in Latin documents it is translated as 'comes', which means 'earl'. The mormaers of Moray had been far more than mere earls, however. They had ruled their rich territories independently, as sub-kings, and they still resented the efforts of the main royal line to treat them as subordinates. Gruoch had therefore married into a powerful, landowning, aristocratic family, a suitable choice for a woman who was herself of royal descent.

During the years when she was Gillecomgain's wife, Gruoch may have come to know his cousin Macbeth, son of Finlay, Mormaer of Moray. Relationships within the family were far from harmonious, however, for Gillecomgain had become involved in a bitter power struggle with his uncle, culminating in his murder of Finlay in 1020.[3] Gruoch's husband was now Mormaer of Moray himself and for the next twelve years he successfully saw off all his rivals. Gruoch and Gillecomgain had one son, Lulach, during those years. There may have been other sons who died, or indeed daughters who survived, but if so their names have not been recorded. Meanwhile, the family feud continued and, in 1032, Gillecomgain's house was set on fire by some of his enemies. Possibly Macbeth was involved, seeking revenge for his father's death. At any rate, Gillecomgain and his men perished in the blaze. Gruoch and her young son somehow escaped. Perhaps they were elsewhere at the time, or they may even have been taken prisoner by the perpetrators of the crime. Not long afterwards, Gruoch married again. Her new husband was Macbeth.

With the memory of Shakespeare's tragedy in mind, it is tempting to imagine a situation in which Gruoch had an affair with her husband's enemy, Macbeth, and urged him to murder Gillecomgain, but any such speculation is fanciful. It is more likely that Macbeth took Gruoch as his wife for practical reasons. By marrying her, he gained control of her young son's lands and prevented any of his own enemies from trying to replace him with Lulach. The marriage would, in theory at least, heal the feud between the two branches of Finlay's family. Moreover, Gruoch was desirable, not necessarily for any personal qualities such as appearance or character, but because she had already shown that she could bear sons. Even more importantly, she was of royal descent. There is still a good deal of argument about Macbeth's own ancestry. At one time it was believed that his mother was a daughter of Malcolm II. This has since been disputed, but there is a distinct possibility that he was the grandson of Kenneth II. Marriage to the granddaughter of Kenneth III would strengthen his claim to the throne, if he had one, or give him one if he did not.

We know nothing of Gruoch's feelings about the death of her first husband, a loss compounded by the murder the following year of one of her close male relatives, probably her only brother, by Malcolm II,[4] nor do we know what she thought about her own remarriage. Usually, widows had a freedom of choice not available to single women in the selection of a partner, but in such violent times they were often in too vulnerable a position to have any say in the matter. There is no evidence that Gruoch was coerced into the marriage, any more than there is any hint of her having fallen in love with Macbeth. What we can say is that Gruoch became Queen of Scots when Duncan was killed near Elgin and her husband seized the throne. There is no hint as to whether Lady Macbeth played any part in Duncan's death, but he was the grandson of Malcolm II, who had murdered her brother,[5] and so she had her own reason for resenting him.

Gruoch and Macbeth had no children. It may be that she was reaching the end of her childbearing years when she married him, and he seems to have accepted the fact that her son Lulach would succeed him. Macbeth's vigorous rule brought peace to the country, and in 1050 he even ventured to make a pilgrimage to Rome, where he visited the Pope and may well have sought absolution for his part in the murder of Duncan. When he returned, he certainly made a generous gift to a Culdee religious foundation on an island in Lochleven. Interestingly, Gruoch was associated with him in making this gift, and part of the property was called after her, 'Gruoch's Well' on Benarty Hill.[6] The lands given to the monks could have belonged to her, but it has been suggested that she, too, might have been doing penance for Duncan's death.[7]

Effective as Macbeth's rule appears to have been, even he could not prevent the endemic feuding from breaking out all over again and in 1054 the English king, Edward the Confessor, ordered the Norse Earl Siward to invade Scotland, with the aim of deposing Macbeth and replacing him with Duncan I's eldest son, Malcolm. Siward won a decisive victory at Dunsinnan Hill, near Scone, on 27 July 1054, and Macbeth fled to Moray, where he spent the next three years. On 15 August 1057, he was killed at Lumphanan, north of the River Dee. His body was taken to Iona, the traditional burying place of the early Scottish kings, and Gruoch's son Lulach claimed the throne. A young married man, he went to Scone to be inaugurated as king, but his reign was brief. Known to the Scots as 'Lulach the Simple', he was no match for the forceful Malcolm, and on 17 March 1058 he was ambushed and killed at Essie in Aberdeenshire.[8]

If Gruoch was still alive by then, this must have been the culminating tragedy of her life. Some historians take the view that the real Lady Macbeth was innocent of any dubious activities, no more than a victim of events, but others have inferred that she really was a powerful woman with a strong influence on those around her. Had she urged her second husband to murder her first, did she inspire Macbeth with the desire to displace Duncan, and was it she who insisted that diffident Lulach claim the throne when Macbeth was killed? We may never know the answer to these questions but, ruthless schemer or passive observer of events, Gruoch lost her brother, both husbands and her only son in violent circumstances and her real life was as dramatic as any of the tales invented about her.

The next Queen of Scots was Gruoch's daughter-in-law, the wife of Lulach. We do not know her name, her parentage or when she married. She and Lulach had a daughter whose name is also unknown. Her husband reigned for only a few months and with his death she vanishes from the pages of history. Her grandson Angus, Mormaer of Moray, was eventually killed at the battle of Stracathro in 1130 while trying to seize the throne. A month after ousting Lulach, Malcolm III was inaugurated at Scone. Although he was now in his late twenties, he was still single. When his father, Duncan I, was killed in 1040, he had been only about nine years old and he had found refuge with his mother's relative, Earl Siward of Northumbria, later receiving a friendly welcome at the English Court from Edward the Confessor. During his years of exile, he would not have attracted offers of a wife of high status. Once he was king, however, a consort became a necessity and he made an interesting choice.

One of Macbeth's greatest enemies had been Thorfinn the Mighty, Earl of Orkney who also owned Caithness, Sutherland and other significant lands in the north in the mid-eleventh century. As his name suggests, Thorfinn was Norse, but his mother was Donada, a daughter of Malcolm II, and he had been brought up at his grandfather's Court after his father's early death in battle. Ever since the Norse had first raided the Scottish mainland, the mormaers of Moray had struggled with them for domination in the north, but when Macbeth decided to oppose Duncan, he and Thorfinn became allies. Indeed, they may even have visited the Pope together in 1050, for although they travelled by different routes, they were in Rome at the same time.

Thorfinn's wife was the Norwegian Ingebjorg, daughter of Earl Finn Arnason, and they had two sons, Paul and Erlend. We do not know Ingebjorg's age, but she must have been a good deal younger than her husband, who was in his mid-fifties when he died in 1064 or 5. She was still young enough to have children, and Malcolm III now chose her as his wife. It has been suggested that the woman Malcolm married was Thorfinn's daughter, on the grounds that his widow would have been too old to be a bride. However, this theory fails to take account of the possibility that Ingebjorg could have been twenty years younger than her first husband, and it has been rejected on the grounds that the *Orkneyinga Saga*, which provides the evidence of Malcolm's first marriage, states specifically that

Ingebjorg was Thorfinn's widow and does not mention his having had a daughter of that name.[9]

It seems likely that Malcolm chose Ingebjorg with a view to extending his own territories southwards. Edward the Confessor was reaching the end of his life. Since he had no children, there was endless speculation about his successor. The three leading candidates for his throne were Harald, son of the Saxon Earl Godwin, William, Duke of Normandy, and King Harald of Norway. If Malcolm could ally himself with the successful claimant, then he could hope to be rewarded for his support with lands in the north of England. He seems to have calculated that the Norwegian King would be the successful contender. Ingebjorg came from an enormously powerful Norwegian family and she was the cousin of King Harald of Norway's wife, Thora, hence Malcolm's decision to marry her.[10]

We know very little about Ingebjorg. She would have spent much of her time as Thorfinn's wife at Birsay, in Orkney, where he had his main stronghold, but as Queen of Scots she would have moved to Dunfermline, Malcolm's preferred residence. He and she had two sons, Duncan and Donald, but by the late 1060s she had gone. It has often been said that Malcolm repudiated her a few years after their marriage, in order to marry Margaret, daughter of the English Edward the Exile. It was far from unusual for a monarch to put away his wife if she failed to produce a son. Indeed, Edward the Confessor had briefly sent away his wife, Edith, for that reason, while the contemporaries of the Emperor Henry II had expressed amazement that he did not repudiate his childless wife, Kunigunde.[11] There was, however, no such problem with Ingebjorg, for she had already satisfied this dynastic necessity.

Malcolm could have had his first marriage dissolved on the pretext of consanguinity, because as great-grandchildren of Malcolm II, he and Ingebjorg were second cousins, but there is no evidence of this. Nor is it likely that Malcolm put away Ingebjorg simply because he had fallen in love with Margaret. Royal marriages were rarely motivated by romantic inclination alone and it is scarcely credible that a mature and highly ambitious man in his forties would select his bride without taking practical considerations into account. It seems much more probable that by 1068-9 Ingebjorg was dead, possibly in childbirth,[12] and that calculation as well as personal attraction dictated Malcolm's second choice.

Margaret, Malcolm's new wife, was the great-granddaughter of King Ethelred II of England but she had been born in Hungary. This was because her father, aptly known as Edward the Exile, had been banished from England by Cnut, who made himself king in 1016. Edward grew up in Sweden, moved on to Kiev and finally settled in Hungary as the close friend of King Andrew I. He married Agatha, probably the daughter of Liudolf, Margrave of Westfriesland and first cousin once removed of the Emperor Henry III. They lived at Castle Reka in the village of Mecseknadard, at the foot of the Mecsek Mountains in South Hungary, about forty kilometres east of Pecs, and had three children, Margaret, Christina and Edgar. Hungary had been converted to Christianity a generation earlier by Stephen I, who was later canonised, and the Court was a notably pious one. Margaret and her sister were taught Latin, so that they could read devotional works, and much of their time was spent in prayer and religious studies. They both decided to become nuns when they grew up. Their peaceful way of life was, however, shattered in 1056 when their father received an urgent message from England. Edward the Confessor's health was very poor, his nephew Edward the Exile was his nearest heir, and he wanted him to return to his native land at once.[13]

Margaret was about ten years old when this unwelcome summons arrived, her young brother only two. Their father had spent almost forty years on the Continent. He was most reluctant to uproot his family, leave his comfortable lifestyle and return to his native land. The Confessor insisted and they set off, taking as much of their wealth with them as they could and a number of religious relics. However, within days of their arrival in London in 1057, Edward the Exile was dead, poisoned, some said, by Earl Godwin's jealous family.[14] Whatever had happened, the Confessor was full of sympathy for Agatha and the children, insisting that they stay on in England. Little Edgar was now his heir, and so Agatha resigned herself to remaining. Margaret and Christina began to learn French, the language the Confessor preferred to speak, took lessons in Court etiquette, deportment and needlework and, above all else, continued their devotional studies. When Edward the Confessor finally died in 1066, Margaret's brother did not however inherit the throne. He was brushed aside by Harald Godwinson, who made himself king, only to be killed on 14 October 1066 at the Battle of Hastings, by William, Duke of Normandy.

The new King William I seemed anxious to enlist Edgar's support, giving him extensive lands in Huntingdonshire, but the resentful teenager was not to be placated. He had been brought up to believe that he would be the Confessor's successor, and within two years he had involved himself in a rebellion against William. It was crushed and he was forced to flee. According to tradition, his mother and sisters went with him, came ashore near Dunfermline and were taken to Malcolm III, who promptly fell in love with Margaret. The actual sequence of events may have been slightly different. Edgar and the other rebels certainly fled to Scotland, but their stay was of short duration and they were soon back in England again. According to one chronicler, it was not until 1069 that Agatha decided to take her children back to Hungary, and was driven ashore at Wearmouth in the north-east of England by a sudden storm. When she learned that Malcolm III was raiding in the area, Agatha supposedly went to him and begged for shelter in Scotland.

Whatever the circumstances of Malcolm's first meeting with Margaret, he no doubt regarded Edgar as a useful pawn. His own support of the Norwegian king as a candidate for the English throne had come to nothing, but by taking up Edgar's cause he would have a pretext for further invasions of England. If he could marry Edgar's sister and then help him to seize the English crown, he would be in a favourable position indeed. Moreover Margaret, in her early twenties, was intelligent and personable.[15] When he broached the subject of marrying her, she rebuffed him, saying that she meant to become a nun, and Edgar and his advisers rejected his proposal. However, as refugees in his kingdom they could hardly ignore his wishes and he no doubt emphasised his intention of helping Edgar to gain the English throne. The following year, Margaret and he were married by Fothad, last Celtic bishop of St Andrews, in a small chapel beside Malcolm's palace in Dunfermline.[16]

Much of our knowledge of Margaret's life in Scotland comes from the biography written after her death by her confessor, Turgot, formerly Prior of Durham. He was, of course, intent on stressing her piety and what he saw as the civilising influence she had on her husband and his subjects. She also emerges from his pages as a clever, headstrong young woman while Malcolm is relegated to the supporting role of illiterate simpleton. The reality was rather different. We know from other sources that Malcolm was a ruthless and highly effective monarch. The marriage was a partnership of two equally strong-minded individuals, and Malcolm indulged his wife from a position of confident maturity, not weakness.

As long as we bear this in mind, Turgot's little stories throw a charming light on the King and Queen's domestic life. When Malcolm saw that Margaret had a favourite book, for instance, he would kiss it, then take it away to have its covers ornamented with gold and jewels as a surprise for her. When he presented gold coins as his offering at High Mass, she surreptitiously extracted some to give to the poor and he enjoyed teasing her afterwards, saying that he would have her arrested and tried for theft.[17] Malcolm allowed her to choose the names for their six sons and two daughters, not one of whom was called after himself or any of his relatives. Instead, the four eldest boys were given English royal names: Edward, Edgar, Edmund and Ethelred. The younger sons were called Alexander, after Alexander II, who was Pope at the time of Margaret's marriage, and David, probably for the younger son of King Andrew I of Hungary. The Hungarian Prince David might well have been Margaret's godfather. Her daughters were named Edith (later known as Matilda or Maud), probably after Edward the Confessor's wife, and Mary, for the Virgin.

The choice of royal English names for the older sons may not simply have been a compliment to Margaret's own family but a reflection of Malcolm's territorial ambitions.[18] He invaded England no fewer than five times during his reign, leading to retaliatory invasions of Scotland by William I and his sons. Meanwhile, Margaret engaged in an energetic round of charitable activities. She imposed a very ascetic way of life upon herself, constantly fasting and spending much time in prayer. Each day she fed nine orphans, taking them on her lap and giving them sups of specially prepared soft food with her own spoon. During Lent, she and Malcolm fed and washed the feet of six poor people, and at least once a year they entertained three hundred of his poorest subjects to a banquet in the royal hall at Dunfermline, serving the food with their own hands.

On the site of the little chapel where she had been married, Margaret built a large church dedicated to the Holy Trinity, endowing it with a valuable crown, solid gold plate and various other expensive gifts. She presented a costly crucifix to St Andrews Cathedral, for she took a special interest in Scotland's patron saint, and gained exemption from ferry tolls for the hundreds of pilgrims who crossed the Forth between what are now North and South Queensferry, on their way to St Andrews. She also built lodgings for them in that city.[19] These were conventional enough activities for a pious queen consort, but Margaret also entered more controversial areas. According to Turgot, she disapproved of the Celtic Church because of the irregularities of its practices. Lent was not observed properly and various allegedly barbarous rites had crept into the celebration of the Mass. Men were being allowed to marry their dead brothers' wives and even their own stepmothers.

Margaret apparently insisted on engaging in public debate with the leaders of the Celtic Church, haranguing them about current abuses while the King obligingly translated her words into the Gaelic which both he and the churchmen spoke. At the same time, she wrote to Lanfranc, Archbishop of Canterbury, asking him to send north from his cathedral of Christ Church, also dedicated to the Holy Trinity, some Benedictine monks. They would be able to demonstrate the correct religious practices. Three arrived, to found a priory at Dunfermline.

Margaret's attitude to the Celtic Church was not, however, as inflexible as Turgot would have us believe. She would never have allowed herself to be married by a Celtic cleric had she really disapproved. She recognised that there was no point in trying to force people to abandon their traditional allegiances and decided instead to encourage spirituality wherever she found it. Hermits had lived near her childhood home in Hungary, and she now made a point of visiting Celtic hermits. When they refused the gifts she pressed on them, because they had embraced a life of poverty, she asked them instead to give her some charitable task to perform. She associated herself with Malcolm in gifts of lands to the Culdees of Lochleven, and she restored the monastic community on Iona, originally established there by St Columba in the sixth century.[20]

Margaret's willingness to learn from her mistakes is nicely illustrated in a story that comes not from Turgot but from a life of St Laurence of Canterbury. Hearing that there was a small church in Fordun, in Angus, dedicated to this saint who had once preached there, she set out to visit it, bearing various gifts. When she arrived, the canons told her that no woman was allowed to enter the building. Undeterred, Margaret replied that she had come to do honour to this sacred place, and marched in. Immediately, she was seized with such dreadful pains throughout her entire body that she had to be helped outside. She blamed herself for ignoring the canons' warnings, and begged them to pray for her. When she had recovered, she presented them with a great silver cross, a beautiful chalice and various other gifts.[21]

Her insistence on fasting eventually took its toll on Margaret's health, and by the autumn of 1093 she was suffering from a serious stomach complaint. Malcolm was set on invading England once more and, leaving her at Edinburgh Castle, he marched south, only to be killed on 13 November besieging Alnwick Castle. Their two eldest sons, Edward and Edgar, were with him. Edward was fatally wounded and died three days later, leaving Edgar to carry the tragic news to their mother. He arrived in Edinburgh to find Margaret at the point of death and could not summon the words to tell her what had happened. Looking at him sadly, she said with a sigh, 'I know it, my boy. I know it. By the Holy Cross, by the bond of our blood, I adjure you to tell the truth'.

When she heard that her husband and her eldest son were dead, she praised God for sending her such sorrow, hoping that by this means she would be cleansed of her sins. Holding her Black Rood, a gold cross set with diamonds and bearing an ivory figure of Christ, she murmured, 'Lord Jesus Christ, who according to the will of the Father, through the Holy Ghost hast by Thy death given life to the world, deliver me . . .', and with those words she died.[22] When Malcolm's brother, Donald Bane, heard that he was dead he prepared to besiege the castle and seize the throne. However, Edgar managed to take his mother's body to Dunfermline, for burial before the high altar in the Church of the Holy Trinity. Twenty years later, Malcolm's body was brought north from Tynemouth Priory and placed beside her.

Turgot may have exaggerated Margaret's role in Scotland, but she had taken an active and very public part in ecclesiastical affairs and she was widely venerated for her devotion to religion. Stories of her holiness and tales of miracles associated with her were circulated throughout the eleventh and twelfth centuries, until in 1249 she was canonised by Pope Innocent IV. 'Once, mere men placed crowns on your head', said the official oration, 'but I, Innocent, Peter's successor, servant of Christ, now place upon your head the greatest crown of sainthood.' On 19 June 1250 her remains were ceremoniously transferred to a newly constructed magnificent gold shrine erected in the Lady Chapel of the Church of the Holy Trinity, Dunfermline. The story goes that when the men carried her coffin past Malcolm's tomb, it suddenly became so heavy that they were forced to put it down. Only when his body too was transferred to the Lady Chapel were they able to move her coffin to its appointed place.

Notes

1. Marjorie O. Anderson, *Kings and Kingship in Early Scotland* (Edinburgh 1980), 63, 284.
2. Arthur Melville Clark, *Murder Under Trust, or the Topical Macbeth and other Jacobean Matters* (Edinburgh 1981), 14–18; James Fergusson, *The Man behind Macbeth* (London 1969), 26–32, 80–1.
3. Duncan, *Making of the Kingdom*, 99.
4. Thomas Owen Clancy and Barbara Crawford, 'The Formation of the Scottish Kingdom', in *New Penguin History*, 78.
5. *New Penguin History*, 78–9; Donaldson, *Shaping of a Nation*, 61.
6. *Liber Cartorum Prioratus S. Andree in Scotia* (Bannatyne Club 1841), 114; I am grateful to Professor Geoffrey Barrow for this reference.
7. *New Penguin History*, 81; Duncan, *Making of the Kingdom*, 99.
8. R.L. Mackie, *A Short History of Scotland*, ed. Gordon Donaldson (Edinburgh and London 1962), 23–4; Lynch, *New History*, 49–50; Donaldson and Morpeth, *Who's Who*, 1–2; David Williamson, *Brewer's British Royalty* (London 1996), 248; *Oxford Companion*, 402.
9. *New Penguin History* 84; *cf.* Donaldson and Morpeth, *Who's Who*, 3.
10. *New Penguin History*, 84–5; Donaldson and Morpeth, *Who's Who*, 2–3.

11. John Carmi Parsons, 'Family, Sex and Power: The Rhythms of Medieval Queenship', in *Medieval Queenship*, 4–5.
12. Wilson, *St Margaret*, 58–9; Donaldson and Morpeth, *Who's Who*, 2–3; *SP*, i, 2; Duncan, *Making of the Kingdom*, 118.
13. Wilson, *St Margaret*, 7–43; Gabriel Ronay, *The Lost King of England: The East European Adventures of Edward the Exile* (Woodbridge 1989), 1–115, 136–43.
14. *Anglo-Saxon Chronicle* ed. D. Whitelock, D.C. Douglas and S.I.Tucker (London 1961), 133.
15. Wilson, *St Margaret*, 43–55.
16. Wilson, *St Margaret*, 46–69; Duncan, *Making of the Kingdom*, 117–20.
17. *Life of St Margaret, Queen of Scotland by Turgot, Bishop of St Andrews*, in *Early Sources*, ii, 59–60.
18. *SP*, i, 2; Duncan, *Making of the Kingdom*, 124.
19. Wilson, *St Margaret*, 49–69; Duncan, *Making of the Kingdom*, 117–20.
20. *Early Sources*, ii, 77–82.
21. Derek Baker, '"A Nursery of Saints": St Margaret of Scotland Reconsidered', in *Medieval Women*, 136; Alan Macquarrie, *The Saints of Scotland* (Edinburgh 1997), 211–23; Denis McKay, 'The four heid pilgrimages of Scotland', in *The Innes Review*, xix, 1 (1968), 76; Wilson, *St Margaret*, 70–94; *Treasurer's Accounts*, i, p.cccii.
22. *Early Sources*, ii, 84–6; Wilson, *St Margaret*, 95–100; W. Moir Bryce, *St Margaret of Scotland and her chapel in the Castle of Edinburgh* (Edinburgh 1914).

CHAPTER TWO

SHADOWY FIGURES AND
FOREIGN BRIDES

B ecause St Margaret was an outstanding personality, stories of her life have been remembered. Her immediate successors as queens consort of Scotland no doubt made their mark, but few details of their achievements have come down to us, and what we do know of them is very much in the context of their husbands' activities. Malcolm III was succeeded by his brother Donald III, better known as Donald Bane (the Fair), who was sixty when he seized the throne. He had a daughter, Bethoc, but we know nothing of his wife, not even her name.[1] Donald was briefly dislodged by his nephew Duncan II, who had married Ethelreda of Dunbar, but Duncan was killed in 1094 and Donald Bane resumed the throne. In 1097 he was deposed again, this time by another of his nephews, Edgar son of Malcolm and Margaret. Edgar never married, and was succeeded in turn by his younger brothers Alexander I and David I. They had fled to England after their parents' death, their sister Edith married Henry I of England, and it was he who found wives for them.[2]

Henry offered Alexander one of his own illegitimate children. The English king had at least twenty of them, five by his favourite mistress, Sybilla Corbet. It was her daughter Sybilla whom Henry suggested for Alexander. There was no dishonour in this. As was the custom, Henry officially acknowledged his children born out of wedlock, and the bridegrooms he selected for his daughters were gratified to be given such close relatives of the King. Alexander accepted Sybilla, took her back to Scotland with him and seems to have loved her. They had no children, or at least none who survived, but when Queen Sybilla died on an island on Loch Tay on 12 July 1122, her husband is said to have mourned her deeply and he founded a church there in her memory.[3]

Two years after that, Alexander was succeeded by his brother

David. Henry I had provided him with a wealthy English widow, Matilda, sometimes known as Maud. She had been married to Simon of Senlis, with whom she had had three sons, but her real significance lay in the fact that she was the eldest daughter and senior heiress of Waltheof, Earl of Huntingdon, and his wife Judith, a niece of William the Conqueror. Better still, Matilda's grandfather had been Siward, Earl of Northumbria. She inherited from him, through her father, the Honour of Huntingdon, which consisted chiefly of extensive properties in the East Midlands, as well as a claim to the earldom of Northumbria. Its lands lay between the Rivers Tees and Tweed, but did not include the bishopric of Durham. David's marriage to Matilda had significant repercussions. Successive Scottish monarchs would become involved in a struggle to acquire all the territories owned by Earl Waltheof and, even more importantly, they would in future owe allegiance to the English king for their southern possessions.[4]

We have no hint of the personal relationship between Matilda and her second husband, who must have been appreciably younger than herself. David I was famously pious and in the secular sphere he was responsible for extending feudal tenure in Scotland, granting land to Anglo-Normans and appointing them as royal officials. We can only speculate that Matilda may have encouraged him in these policies. He and she had two daughters, Claricia and Hodierna, who never married, and a son, Henry, Earl of Northumberland and Huntingdon, who was himself to become the father of two Scottish kings. According to the chronicler Fordun, Matilda died in 1130–1 and was buried at Scone.[5]

When David died in 1153 at the age of about seventy-three he was succeeded by his grandson, Malcolm IV. Known to later medieval writers as 'the Maiden', Malcolm had taken a vow of chastity and died unmarried in 1165 at the age of twenty-three. His younger brother William I then became king. William the Lion, as he is usually known,[6] invaded the north of England in 1174 and was captured at Alnwick. He was released only after he had sworn fealty to Henry II, not merely for his English lands but for his kingdom of Scotland. The terms of the Treaty of Falaise,[7] by which he was released, not only had grave implications for Scotland's independence, but they complicated William's personal life. He would now need the permission of his feudal lord, the English King, before he could marry.

According to Walter Bower, William had earlier married a daughter of Adam de Whitsome, but the chronicler was mistaken. Adam's daughter was one of the King's mistresses, and their child, Margaret, was illegitimate.[8] William had at least three other illegitimate daughters, Isabel, Ada and Aufrica, as well as various illegitimate sons.[9] To the surprise and dismay of his contemporaries, he remained a bachelor for the first twenty years of his reign,[10] and not until 1184 did he decide that Henry's granddaughter Matilda, the daughter of the powerful Henry, Duke of Saxony, would be a suitable wife. He set off for England to ask Henry II to give his consent, but Henry did not wish to see William married into such an influential family and seems to have indicated that he would provide a substitute.[11] Two years later, he announced that he had identified an appropriate Frenchwoman, Ermengarde, daughter of Richard, Viscount of Beaumont sur Sarthe in Maine.

William and his advisers received the news with less than enthusiasm. Ermengarde was not nearly important enough. Although she was the great-granddaughter of Constance de Beaumont, one of the many illegitimate daughters of Henry I, the connection with royalty was tenuous. Ermengarde might be aristocratic, but her father's status was negligible compared with that of the King of Scots.[12] Perfectly well aware of the problem, Henry set out to make the prospect of marriage with Ermengarde more alluring. He would provide part of her dowry, he said, giving back to William Edinburgh Castle, which had been under his control ever since the Treaty of Falaise. He would also supply land to the value of a hundred merks and forty knights' fees, not to mention paying for a suitably lavish wedding.

The offer of Edinburgh Castle was probably the deciding factor for William, along with the knowledge that it was high time he married and produced heirs. He therefore accepted Ermengarde and made provision for her future, settling on her lands including Crail and Kinghorn in Fife. Ermengarde must have been much younger than her bridegroom, whom she may never have seen before, but her parents brought her to England and she and William were married a few days later, on 5 September 1186, in the royal chapel at Woodstock, near Oxford. Baldwin, Archbishop of Canterbury,

[17]

celebrated the nuptial Mass.[13] A year after her marriage, Queen Ermengarde had a daughter who was named Margaret, after her husband's illustrious ancestor. She then had two more daughters, Isabella and Marjory, but there was no sign of the required son.

After Henry II's death in 1189, William managed to have the Treaty of Falaise cancelled by Richard I in return for the payment of the considerable sum of 10,000 merks. William was aware, however, that England's territorial ambitions with regard to Scotland were not so easily ended, and when he fell seriously ill in the summer of 1195, he was tormented by anxiety about the succession. Perhaps his eldest daughter could marry the Duke of Saxony's son Otto, and they could rule Scotland together. His lords were indignant when he told them about his plan. Why should they be ruled by a woman, they demanded, when William had a perfectly good brother, David, and a nephew, Henry, both of whom were much better fitted for the supreme responsibility? The problem was solved on 24 August 1198 when Ermengarde gave birth to a son, Alexander.[14]

According to his recent biographer, William was 'a good family man' in spite of all his earlier liaisons,[15] and there are indications that he relied on Queen Ermengarde and allowed her to play an increasingly influential part in public affairs. A resentful Glasgow canon was to allege that in 1207 Walter, a royal chaplain, obtained the position of bishop of Glasgow after bribing not only the King's chamberlain but the Queen herself.[16] There are signs that her relatives also profited from their relationship with her: Richard de Beaumont, possibly a brother or nephew, acquired a sizeable estate in the Crail area.[17] Ermengarde appears to have acted as mediator when William was negotiating with King John of England in 1209,[18] and she certainly did so with great aplomb when her husband met John at Durham in February 1212. According to Bower, she showed herself in their discussions to be 'an extraordinary woman, gifted with a charming and witty eloquence'. As a result of her efforts, the peace between the two countries was renewed, and it was agreed that her son Prince Alexander should be given an English wife.[19]

That same summer, William fell ill, and there are signs that Ermengarde exercised considerable influence during his sickness.[20] The King was nearly seventy by now, and although he recovered, his health remained poor. He was well enough to travel as far north as Elgin in the summer of 1214, but the lengthy journey brought on some sort of collapse and he was taken south again to Stirling by very easy stages. Ermengarde was probably with him when he saw his lords for the last time and urged them to accept his sixteen-year-old son Alexander as king. He died in Stirling Castle at the beginning of December 1214.[21]

Next morning, the prelates and nobles urged the Queen to supervise the arrangements for the funeral, but she was 'in a state of extreme mourning and worn out with grief'. Try as they might, they could not rouse her from her sorrow and so they hastily took Prince Alexander to be crowned at Scone while Ermengarde remained with her husband's body. William was then buried in his abbey of Arbroath.[22] Ermengarde lived for another twenty years, devoting her considerable energies to raising money to found a Cistercian abbey at Balmerino in Fife. She purchased the necessary land for a thousand merks and oversaw the construction of the building, which was made of local red stone. Monks from Melrose settled at the abbey on St Lucy's Day, 13 December 1229 and both Ermengarde and her son Alexander frequently stayed there. When Ermengarde died on 11 February 1233, she was buried before the high altar at Balmerino. It is a pity that the records do not tell us more about this effective and influential Queen Consort.[23]

From Alexander's earliest years, his father had been determined to marry him to King John of England's daughter, Joan. The Prince had been knighted by John on 4 March 1212, during a visit to London, and he always insisted afterwards that John had on that occasion promised him that he could have Joan, with Northumberland as her dowry. It seems most unlikely that John would ever have considered parting with Northumberland but, once he had inherited the throne of Scotland, Alexander persisted with the scheme. John himself died in 1216, Alexander continued his negotiations, and on 15 June 1220 the English finally agreed to the match. Joan's mother had remarried and ten-year-old Joan was currently living in the custody of her stepfather, Hugh de Lusignan, in Gascony. On 18 June 1221, Alexander formally settled on his bride lands worth £1000, including Jedburgh, Hassendean, Kinghorn and Crail. Kinghorn and Crail were part of Queen Ermengarde's jointure lands, and so if she was unwilling to part with them, Joan would be given properties in Ayrshire and Lanarkshire instead, until Crail and Kinghorn became available. The wedding took place the following day.[24]

Joan and Alexander were married for over sixteen years, but they had no children. When Alexander travelled to York in September 1237 to discuss with Henry III the vexed question of the northern counties of England, Joan went too. The kings sealed a treaty on 25 September, with Alexander giving up his claims to the disputed territories. He then returned home, but Joan and her sister-in-law, Eleanor of Provence, decided to make a pilgrimage to Canterbury together. Joan fell ill on the way, and died near London on 4 March 1238, in the arms of her brothers King Henry and Richard, Earl of Cornwall. She was twenty-seven. She was buried in the recently founded Cistercian nunnery at Tarrant Crawford, immediately south of Tarrant Keynston in Dorset, and Henry ordered an effigy of her to be carved for her tomb.[25] Historians sometimes infer that Joan had not simply been going on a pilgrimage, but had separated from her husband. It could be that in exchange for giving up his claims to the north of England, Alexander gained Henry III's agreement that he should part from his childless wife, but there is no written evidence to confirm this theory.

Free now to find a partner who could give him sons, Alexander married again the following year. This time he did not seek the approval of his former brother-in-law, and indeed his choice suggests that he was deliberately setting out to irritate Henry III, for Marie de Coucy was the second daughter of Enguerrand, 3rd Baron de Coucy, one of Henry's enemies. She was also a great-great-granddaughter of Louis VI of France, wealthy and of considerable status. She arrived in Scotland with an impressive train of French followers, and her wedding took place at Roxburgh on Whit Sunday 1239.[26] Alexander was now forty-one, Marie about twenty. Two years after that, on 4 September 1241, she gave birth to a son, Alexander, and she is also believed to have had a short-lived daughter named Ermengarde, after her mother-in-law.[27] Alexander met Henry III again at Newcastle in 1244. He was in a conciliatory mood once more, ready to renew the peace between the two countries, and it is likely that it was also agreed at this point that his little son Prince Alexander should marry Henry's daughter Margaret.[28]

Four years after that, Alexander fell ill and was forced to obtain from the Pope a dispensation allowing him not to eat fish during Lent, for it always made him unwell. He was allowed to have eggs and cheese instead, but his health did not improve and he collapsed and died on the island of Kerrera on 8 July 1249, while leading an expedition against the Lord of Argyll.[29] The Queen and her seven-year-old son were probably together at one of the royal residences when news of the king's death reached them, and Marie made sure that the Prince was immediately taken to Scone for his inauguration as Alexander III. The following year they were both in Dunfermline on 19 June for the celebrations marking the canonisation of St Margaret and the translation of her body to the new shrine.[30]

That autumn, Marie visited France, and for the rest of her life she divided her time between the two countries. She had inherited property from her father, and Alexander's provisions for her had been unusually generous, with the result that she was a very wealthy woman. It was noticed that when she attended her son's wedding in York in 1252, she 'proceeded exceedingly loftily, with a magnificent and numerous retinue' and was accompanied by 'many nobles . . . not of Scotland only but also of France'.[31] Still young, Queen Marie was obviously a highly eligible widow, and during one of her regular visits to France in 1256–7 she married Jean de Brienne, a widower who bore the empty but impressive title of King of Acre, his father having been a famous crusader. Jean had been brought up at the French Court with Louis IX and his brothers and he had been made Grand Butler of France.[32]

Henry III was extremely annoyed when he heard about the marriage, for he certainly did not wish to see an increase of French influence in Scotland. When Marie and Jean asked for a safe-conduct to travel through England on their way north, he insisted that as soon as they arrived in Dover they must swear not to harm him or his kingdom.[33] The situation in Scotland was unstable, with powerful nobles competing for control of the young king, but Marie and her husband became members of the ruling council and she received a re-grant of all her jointure lands so that her Scottish revenues were secure. The following year, Alexander was old enough to rule for himself.

According to some sources, Queen Marie had a daughter, Blanche, by her second husband. In the autumn of 1276 she went to Coucy by way of Canterbury, so that she could visit Thomas Becket's shrine just as her predecessor, Queen Joan, had hoped to do all those years before. Marie was in her sixties when she died in the summer of 1285 but her body was not taken back to France. Instead, she was buried at Newbattle, where her tomb had already been prepared, presumably on her own instructions.[34] Because of the lack of evidence, it is difficult to estimate the influence of Marie de Coucy in Scotland, but she appears to have enjoyed considerable prestige, in part because of her own personality and her important French connections, but also because she had given her husband his much needed son and heir.

Very different was the situation of her daughter-in-law Princess Margaret of England, one of those small girls plucked from familiar surroundings to become a child bride in a foreign land. The eldest daughter of Henry III and his wife Eleanor of Provence, Margaret was born on 1 or 2 October 1240. She made her first recorded public appearance at the age of three, when she and her brother, the future Edward I, were presented by the citizens of London with expensive scarlet robes and hoods trimmed with ermine.[35] A year later came her betrothal to Prince Alexander.[36] At four she was far too young to be married and she remained with her parents.

Unlike many royal families, Henry III, his wife and their children seem to have enjoyed a close and affectionate relationship. When Margaret was eleven, Henry began to make careful arrangements for her wedding. The ceremony would take place at Christmas 1251 in York, and Henry gave a great deal of attention to the clothing and jewellery he and his family would wear, as well as to the wine and the catering arrangements.[37] Alexander, a few months older than his bride, arrived in York with his mother on Christmas Eve and was knighted by his future father-in-law on Christmas Day.[38] The wedding took place in York Minster on 26 December,[39] and the following day Henry bound himself to pay Alexander 5000 silver merks as Margaret's dowry.[40]

The royal party stayed at York Castle until the end of January, when the young couple set out for Scotland. Margaret's anxious father had taken the precaution of appointing special representatives, led by Robert de Noreis and Stephen Bauzan, to travel with her and safeguard her interests. Margaret also took her own household of green-clad attendants, with Mathilda de Cantiloupe, widow of a steward of Henry's household, as her chief lady. Travelling by Berwick-upon-Tweed to Roxburgh, they were in Linlithgow in April 1252 before moving to Edinburgh Castle, which would be their principal residence. De Noreis and Bauzan were soon recalled to the English Court, and Henry replaced them with John Balliol and Robert de Ros, whose mother had been an illegitimate daughter of William the Lion.

Margaret hated Edinburgh Castle. She hated the grim building perched on its rock, she hated the weather, she hated being away from her own family and she hated the fact that she was, for the most part, separated from Alexander. She was very fond of her young husband, but Ros apparently had strict instructions that the King and Queen were not to sleep together because of their tender age. Although child marriages were a normal occurrence, people believed that cohabiting too early would destroy the health of both bride and groom, and so it was customary for a very young couple to live in the same household like brother and sister until they were mature enough to have sexual relations. Margaret poured out her misery in anguished letters home and her parents were naturally upset. They urged the Scots to allow her to come and visit her mother, but the request was refused. The Scottish lords presumably felt that if she were allowed to vanish south, they might never see her again.

In 1255, Queen Eleanor sent Reginald of Bath, one of her physicians, to her daughter. He found Margaret pale, depressed and complaining of neglect and loneliness, and he had a series of bitter arguments with Ros and Balliol, whom he blamed for her plight. He sympathised deeply with the young Queen, all the more so as his own health gave way in the Scottish climate. Terminally ill, he retreated south again, just managing on his deathbed to put in writing his allegations that Margaret was being 'unfaithfully and inhumanly treated by those unworthy Scots'.[41] When he read the report, Henry III was furious and lost no time in sending a new set of representatives to find out what was really going on. He also wrote angrily to the Earls of Dunbar, Strathearn and Carrick, demanding that they redress the situation, and then he marched to Newcastle with an army. From there he sent special envoys to Edinburgh Castle.[42]

As soon as they arrived, Margaret told them that she was a virtual prisoner, not allowed to go about her realm or choose her own attendants. Worse still, she and Alexander were kept apart and 'forbidden the comfort of mutual embraces'. They were fourteen now, and the English envoys decided that they were old enough to live together properly. Ros was blamed for all the difficulties, removed from his position and Margaret and Alexander were brought to Henry at Wark, where he saw them on 7 September 1255. Alexander went back to Scotland that same day, but Margaret was allowed some time with her family. Her mother and her young sister Beatrix had come north too, and they stayed together at Morpeth while Henry told the Scots that a council of fifteen should govern Scotland for the next seven years. After that, Alexander would be old enough to rule for himself. At the same time, a declaration was issued on the young King's behalf, promising to treat Margaret 'with matrimonial affection and every consideration befitting our Queen and the daughter of so great a prince'. She was to be allowed to make regular visits south. Happy with that assurance, she rejoined her husband.[43]

In the summer of 1257, she received a visit from her brother Edward. That same October, there was an alarming episode when Margaret and Alexander were seized by members of the powerful Comyn family while visiting Lochleven. Margaret was held separately and closely watched in case she showed any signs of returning to England. The Comyns reproached her for having sent for her father in 1255 and wanted all foreigners removed from Scotland. Henry III quickly intervened, the council of regency that included Marie de Coucy was set up and the power of the Comyns ebbed away after the death of their leader, Walter, Earl of Menteith.[44]

In November 1260, Margaret and Alexander visited her parents. By that time, she was nineteen, had been married for almost nine years and was five months pregnant. This fact was not disclosed to the Scots in case they objected to her leaving now that she was carrying a possible heir to their throne. Before she and Alexander set out, Henry III had to swear that if she gave birth in England, he would not try to keep either her or the child. He persuaded Alexander to allow her to stay in the south for the birth, promising to let her go home forty days after her delivery or by Easter at the very latest. If she died in childbirth, he would send her baby to Scotland, and if Alexander himself were dead by then, a specified group of bishops and noblemen would take the infant north.

Every eventuality covered, Alexander went home and on 28 February 1261 Margaret gave birth to a daughter, Margaret, at Windsor Castle. The christening took place on Easter Sunday, 24 April 1261 and mother and baby set off for Scotland in late May.[45] Three years after that, on 21 January 1264, Queen Margaret gave birth at Jedburgh to a son, Alexander. No doubt delighted at having an heir, the King kept his promise to allow her regular visits to her parents, and in October 1269 he and she were in Westminster Abbey to see her father and brothers moving the relics of Edward the Confessor to a splendid new shrine. Her father died in November 1272, but she was unable to travel south to console her mother because she was pregnant again. Her second son, David, was born on 20 March 1273. Nine years had elapsed since the birth of her first boy, and during that interlude, when she was still in her twenties, she must almost certainly have suffered miscarriages or stillbirths.[46]

David was a delicate child, and Margaret was slow to recover from his birth. According to the Chronicle of Lanercost, she went to Kinclaven Castle, near Perth, that summer to recuperate, and the chronicler tells a curious tale about an incident that took place there. One evening after supper, the Queen and some of her retinue strolled by the banks of the River Tay. They were in high spirits, and when they noticed a young English squire bend down to wash his hands in the water, the Queen laughingly urged one of her ladies to give him a push. Everyone laughed and applauded when he toppled over into the water. He splashed about frantically and shouted to them but they assumed he was simply joining in the fun, not realising that he was being dragged under by a strong current. Only his little servant boy saw that he was in difficulties and jumped in to help, but they were both swept away and drowned.

Claiming that he had had the story from the Queen's confessor, the chronicler alleged she was so upset that everyone realised that she had been secretly in love with the young man. It is impossible to tell if this was true. The Lanercost chronicler was a notorious misogynist and he may well have put his own sour interpretation on a tragedy that began as innocent fun. His anecdote does, however, give us a sudden vivid glimpse of Margaret's adult life.[47] There is no other hint that she may have been unhappy in her marriage, and on 19 August 1274 she and Alexander went south again together to attend the coronation of her brother Edward I in Westminster Abbey. She had always been close to him, and it was an occasion for great rejoicing.

Eighteen months later, in February 1275, Margaret fell seriously ill during a visit to Fife. There were rumours that she had been poisoned. Many churchmen came to visit her, but she would see only her husband and her confessor. She died on 26 February in Cupar Castle, and Alexander buried her beside David I in Dunfermline Abbey. She was thirty-four and had been Queen of Scots for more than twenty-three years.[48] After her death, Alexander showed no sign of wanting to marry again. He was only thirty-four but he had two sons and a daughter, and so there was no dynastic pressure. In the early 1280s, that all changed. His younger son David, who had always been delicate, died at Lindores in June 1281,[49] and less than two years later both his other children were dead, Alexander after a lengthy illness, Margaret, who had married King Eric II of Norway, in childbirth. Her infant daughter, Margaret, the Maid of Norway, was now Alexander III's only immediate heir.[50]

In February 1284, Alexander persuaded the Scottish magnates to recognise the Maid as his successor, but he needed to marry again and have more sons. His mother, Marie de Coucy, found him his second bride. Eighteen-year-old Yolande, Countess of Montfort, was a member of a prominent French family and a descendant of King Louis VI. She must have been well known to Marie, for she was the stepdaughter of the Queen's second husband, Jean de Brienne. Alexander III sent ambassadors to France in the spring of 1285 to negotiate the match. Edward I raised no objection, for Yolande's father, Robert IV, Count de Dreux, was one of his vassals. Queen Marie died that summer, but the marriage plans went ahead and on 19 August 1285 Edward I issued a safe conduct for Yolande and her brother Jean to travel north through England.

The wedding took place at Jedburgh on 14 October 1285.[51] The following spring, the royal couple spent some time at Kinghorn in Fife. On Monday, 18 March 1286, Alexander crossed to Edinburgh to attend a meeting with his lords of council. The weather was very stormy and over dinner the King joked that perhaps his subjects had been right in predicting that this would be the Day of Judgment. He intended to ride back to Yolande that evening, for the next day was her birthday and he had promised to be there. His lords urged him to wait until morning rather than cross the Forth in such bad weather, but he brushed aside their advice.

He sailed safely over to Fife, but as he rode from Inverkeithing with only three esquires for company and two local men to guide him, he somehow became separated from them. His horse, so the story goes, stumbled on the edge of a cliff, hurling him to his death on the beach below. His body was found the next morning, his neck broken. Alexander was buried in Dunfermline on 29 March, Yolande moved to Stirling Castle, and a meeting was called to discuss the succession crisis.[52] Yolande might be pregnant, but even if she was, there was no knowing whether she would carry the baby to full term or give birth to the desired son. The nobles and churchmen who met at Scone on about 28 April therefore swore fealty to Princess Margaret of Norway, taking a solemn oath to guard and preserve Scotland for her, but acknowledging that if Yolande did have a son, then the throne would go to him. During the royal minority the country would be governed by six guardians acting with a council. It was also agreed that three envoys would be sent to Edward I to ask his advice about the situation.[53]

The truth about Yolande's pregnancy remains unclear. According to the Lanercost chronicler, there were rumours that the Queen pretended to be expecting a child, with the intention of passing off some other woman's son as her own in order to maintain her position in Scotland. The chronicler alleged that, when her deception was uncovered, Yolande was sent back to France in disgrace. However, since in 1288 the royal exchequer was still paying her the revenues from her jointure lands, this seems unlikely. Historians are now more inclined to believe that she suffered a miscarriage or gave birth that autumn to a son, who was either stillborn or died shortly afterwards.

According to tradition, the baby was buried at Cambuskenneth.

When she had recovered, Yolande returned to France. Eight years passed, and in May 1294 she married a wealthy and important French nobleman, Arthur II, Duke of Brittany. His mother, Princess Beatrix of England, had been the sister of Alexander III's first wife. Yolande had six children with Arthur. She outlived him, and was still alive in the late 1320s, her brief time as Queen of Scots presumably by then a distant memory.[54]

Notes

1. *SP*, i, 3.
2. Duncan, *Making of the Kingdom*, 124–6.
3. Given-Wilson and Curteis, *Royal Bastards*, 62–4, 71–2; *SP*, i, 3.
4. Duncan, *Making of the Kingdom*, 134; *SP*, i, 3–4.
5. *Fordun's Chronicle*, i, 233; G.W.S. Barrow, *Charters of King David I* (London 1999), nos. 46, 47.
6. *SP*, i, 5.
7. Donaldson, *Scottish Historical Documents*, 27–8; Owen, *William the Lion*, 1–56.
8. *Scotichronicon*, iv, 369.
9. Owen, *William the Lion*, 67.
10. Anderson, *Scottish Annals*, 244.
11. *Ibid.*, 68–9; Duncan, *Making of the Kingdom*, 231.
12. Given-Wilson and Curteis, *Royal Bastards*, 63; Owen, *William the Lion*, 71.
13. Anderson, *Early Sources*, ii, 210, 211; Wyntoun, *Chronicle*, v, 31; *Scotichronicon*, iv, 318–19; Duncan, *Making of the Kingdom*, 231–2; Campbell, *Alexander III*, 45, n.17.
14. *Scotichronicon*, iv, 419; *SP*, i, 5; Owen, *William the Lion*, 85–7.
15. Owen, *William the Lion*, 112.
16. Anderson, *Early Sources*, ii, 489.
17. Charter of Richard de Beaumont in National Library of Scotland, MS 8487: *CDS*, ii, 449–50.
18. Owen, *William the Lion*, 179; Duncan, *Making of the Kingdom*, 251.
19. *Scotichronicon*, iv, 467–9.
20. Duncan, *Making of the Kingdom*, 253.
21. Anderson, *Early Sources*, ii, 488–9.
22. *Scotichronicon*, v, 3.
23. Anderson, *Early Sources*, ii, 469; *Scotichronicon*, v, 143, 147; Owen, *William the Lion*, 90, 108–13, 186; Duncan, *Making of the Kingdom*, 413, 552; John Geddie, *The Fringes of Fife* (Edinburgh n.d.), 239, 241–4.

24. CDS, i, 142, 144; Anderson, *Early Sources*, ii, 403.
25. *Scotichronicon*, v, 161; Duncan, *Making of the Kingdom*, 534; *SP*, i, 6; Campbell, *Alexander III*, 13.
26. Anderson, *Early Sources*, ii, 403, 514; Barrow, *Bruce*, 18; *SP*, i, 6.
27. Duncan, *Making of the Kingdom*, 534; Campbell, *Alexander III*, 13.
28. Duncan, *Making of the Kingdom*, 535–6.
29. Duncan, *Making of the Kingdom*, 551; Campbell, *Alexander III*, 5–8.
30. Duncan, *Making of the Kingdom*, 558.
31. Anderson, *Scottish Annals*, 363–7.
32. *SP*, i, 6; Campbell, *Alexander III*, 83–5.
33. Anderson, *Early Sources*, ii, 588, n. 5.
34. Anderson, *Early Sources*, ii, 570 n. 2; Campbell, *Alexander III*, 221; *SP*, i, 6.
35. *CDS*, i, 292–3.
36. Duncan, *Making of the Kingdom*, 536.
37. *CDS*, i, 338–46.
38. Duncan, *Making of the Kingdom*, 560.
39. *CDS*, i, 341; Anderson, *Early Sources*, ii, 557; Anderson, *Scottish Annals*, 348–9; Campbell, *Alexander III*, 36.
40. *CDS*, i, 346.
41. Anderson, *Scottish Annals*, 370–1.
42. *CDS*, i, 381.
43. E.L.G. Stones, *Anglo-Scottish Relations* (Oxford 1965), 61–9; Campbell, *Alexander III*, 59–70; Duncan, *Making of the Kingdom*, 563; Barrow, *Bruce*, 569.
44. Alan Young, *Robert the Bruce's Rivals: The Comyns, 1212–1314* (East Linton 1997), 59.
45. *CDS*, i, 438; Campbell, *Alexander III*, 120–6.
46. *SP*, i, 6; Campbell, *Alexander III*, 144, 177.
47. Campbell, *Alexander III*, 192–3; *Chronicon de Lanercost*, 96.
48. *SP*, i, 6; Campbell, *Alexander III*, 199.
49. *SP*, i, 6.
50. Campbell, *Alexander III*, 217–9; *CSP Scot.*, ii, 222; G.W.S. Barrow, 'A Kingdom in Crisis: Scotland and the Maid of Norway', in *SHR*, lxix, no 2 (1990), 121; *Fordun's Chronicle*, ii, 301–4.
51. *CDS*, ii, 78; Anderson, *Scottish Annals*, 293–4; Anderson, *Early Sources*, ii, 686 and n. 2; *SP*, i, 6; Campbell, *Alexander III*, 222–3.
52. *Scotichronicon*, v, 419–21; Anderson, *Early Sources*, ii, 691–2.
53. *Chronicon de Lanercost*, 96, 117–8; Barrow, *Bruce*, 21–2.
54. Anderson, *Scottish Annals*, 384; Anderson, *Early Sources*, ii, 693–4; Norman Reid, 'Margaret, "Maid of Norway" and Scottish Queenship', in *Reading Medieval Studies*, viii (1982), 75–6; *SP*, i, 6; *ER*, i, 39; Campbell, *Alexander III*, 235–8.

CHAPTER THREE

THE MAID OF NORWAY
AND THE BRUCE QUEENS

With no baby prince to save the situation, the thoughts of the Scottish magnates once more turned to the Maid of Norway. Not only was the new Queen Margaret only three years old, but she would be something very unusual for Scotland, a queen in her own right. It is fascinating to note that there seems to have been no opposition to her inheriting the throne. The lords had, of course, already acknowledged the Maid as heir in 1284, after the death of Prince Alexander,[1] but the implications were enormous. Even when she grew up, this new queen could not be expected to lead her army in time of war and she would have the greatest difficulty in controlling her headstrong nobility.

Worse still, a woman, no matter how highly born, would take second place to her husband as soon as she married. 'So long as the husband is living, the wife is under his power and he was lord of all that pertained to his wife', as *Regiam Majestatem*, the great medieval legal authority, put it.[2] Were she to marry one of her own nobles, all the others would be bitterly jealous, and if she married someone from another country, Scotland would almost inevitably fall under the influence of a foreign power. William I had confronted this problem when he became ill in the summer of 1195 and tried in vain to persuade his lords to recognise his daughter as his successor. In the end, the situation was remedied when Queen Ermengarde gave birth to a son, but this time there could be no such solution.[3]

The Guardians were now anxious for the Maid to come to Scotland for her coronation as soon as possible,[4] but her father, King Eric, was understandably reluctant to part with her, and not simply from reasons of affection. Still only in his teens, he would inevitably marry again, but for the moment Margaret was his heir. Her safety was vital, as long as she was in his hands he had an excuse to take a prominent part in Scottish affairs and he naturally wanted to choose her husband himself. Someone else was equally interested in the little girl's fate. Edward I of England was her great-uncle, and he saw his opportunity to gain control of Scotland at last. He had a five-year-old son and heir, Edward of Caernarvon. He would marry the boy to her, and then Scotland would be within his grasp. He evidently made an approach to Eric soon after he heard the news of Alexander's death, and finally on 1 April 1289 Eric appointed an embassy to go to England for discussions. At the beginning of May, Edward sent a major embassy to Pope Nicholas IV. As well as requesting the grant of a tax to finance a crusade, his envoys were to ask for a papal dispensation allowing his son to marry the Maid.[5]

In the autumn of 1289, it was arranged that three Norwegian envoys should meet four leading Scots in Salisbury to discuss the Maid's future. Edward would be represented at the meeting by two of his bishops and two of his barons, who would give advice and counsel. On 6 November, the Treaty of Salisbury was agreed. The Maid was to leave Norway on 1 November 1290, the Norwegians giving assurances that she was free of any other contract of marriage and betrothal. If she landed in England, Edward I was to send her on to Scotland, provided that kingdom was at peace and it was safe for her to go there. The Scots undertook not to marry her off without the advice of Edward and the consent of her father and they promised to ensure that she could safely come to Scotland and stay there 'of her own will, as true lady, queen and heir of that land'.[6]

When the Pope issued the necessary bull on 16 November 1289, declaring the marriage to be necessary because of various past difficulties between Scotland and England and the threat to future peace, the Scots were still unaware that Edward had actually requested the dispensation.[7] However, in a letter of 17 March 1290 the Scottish nobles and leading churchmen spoke of the joyous news and gave their cordial agreement to the marriage.[8] On 17 April, Edward I wrote to King Eric asking that the Maid be sent to England,[9] and in July 1290 the Treaty of Birgham between the Scots and the English was drawn up near Roxburgh.

It was an elaborate and complicated document, for it was not simply the usual marriage alliance, settling details of dowry, jointure and the date of the wedding. Those who drew it up had to try to regulate the future relationship between Scotland and England. It stated that Scotland would remain 'separated and divided and free in itself, without subjection to the realm of England', its rights, laws, liberties and customs 'preserved in every respect and in all time coming ... completely and without being impaired'. When Margaret arrived and was crowned, a new seal would be struck. It would not mention her husband, but would have only the 'arms and title of the name of the kings of Scotland'. Until Margaret settled down with her husband and gave birth to a living child, all the archives relating to the crown were to remain in Scotland under a strong guard.[10] These efforts at securing the country's position were, however, cast in doubt by clauses reserving Edward I's rights. In other words, he could interfere in Scottish affairs whenever he chose to do so.

The Treaty of Birgham was confirmed at Northampton by Edward I on 28 August 1290. At the same time, Edward appointed Bishop Anthony Bek of Durham to represent the interests of the Maid in Scotland. He instructed the Scottish Guardians to obey Bek, and announced that the Bishop would implement 'a reform of the Scottish realm'. Bek promptly demanded custody of the Scottish castles; the Guardians could only play for time, delaying the handing over of the castles until the Maid arrived.[11] Ever more eager for this event to take place, Edward I on 20 May 1290 sent a ship from Yarmouth to collect her. It was expensively fitted out with a variety of luxurious provisions, including sturgeon, rice, whale meat and ginger, for the benefit of the dignitaries who would accompany the little Queen. The vessel reached Bergen on 26 May, but the English envoys discovered that King Eric was away fighting the Danes. Nothing could be done, and so they returned, empty-handed, twelve days later. If a second voyage was planned, it did not take place.[12]

On 8 August 1290, a joint Scottish and English embassy was appointed to negotiate with King Eric, who announced that he would bring his daughter to Scotland himself. Bishop Bek and Elias de Hauville were sent north at the beginning of September to greet them, but Eric did not come. Instead, he prepared to send the Maid to Orkney, possibly with the intention that the final arrangements should be made there. Two Scottish representatives, the knights

Sir Michael Wemyss and Sir Michael Scot, sailed to Norway to escort her, perhaps in company with an English envoy. Queen Margaret's own retinue was led by Bishop Narve of Bergen, Baron Tore Haakonsson was another of the prominent members of her suite, and Tore's wife Ingebjorg was her principal lady-in-waiting.

We can only imagine the Maid's feelings as she parted from her father and set out on her long journey to her distant kingdom that September. During the voyage, she fell ill. She was carried ashore when her vessels reached Orkney, but she died there, in the arms of Bishop Narve.[13] Sadly he took her body back to Bergen, where King Eric ordered her coffin to be opened so that he could have one last sight of his daughter and assure himself that she really was dead. He then had her buried in the north aisle of the choir of Bergen Cathedral, beside her mother. The Scottish lords had been gathering at Scone in readiness for her coronation, but instead of welcoming their new monarch, they found themselves plunged into a major dynastic crisis. Thirteen competitors claimed the Scottish crown and began gathering their armies.

In accounts of the epic events of the next three decades, little space has been devoted to the Scottish queens who found themselves caught up in the turmoil. Fearing civil war, one of the Guardians, William Fraser, Bishop of St Andrews, wrote to Edward I seeking his advice, and Edward offered to act as arbitrator. He chose as next King of Scots John Balliol, a descendant of David, Earl of Huntingdon's eldest daughter. Balliol was inaugurated at Scone on St Andrew's Day, 30 November 1280 and obediently did homage to Edward for the kingdom of Scotland. Balliol's wife, the mother of his two sons, was Isabella, daughter of John de Warenne, Earl of Surrey, but their time in Scotland was to be short. Edward I made it plain that he regarded the country as his vassal state, and the Scots made a defensive alliance with Philip IV of France. In 1296 Balliol renounced his fealty to Edward, surrendered three months later after a military campaign and was taken south as a prisoner. In 1299 he was allowed to go and live first at the Pope's castle of Gevrey-Chambertin in Burgundy and then on his own family estates at Bailleul-en-Vimeu in Picardy. If Isabella was still alive, she presumably went with him.

Meanwhile the Scots, led by William Wallace and Sir Andrew

Moray, continued their resistance against Edward. In 1306 they turned to Robert Bruce to carry on the struggle. He was crowned king at Scone in March and his Irish wife became Queen of Scots. Robert had previously been married to a Scotswoman, Isabella, the daughter of Donald, 10th Earl of Mar, but she had died young, leaving him with an only daughter, Marjorie.[14] In 1302, he had married again. At that time he was supporting Edward I, and his new wife was Elizabeth de Burgh, the daughter of one of Edward's most prominent Anglo-Irish supporters, Richard, Earl of Ulster. Possibly Edward chose Bruce's bride for him, but it may be that Robert had transferred his allegiance to the English King in the hope of allying himself with the Earl of Ulster.[15] At any rate, Elizabeth seems to have been a person of mature and resolute character. According to one account, she rebuked her husband at his coronation for playing kings and queens like children, presumably a reference to the well-known custom of children pretending to be kings and queens at midsummer revels.[16]

Within weeks of his coronation, Robert I was defeated by John of Lorne on the borders of Argyll and Perthshire. His situation looked very bad, and so Elizabeth took her young step-daughter Marjorie, who was less than twelve years old, and fled north with Robert's sisters, Christian and Mary. Neil Bruce, one of the King's brothers, and the Earl of Atholl escorted them to Kildrummy Castle, where they found refuge, but the castle was almost immediately besieged by the English. A traitor inside set fire to the grain that was stored in the great hall and the garrison was forced to surrender. Neil Bruce was captured, but Elizabeth and her other companions had managed to escape as the English army approached, desperately riding further north, pursued by William, Earl of Ross, one of Balliol's supporters. They may have meant to sail to Orkney, but when they stopped for shelter in the sanctuary of St Duthac at Tain, Ross forced his way in and seized them.

Queen Elizabeth was held in the manor house of Burstwick in Holderness with only two elderly women as her attendants. Christian was sent to a Lincolnshire nunnery, Mary was imprisoned in a cage of timber and iron at Roxburgh Castle, and Marjorie was held first in the Tower of London and then in a Yorkshire nunnery.[17] They remained prisoners for the next eight years. Elizabeth was moved from time to time to other places, including the Tower of London and Shaftesbury in Dorset. She had written an undated letter from Holderness to the English king to complain that she was allowed only three changes of clothing a year, no headgear and nothing for her bed. By the time she was in the Tower in 1312, however, her conditions had improved, for she had six attendants and received an allowance to pay for them.[18] At long last, on 24 June 1314, Robert I defeated the English at the Battle of Bannockburn. Edward I was dead by that time, and Edward II's commander Humphrey de Bohun, Earl of Hereford, was captured immediately afterwards. Negotiations for an exchange of prisoners began, and in the end Elizabeth, the other royal ladies and the aged Robert Wishart, Bishop of Glasgow, were released on condition that Hereford was given his freedom.[19] Queen Elizabeth could now take up her rightful place at the centre of her powerful and successful husband's Court.

Elizabeth and Robert then had two daughters, Matilda and Margaret, but as yet no son.[20] Marjorie, Robert's daughter by his first wife, married Queen Elizabeth's cousin, Walter, High Steward of Scotland, the year after Bannockburn, and in 1316, while heavily pregnant, she suffered a fall from her horse. Her baby was born safely, but she died as a result of the accident. The child, a boy, was christened Robert, after his grandfather, and in 1318 he was declared heir presumptive to the throne. However, on 5 March 1324 Queen Elizabeth gave birth at Dunfermline to a son, David. She had by then been married for almost twenty-two years. She later had a second son, John, who died in childhood. She herself died in the royal residence at Cullen on 26 October 1327. Her body was embalmed and her entrails were buried in the Church of St Mary the Virgin at Cullen. A chaplainry was established there to celebrate masses for her soul. Her body was taken to Dunfermline for burial.[21]

The victory at Bannockburn in 1314 had not ended the war between Scotland and England, and when Elizabeth died, negotiations for peace were still under way. Finally, on 1 March 1328, Edward III issued letters patent recognising Robert I as King of Scots and agreeing that the boundaries of Scotland should be as they were in the reign of Alexander III. At the same time, English envoys were given the power to negotiate a marriage between Robert's son and heir, David, and Edward's younger sister, Joan of the Tower, so called because she had been born in the Tower of London.[22] The Treaty of Edinburgh-Northampton was concluded at Holyrood on 17 March 1328 and confirmed by Edward at Northampton on 4 May 1329. David was only four years old and Joan was six. Should Joan die before the wedding, Edward would supply an appropriate replacement, and were David to die, then Joan was to become the wife of King Robert's next heir instead. The Scots would settle on her lands to the value of £2000 a year. Nothing was said in the treaty about her dowry.

Joan was to be taken to Berwick-upon-Tweed by 15 July 1328 and married 'as soon as can properly be', Robert agreeing to pay a penalty of no less than £100,000 if the ceremony did not take place before Michaelmas 1338.[23] This was a huge sum of money, but the English were afraid that the Scots might change their minds and repudiate the marriage arrangements, which they could do at any time before David's fourteenth birthday, when he would be old enough to give his own consent to the match. For his part, Robert was seriously ill and he needed to settle his son's future. Isabella, the English Queen Mother, took her small daughter to Berwick-upon-Tweed that summer, and Joan married David there before a great gathering of the Scottish and English nobles. Neither Edward III nor Robert I attended in person. Robert was said to be too ill to travel, but he spent almost £1000 on the wedding celebrations and the bride and groom were taken to Cardross soon afterwards to see him.[24] Some of the ladies who had accompanied the new Queen north then returned to England.[25]

When King Robert died on 7 June 1329, David was only five and the royal minority gave Edward III the opportunity to interfere in Scottish affairs. Joan was with her husband when he was crowned and anointed at Scone as David II, probably on 24 November 1331, but within the year his throne was being claimed by John Balliol's son, Edward, with the support of Edward III. Edward III was very conscious of the fact that Joan would not be old enough to give formal consent to her own marriage until 1333. If he could dislodge David before then, Joan could simply repudiate her husband and marry Balliol instead. Edward Balliol defeated the Scots at Dupplin

Moor, near Perth, on 12 August 1332 and was enthroned at Scone on 24 September. However, his fortunes suffered a sudden reverse, and the supporters of David II gathered a force and surprised Balliol by night, forcing him to flee over the Border. Edward III intervened, marching north with an army to defeat the Scots at the Battle of Halidon Hill on 19 July 1333. At the invitation of Philip VI of France, David and Joan were sent to the safety of Normandy in May 1334.[26] David's nephew, Robert, who had succeeded his father as High Steward of Scotland in 1326, had been one of the commanders at Halidon Hill, and in David's absence he and John Randolph, Earl of Moray, were made joint Guardians of the realm.[27]

The move to France must have been a pleasing one for Joan, for her mother was French and her grandfather had been King Philip IV of France. Philip VI made the royal visitors very welcome and installed them with their household in the Château Gaillard, an imposing fortress on a hill overlooking the River Seine, about 40 kilometres upstream from Rouen. Originally built by Richard I of England, it had been captured by the French in 1204 and had been a royal residence ever since. Twenty years before Joan and David's arrival, it had been the prison of Louis X's disgraced wife, Marguerite of Burgundy, who had committed adultery and, people said, had actually been murdered in the castle.[28] In spite of this somewhat offputting episode, the Château Gaillard provided a pleasant home for Joan and David during their adolescence, and there they spent the next seven years. It was only at the end of May 1341 that they were able to return to Scotland, after Edward Balliol had fallen from power.

They landed at Inverbervie on 2 June 1341. David was seventeen now, Joan almost twenty. She had, according to Bower, grown up to be 'seemly, very attractive and beautiful',[29] but as the years went by, there was no sign of her becoming pregnant.[30] On 26 August 1346 Edward III defeated the French at the Battle of Crécy and David decided to invade England in support of his ally. He carried with him the Black Rood, St Margaret's crucifix, but in spite of this precaution he was defeated and captured on 17 October 1346 at the Battle of Neville's Cross, near Durham. He spent the next eleven years as a prisoner in England, and to his intense annoyance Robert the Steward ruled Scotland for him.

David had never liked his nephew, and now he was convinced that Robert, who had been one of the commanders at Neville's Cross, had not tried to prevent him from being captured. Because of his own lack of a son, Robert was still his heir. Although the Steward was eight years older than David and therefore unlikely to succeed him, he did have sons who could inherit. Edward III allowed Joan to visit her husband in the Tower from time to time, but when David was finally released and allowed to return to Scotland in 1357, his Queen decided to remain in England. It seems likely that they separated by mutual consent. After they parted, David took as his mistress Katherine Mortimer, described by Sir Thomas Gray of Heton as 'a young lady of London', but she was murdered in the summer of 1360, stabbed to death on the road near Soutra, at the instigation of the jealous lords.[31]

David then found a new partner, Margaret, the beautiful and ambitious widow of Sir John Logie of Logie and daughter of Sir Malcolm Drummond. David seems to have fallen passionately in love with her, and whether or not she returned his feelings, she no doubt saw the relationship as a good way of improving her own position and that of her many relatives. When Queen Joan died on 7 September 1362,[32] David resolved to marry Margaret. She was far from being acceptable to many Scots, for she was the daughter of a mere knight, and Robert the Steward was furious at the relationship. Not only was there suddenly the prospect of David having a son, but Robert's own relatives were involved in a fierce feud with Margaret's brothers, John and Maurice Drummond. Now, the whole Drummond family were set to enjoy an increase of both property and status.

Ignoring the general discontent, David openly acknowledged his interest in Margaret by making a grant of lands to her on 20 January 1363, and he may well have forced the Steward to pass various lands and offices to Maurice Drummond. This could account for a rebellion led by Robert early that same year, when the King was presented with a petition demanding that he dismiss Margaret as well as his current advisers. David paid no attention. He married Margaret in April 1363, at Inchmurdoch, a Fife manor house of the Bishop of St Andrews, and so she became Queen of Scots.[33] Predictably, David then showered favours upon her relatives, granting them lands and finding them important marriage partners. Margaret already had a son by her first husband, but she had no children by the King. One chronicle claimed that she went so far as to pretend to be pregnant in an attempt to secure her position, but the writer may have been confusing her with Queen Yolande.[34] Since David had no children at all, legitimate or illegitimate, Margaret's failure to conceive probably lay with him.

In spite of that particular problem, Margaret continued to exert a strong influence over her husband and she no doubt inspired the marriage of Robert the Steward's eldest son, John, to her own niece, Annabella Drummond. If she could not produce a son who would be king, at least she would give Annabella the chance of becoming queen, once both David and Robert were dead. The Drummond feud with the Steward was not yet an end, however, and in the winter of 1368 the Queen seems to have persuaded David to arrest and imprison Robert and some of his sons. He released them soon afterwards, however. He was beginning to tire of his arrogant, demanding wife. At about that time he began an affair with Agnes Dunbar, sister of George, Earl of March, and in 1369 he divorced Margaret, relegating her to the position of 'Lady Margaret Logie, onetime Queen'. He then prepared to marry Agnes, granting her a huge annual income of 1000 merks from the customs of Aberdeen and Haddington.[35]

David had reckoned without his former wife's determination, however, and if he had expected her to live quietly in retirement on the pension of £100 a year he had granted her, he was to be sadly disappointed. Furious at having been set aside, Margaret decided to take her case to the highest authority. She secretly boarded a ship in the Firth of Forth, sailed to France and made her way to Avignon, where Pope Gregory XI lived. She engaged the sympathy of the Pope and submitted an appeal against her divorce to the papal curia. David was forced to send out his own legal representatives, the arguments were complex, and the case dragged on for several years. David died in Edinburgh Castle on 22 February 1371 but Margaret persisted with her lawsuit. It seemed as though Scotland would be placed under a papal interdict as a result of her representations, but she died on a pilgrimage to Rome, some time after January 1375.[36]

Notes

1. Donaldson, *Scottish Documents*, 37–8.
2. *Regiam Majestatem and Quoniam Attachiamenta*, ed. Lord Cooper (Stair Society 1947), 126–30, 148, 291, 328; Marshall, *Virgins and Viragos*, 33–6.
3. See Chapter 2, p.18.
4. Reid, in *Reading Medieval Studies*, viii (1982), 82–6.
5. Prestwich, 'Edward I and the Maid', 164–5; Helle, 'Norwegian Foreign Policy', 149; Barrow, 'A Kingdom in Crisis', 130; Barrow, *Bruce*, 39; Nicholson, *Later Middle Ages*, 30.
6. Donaldson, *Scottish Historical Documents*, 39; Prestwich, 'Edward I and the Maid', n.5, 165–6.
7. Nicholson, *Later Middle Ages*, 31; Prestwich, 'Edward I and the Maid', 165.
8. Dickinson, Donaldson and Milne, i, 107.
9. Prestwich, 'Edward I and the Maid', 168.
10. Text printed in Barrow, 'A Kingdom in Crisis', 137–41.
11. Nicholson, *Later Middle Ages*, 34.
12. Prestwich, 'Edward I and the Maid', 169–70.
13. Prestwich, 'Edward I and the Maid', 171–3; Helle, 'Norwegian Foreign Policy', 151; Barbara E. Crawford, 'North Sea Kingdoms, North Sea Bureaucrat: A Royal Official who Transcended National Boundaries', in *SHR*, lxix, no 2 (1990), 175–6; Barrow, *Bruce*, 42.
14. *Ibid.*, 199–200.
15. Alan Young, *Robert the Bruce's Rivals: The Comyns, 1212–1314* (East Linton, 1998), 171–2; Nicholson, *Later Middle Ages*, 70; Barrow, Bruce, 174–5, 200.
16. Barrow, *Bruce*, 230.
17. *Scotichronicon*, 323, 353; Nicholson, *Later Middle Ages*, 74–5; Barrow, *Bruce*, 230.
18. Geoffrey Barrow, 'Elizabeth de Burgh', in forthcoming *Oxford Dictionary of National Biography* (Oxford 2004).
19. Barrow, *Bruce*, 330.
20. *Scotichronicon*, vi, 37, 377.
21. *Ibid.*, 411; *SP*, i, 8; *Fordun's Chronicle*, i, 318; ii, 312; *HMC Report* iii, 404.
22. Nicholson, *Edward III and the Scots*, 48.
23. Donaldson, *Scottish Documents*, 61–2; Nicholson, *Later Middle Ages*, 120; Barrow, *Bruce*, 361, 366–8.
24. Barrow, Bruce, 368; Nicholson, *Edward III and the Scots*, 368.
25. Nicholson, *Edward III and the Scots*, 53.

26. *Ibid.*, 73, 99, 149; Nicholson, *Later Middle Ages*, 130.
27. Nicholson, *Edward III and the Scots*, 75–118.
28. Bouyer, *Dictionnaire*, 192–3.
29. *Scotichronicon*, v, 105.
30. Nicholson, *Later Middle Ages*, 130, 140.
31. Sir Thomas Gray, *Scalacronica* (Maitland Club 1836), 196; *Scotichronicon*, ii, 365–6; Nicholson, *Later Middle Ages*, 168; Michael Penman, 'The Earl, the King, his Lover and the Ransom', in *History Scotland* ii, no.2 (Jan/Feb 2002), 26–8.
32. *SP*, i, 9; Boardman, *Early Stewart Kings*, 15.
33. Wyntoun, *Chronicle*, vi, 506; *Fordun's Chronicle*, i, 382; Boardman, *Early Stewart Kings*, 15–16.
34. *Liber Pluscardensis*, ed. Felix J.H. Skene (Edinburgh 1877), i, 307; Boardman, *Early Stewart Kings*, 22.
35. Boardman, *Early Stewart Kings*, 24.
36. *Scotichronicon*, vii, 359; Boardman, *Early Stewart Kings*, 23–5; *SP*, i, 9; Nicholson, *Later Middle Ages*, 182.

CHAPTER FOUR

THE EARLY STEWART QUEENS:
EUPHEMIA ROSS TO JOAN BEAUFORT

When David II died, his nephew Robert the Steward did inherit the throne, becoming the first Stewart monarch. He and his wife, Euphemia Ross, were an elderly couple by medieval standards, he fifty-five and suffering from serious eye problems, possibly glaucoma or cataract, she in her later forties. Both had been married before. Euphemia was the daughter of Hugh, 4ᵗʰ Earl of Ross, and his second wife, Margaret Graham. Born about 1322, she would have been brought up at Dingwall Castle, their principal residence in the north of Scotland. It was a large and imposing building surrounding a courtyard, with a tower at each corner. The family lived in the west wing and Euphemia must have shared the nurseries with her elder brother Hugh and her younger sisters, Janet and Lilias. Although they lived far from the Court, their father was a friend of Robert I. Indeed, his first wife had been Maud Bruce, the King's sister, and after Maud's death he remained a member of the royal family circle.[1]

Euphemia was betrothed when she was still a young child, and it may well be that it was Robert I himself who made the arrangements, for her bridegroom was to be the King's great-nephew, John, second son of Thomas Randolph, 1ˢᵗ Earl of Moray. A staunch Bruce supporter, Moray led the army that took the field against Edward Balliol in the summer of 1332, his two eldest sons going with him. He was taken ill at Musselburgh and died there. Three weeks later, his elder son was killed at the Battle of Dupplin, John inherited the earldom and, emerging unscathed from the conflict, escaped to France. Less than a year after that, on 19 July 1333, Euphemia's own father was killed fighting the English at the Battle of Halidon Hill.

After a few months' absence, John returned to Scotland and was chosen to be joint Guardian of the country for the young David

II. The other Guardian was Robert the Steward. Both were only seventeen years of age, reckless and energetic, and it was not long before they quarrelled. Their guardianship was dissolved in 1335 and Sir Andrew Moray took up the position instead. That same year John was captured by the English on the Borders and imprisoned in the Tower of London. When he was set free in February 1341, he retreated to France once more. Euphemia must have wondered if her wedding would ever take place. By 1343, however, John was back in Scotland and it was probably soon after his return that the two were married at last.[2]

As a bride of about twenty-one, Euphemia would have lived in her husband's castle at Darnaway, in Moray, and on his estates in Dumfriesshire. Because the past turmoil had delayed her marriage, she was older than most girls were when they married, and so there was all the more pressure on her to produce a son. Time passed, but there was no sign of her becoming pregnant. In 1346, Euphemia's husband and Robert the Steward marched into England with David II as commanders of the royal army. John was killed at the Battle of Neville's Cross and Euphemia became a widow at not yet twenty-five. She remained so for the next eleven years. Although her childlessness was an obvious disadvantage, she was wealthy and highly eligible and she must have had proposals, but it seems that she preferred to remain single.

Meanwhile, Robert the Steward was ruling the country once more as Guardian and worrying about the future. He had married Elizabeth Mure, daughter of Sir Adam Mure of Rowallan, in 1336, when he was twenty. She had already been pregnant with their first child, and they went on to have four sons and five daughters. Robert would also have no fewer than eight illegitimate sons by his various mistresses, and presumably daughters too.[3] This was no doubt a matter of pride for him, not least because he was still the heir to David II's throne, but unfortunately his enemies were taking great pleasure in saying that all his children were illegitimate, even his wife's, for Robert and Elizabeth had been within the forbidden degrees when they married and they had omitted to obtain a dispensation. To remedy the situation, Robert now made an application to Pope Clement VI, who obligingly granted it and declared Elizabeth's children to be legitimate.[4]

Elizabeth died in 1353 and two years later Robert married Euphemia. Perhaps she had always been attracted to him. He was tall and dignified, 'witty in his responses', with a friendly, cheerful manner.[5] They knew each other well, for Euphemia's husband and Robert had soon made up their early quarrel and the two families had been close ever since. Euphemia was probably concerned for Elizabeth's young children. For his part Robert was eager to acquire Euphemia's lands in the north and, having a large family already, her childlessness did not matter to him. According to the Clan Fraser chronicler, her uncle the Lord of Lovat and a splendid retinue escorted her south to her wedding, which probably took place at Robert's castle of Dundonald, in Ayrshire.[6]

Dundonald now became Euphemia's home. Set on top of a hill, the thirteenth-century castle had been copied by one of her husband's ancestors from the Norman fortress of Couch-le-Château, which he had seen during a pilgrimage to Santiago de Compostella in Spain. This second marriage must have brought her unexpected happiness and fulfilment, for although she was now in her thirties, she went on to have children of her own. Her first son was named David, after the King, her second was called Walter, for her husband's father, and she had two daughters, Jean and Egidia.[7] As stepmother to Robert's nine children and the person who had to run his estates during his frequent absences, she had much to occupy her attention

Euphemia had been Robert's wife for sixteen years when he finally inherited his uncle's throne in 1371. She was crowned at Scone by Alexander Kinninmonth, Bishop of Aberdeen, a few months after her husband's coronation.[8] Robert had long since left his rash youth behind him and, characterised by one chronicler as 'the peacemaker, the son of peace',[9] he managed to maintain harmonious relations with England. Thanks to lavish gifts and his own genial personality he was also on good terms with his nobility. His own children proved more of a problem, however, for the ambitious sons of his first marriage vied with each other for power. 'Some of them were peaceable and benign,' said Walter Bower, 'some insolent and malign.'[10] Alexander, the third son, earned for himself the picturesque nickname, 'the Wolf of Badenoch', for his marauding activities in the north.

We have no knowledge of Euphemia's relationship with these turbulent stepchildren during their adult years, but there is some evidence that she was naturally eager to promote the interests of her own sons. In about 1377, David was created Earl Palatine of Caithness, no doubt through her influence, and he began to claim that he was the rightful heir to the throne, reviving the old allegation that his half-brothers and sisters were illegitimate.[11] Euphemia may or may not have supported this move. By 1384 her husband's former vigour was fading fast, and his sight was seriously impaired. His eldest son, John, Earl of Carrick, took over many of his responsibilities, and Robert retired to Dundonald Castle. Euphemia died in 1387 at the age of about sixty-five, he three years later. They both seem to have been buried at Scone.[12]

When John, Earl of Carrick, succeeded to the throne in 1390, he was fifty-three years old and had been married since 1367 to Queen Margaret Logie's niece Annabella, daughter of Sir John Drummond of Stobhall in Perthshire.[13] According to Bower, John was tall, like his father, with very handsome features and a luxuriant beard. He also seems to have inherited his father's genial personality, 'with lively eyes which always spread good humour and rather long and ruddy cheeks, blooming with every mark of handsome amiability'.[14] We have no description of Annabella, but the glimpses we have of her activities suggest that she was a much more assertive character, perhaps sharing her aunt's qualities of persistence and determination.

John's gentle nature put him at a disadvantage with his more savage and ambitious brothers, and there are indications that within a few years of her marriage Annabella engaged in a vigorous power struggle with her eldest brother-in-law Robert, later Duke of Albany. Not only did Robert have a royal name. He also had designs on the throne. By 1373, when they had been married for six years, John and Annabella had two children, Margaret, named after Annabella's aunt, and Mary.[15] Encouraged by their lack of sons, Robert seems to have decided to do all he could to push John aside in the succession, and it was almost certainly he who inspired the piece of legislation by which parliament entailed the descent of kingship on the male line. This meant that neither Margaret nor Mary could succeed to the throne, and if Annabella and John never did have a son, John's heir would be the unpleasant Robert.

John and Annabella were anxious about the future of their two little girls, and it may well have been Annabella who devised the plan to secure their inheritance. In 1374 John resigned his earldom of Carrick to his father the King and received it back jointly with Annabella, the new grant confirming that if they had no sons the earldom itself could descend through the female line.[16]

Four years later, on 24 October 1378, and more than eleven years after her marriage, Annabella triumphantly gave birth to her first son, David. She then had two more daughters, Elizabeth and Egidia, followed by a second son, Robert, who died in infancy.[17] Her brother-in-law was not to be deterred, however, and after John suffered a serious injury when he was kicked by a horse and left permanently lame, Robert seized the opportunity of making himself their father's chief adviser but he did not manage to dislodge John from the succession, and when Robert II died, John inherited, taking the title of Robert III. He was crowned and anointed at Scone by Walter Trail, Bishop of St Andrews, on 14 August 1390, and Annabella, 'a lady of great distinction', was crowned there the following day by the Bishop of Dunkeld.[18] A huge crowd had gathered from all over Scotland to take part in the festivities. Four years after that, Queen Annabella gave birth to her third and last son, James. She must have been about forty by then.[19]

A letter from her survives from that time. Annabella did not write or even sign it herself. Very few women of her time could write, although they were taught to read so that they could study devotional works. The Queen would have dictated it to a secretary. She had apparently received a letter from Richard II of England who was engaged in negotiations with her husband for marriages between members of their two families. Queens usually were involved in the arrangements for their daughters, and so we can assume that this was why Richard wrote to her. His letter has not survived, but she replied from Dunfermline Abbey on 1 August 1394, telling him that the prospect pleased her. She excused herself for not having answered sooner. She had been pregnant, but had now been safely delivered of her son, James, 'thanks to God and

Our Lady'. Her letter is in Norman French, but even if she did not speak that language and had left it to her scribe to translate her spoken words, the personal allusion to her state of health gives us a fleeting feeling of connection with this early Scottish Queen.[20]

None of Annabella's children did marry into the English royal family, but it is intriguing to see this daughter of a Perthshire knight corresponding in assured manner with a foreign monarch, even if she did only dictate the letter. There are also other signs of her abilities and her influence. She obviously liked to live in suitably regal style, for in March 1391 she was granted by parliament an enormous pension of 2,500 merks a year for 'her adornment and other things necessary for her rank and livelihood'.[21] We have no details of her household, costume or jewels, but had she not been well regarded, parliament would never have made her this grant.

Apart from making sure that she maintained her own status, Annabella energetically promoted the interests of her eldest son. As early as 1392, when he was only fourteen, David, Earl of Carrick, was playing an active part in the royal administration, and it is noticeable that his first two chamberlains were William Drummond and John Logie, both relatives of his mother. Again, it was Queen Annabella rather than King Robert who arranged a grand tournament in Edinburgh in 1398 when David was knighted. He and eleven other knights took part in the jousting, which was held at the west side of the castle, in the area where King's Stables Road is now.[22] Anglo-Scottish tournaments in the 1390s played an important part in fostering good relations between the two countries, and it seems that the Queen took a significant part in these diplomatic interchanges.[23] On 28 April that same year, she and her husband were present at Scone when David was created Duke of Rothesay. It was on that occasion also that the King's brother Robert became Duke of Albany. William Trail, Bishop of St Andrews, celebrated Mass and preached a sermon about the state of the realm before the King, Queen Annabella and the assembled courtiers.[24]

As the King's health increasingly failed, Albany secured for himself the place of Robert III's chief adviser. However, the Queen was evidently determined to fight his efforts to gain complete control and, on 27 January 1399, Prince David was made Lieutenant of the

Realm. His father, King Robert, it was said, was 'unable to govern', and so David was to rule the country for the next three years.[25] Albany was effectively excluded from power, and soon afterwards Annabella was making a formal complaint that his deputies as chamberlain had been obstructing the collection of her revenues. He was ordered to remedy the situation.

Towards the end of his life, Queen Annabella asked the King what epitaph he would like to be inscribed on his monument. His predecessors had all been honoured in this way and he should be making the necessary arrangements. 'You have spoken like a worldly woman,' her mild husband replied, 'for if I think carefully over what, who and what kind I am ... I should as a result have no desire to erect a proud tomb. Therefore let those men who strive in this world for the pleasures of honour have shining monuments. I on the other hand should prefer to be buried at the bottom of a midden so that my soul may be saved in the day of the Lord. Bury me, therefore, I beg you, in a midden, and write for my epitaph, "Here lies the worst of kings and the most wretched of men in the whole kingdom."' Bower, who gives us this conversation, does not record Annabella's reply, which was no doubt brisk and to the point.[26]

Taking advantage of the weakness of the Scottish king, Henry IV of England invaded Scotland in August 1400, saying that the Scots had slandered him to the King of France. He besieged Prince David in Edinburgh Castle, but in September he retired south again, having caused singularly little damage. This was out of respect, so it was said, for Queen Annabella.[27] The following autumn, Annabella died at Scone and was buried in Dunfermline. Walter Trail, the influential Bishop of St Andrews, had died a few weeks earlier. 'While these two lived,' wrote Bower, 'they raised high the honour of the kingdom' by making peace between princes and noblemen, by entertaining 'foreigners and strangers brilliantly, with feasting', and by delighting them with generous gifts when they left.[28]

'Fair, honourable and pleasant' was the verdict of another chronicler, Andrew of Wyntoun, on Annabella. 'Cunning [meaning intelligent], courteous in her affairs/Loving and large [generous] to strangers/ They she treated honourably/And them rewarded largely.'[29] Some historians thought that she propelled her son forward at the expense of her husband, but Robert III was very obviously unable to rule effectively for himself and Annabella may have acted to protect his interests as well as their son's when she opposed the rapacious Albany.

Prince David, undoubtedly spoiled by his mother, features in the chronicles as a dissolute and erratic figure. After Queen Annabella had gone, he was arrested and imprisoned by Albany. His mysterious demise at Falkland Palace in 1402 gave rise to widespread rumours that he had been starved to death by his uncle. Unable to do anything about it, Robert III endowed masses for the souls of his dead wife and son[30] and then, fearing for his own life and that of his younger boy, Prince James, took refuge in the greater safety of Rothesay Castle and arranged to send James to France. The Prince was captured by English pirates off Flamborough Head on 22 March 1404, and when the news was brought to Robert he was unable to recover from the shock. He died on 29 March 1404.[31]

Devastating as his capture seemed at the time, it was to bring James I an excellent, cosmopolitan education, a first-hand knowledge of other courts, and a politically important bride. After his capture, he spent eighteen years as the prisoner of the English. He was treated honourably, on more than one occasion travelled to France with the English Court, attended the wedding of Henry V and Katherine de Valois in Troyes Cathedral in 1420 and returned to London for the King's coronation. Henry knighted him on St George's Day, 23 April 1421, making him a member of the Order of the Garter. However, these honours did little to ease his frustration at being kept captive when he should have been ruling his own kingdom.[32] 'The bird, the beast, the fish eke in the sea/They live in freedom, everyone in his kind/And I, a man, and lacketh liberty!' he wrote in the long autobiographical poem, *The Kingis Quair*, reliably believed to be his.[33]

One spring day in May 1423, shortly before the poem was written, he was at Windsor Castle. Looking down from a window in the tower, he suddenly saw a young woman strolling in the gardens. She was so beautiful that he was enthralled, noting her sweet expression, her golden hair and the richness of her attire. Her quilted dress was sewn with pearls, rubies, emeralds and sapphires, she had a head-dress of red, white and blue feathers shimmering with gold spangles, and round her neck was a gold chain with a heart-shaped ruby pendant. He fell instantly in love with her.[34] His poem does not tell us the details of his courtship, concentrating instead on his agonising over whether he, a poor prisoner, will ever be able to have his love. However, he had made a fortunate choice.

The young woman in the garden was Lady Joan Beaufort, who was not only unmarried but very well connected. Her mother, Lady Catherine de Holand, was a niece of Richard II. Her father, John Beaufort, 1st Earl of Somerset, was Henry IV's half-brother. His parents had been the famous John of Gaunt and his mistress Catherine Swynford. Henry IV had declared the Beauforts legitimate in a charter of 1407, but he had banned them from the succession.[35] Naturally they resented this, and so they were all the more ready to welcome James's interest in Joan as an opportunity for improving their own position. Henry V and his wife were on good terms with James, and there was every prospect that the King of Scots might soon be allowed to return home.

Joan's own feelings towards the Scots may not have been particularly warm, for two of her brothers had recently been captured by the Scottish forces who were fighting the English near Baugé in France. However, it seems that when she and James met, she was charmed with him. As a captive monarch, he was a romantic figure, and a personable one at that. According to the chronicler Bower, James was of medium height, a little on the short side, with a well-proportioned body and large bones, strong-limbed and full of pent-up energy.[36] *The King's Quair* tells us that his love for Joan made him feel his imprisonment all the more keenly, but it was to lead to his release. The Beauforts put pressure on Henry V to set James free so that he could marry Joan, and Henry's French wife Katherine de Valois also interceded on his behalf.[37]

Intense diplomatic activity resulted. Murdoch, Duke of Albany, James's heir presumptive, was ruling Scotland as Governor and on 19 August 1423 he issued letters appointing an impressive embassy to negotiate James's release. A draft treaty was agreed at York on 10 September and on 4 December the finalised document was sealed at London. The Scots were to pay a ransom of 60,000 merks (£40,000) for their King. Joan would receive a dowry of 10,000 merks, but that sum would not be given to the Scots. Instead, the amount would be subtracted from the ransom. Twenty-one Scottish hostages would come to England in surety for payment of the rest of the money.[38] James and Joan were married on 2 February 1424 in the Church of St Mary Overy (now Southwark Cathedral) in London, and when the festivities were over they set off for the north.[39]

A large number of Scottish nobles had gathered in York to escort them home.[40] By 28 March they were in Durham, where James signed an indenture agreeing a seven-year truce between Scotland and England, and James and Joan were both crowned at Scone on 21 May by Henry de Wardlaw, Bishop of St Andrews.[41] The Queen was already pregnant, and she gave birth to their first child at Christmas 1424, a daughter, whom they called Margaret. They would have five more daughters, all of whom were debarred from the succession by the 1373 entail on heirs male, but on 16 October 1430 Joan gave birth to twin sons at Holyrood Abbey. This was a cause for great rejoicing. Bonfires were lit, wine flowed and food was distributed to the people of Edinburgh. The delighted King knighted both babies at their baptism. The elder, Alexander, died in infancy, but Prince James survived.[42]

For Joan, life with her husband could never have been dull. After his long captivity, James seemed to be charged with energy, desperate to make up for the long years of captivity. According to Bower, he was a great wrestler, archer and jouster, a very fast runner, an energetic rider and traveller and a musician of professional ability, skilled on the drum, fiddle, psaltery, organ, flute and lyre, trumpet and pipe. He composed more poetry, drew, painted, laid out herb gardens, planted and grafted fruit trees and was willing to turn his hand to almost any practical task.[43] Moreover he loved his wife and obviously trusted her. In 1428 and again in 1435, when he was about to visit the northern parts of his kingdom, he made his nobles swear oaths of fealty to her in case anything happened to him.[44]

Apart from the occasions when she had their children, Joan features scarcely at all in the records, and when she does, she is undertaking the conventional female role of intercession. Alexander Macdonald, Lord of the Isles, seized in 1429 for burning and pillaging in the Highlands, was brought to Edinburgh and made to appear before the high altar in Holyrood Abbey dressed as a penitent. Joan and the nobles pleaded for his life, and he was imprisoned in Tantallon Castle instead of being executed. This did not necessarily mean that the Queen was acting on her own initiative, of course. The scene had obviously been stage-managed to allow James to exercise mercy without losing face.[45] He was, in fact, becoming increasingly autocratic. No matter was too great or too trivial for his attention and his intrusive control contrasted sharply with the freedom his nobles had enjoyed during his absence.[46]

James was also ambitious for recognition on the European stage, and on 24 June 1436 his eldest daughter, aged twelve, was married to the Dauphin Louis, heir to the French king. James decided to spend Christmas that year at Perth. He and Joan stayed in the Dominican Friary and remained there after the festivities were over. On the evening of 21 February 1437, the King and Queen were sitting with Joan's ladies when they heard a sudden commotion outside the royal apartments. Seizing a poker, James wrenched up some of the floorboards and let himself down into the sewer beneath. He knew that it had an opening at the other end, beside his tennis court, but he had forgotten that he had given orders for it to be blocked up because the tennis balls had been rolling into it. He was trapped.

Joan and her ladies hastily replaced the floorboards and Katherine Douglas, one of the Queen's ladies, tried to bar the door by putting her arm through the hasps of the great lock, but the conspirators burst in, led by Sir Robert Graham and Sir Robert Stewart, Chamberlain of the Royal Household. In the mêlée, Joan was seriously wounded in the shoulder, but she managed to flee outside in great distress while her ladies huddled in a corner of the room, weeping in terror. After what must have seemed an eternity, the conspirators gave up their search for James and left but, just as they were about to ride away from the Friary, one of them remembered the sewer. Back they came, forced up the floorboards and, by the light of a flaming torch, they glimpsed the King huddled below. He fought savagely, but he was unarmed, and they stabbed him to death.[47]

The assassins fled north. In the resulting chaos and confusion, Queen Joan managed to reach Edinburgh, where her children were staying. It would have been far too dangerous to take her six-year-old son, James II, to Scone, and so on 25 March 1437 he was crowned and anointed at Holyrood Abbey by Michael Ochiltree, Bishop of Dunblane. The various assassins were then hunted down, seized and executed after terrible tortures, ordered, so it was said, by the Queen herself. Parliament gave Joan custody of the young King and his sisters, appointing a council to advise her and allocating her a yearly allowance of 4000 merks. Stirling Castle would be her main residence. Meanwhile, James I's nephew, Archibald Douglas, Duke of Touraine and Earl of Douglas, would head the government of the kingdom as Lieutenant-General.[48]

Satisfactory as those arrangements may have seemed, it soon became clear that ambitious men would stop at nothing to gain possession of the young King. Desperate to keep him herself, Joan announced that she was going on a pilgrimage to Whitekirk, in East Lothian, and then, eluding Sir William Crichton, Keeper of Edinburgh Castle, she smuggled her son out of the castle in one of her trunks. Instead of sailing from Leith to Dunbar, she set off in the opposite direction, up the River Forth to Stirling Castle. There she was welcomed by Sir Alexander Livingston of Callendar, Keeper of the Castle.[49] That was the story told by Robert Lindsay of Pitscottie, a sixteenth-century chronicler of varying reliability. It is difficult to know how accurate it is, but the summer's events certainly marked the beginning of a bitter power struggle between the Crichtons and the Livingstons while Queen Joan looked on helplessly.[50]

In June 1439 the Queen married James Stewart, 'the Black Knight of Lorne'. She needed a masculine protector, and although little is known about him, he was apparently 'a handsome, graceful young man'.[51] The nobles were extremely jealous of the Black Knight for having advanced himself in this way and Sir Alexander Livingston imprisoned Queen Joan, her new husband and his brother.[52] On 4 September 1439, however, a general council met at Stirling and the members of parliament negotiated Joan's release. A document known as 'the Appointment' was drawn up, laying down the terms for her freedom. Joan was to allow the Livingstons to have the keeping of James II until he came of age, with the annuity parliament had given her, but she would have access to her son.[53]

The struggle between the Livingstons and the Crichtons was not yet over, however. One morning, not long after the Appointment had been agreed, the King was hunting in Stirling Park when William Crichton, by now Lord Chancellor, appeared before him at the head of a hundred armed men. Apparently delighted to be rescued from the Livingstons, James willingly went with them to Edinburgh. After that, a general reconciliation was arranged and it was agreed that Livingston should have custody of James once more, while Crichton would continue as Chancellor.[54] The rivalry between the Crichtons and the Livingstons flared up yet again in 1444, and Sir William Crichton was outlawed.

James II reached the age of fourteen on 16 October 1444, but he was still in the hands of the Livingstons. Queen Joan and her husband sided with Sir William Crichton and his main ally, James Kennedy, Bishop of St Andrews, and civil war broke out that November. In July 1445, the Black Knight was arraigned before parliament because he had allegedly been saying that the country was being ruled badly. Joan took refuge in Dunbar Castle, which was then besieged by the Livingstons.[55] The Queen and its keeper, Adam Hepburn of Hailes, defended the castle, but Joan died during the siege, on 15 July 1445. Her body was taken to Perth, and buried beside James I in the Charterhouse.[56]

Queen Joan, gently brought up and presumably happy with James I, had been forced to struggle desperately to protect herself and her children in the years of turmoil after the murder at Perth. Perhaps she found some consolation in her second marriage. She and the Black Knight had three sons, John, later created Earl of Atholl, James, who became Earl of Buchan, and Andrew, who entered the church and would be Bishop of Moray.[57] After Joan's death, the Black Knight left the country. Despite the Auchinleck Chronicler's assertion that he was captured at sea by the Flemings and put to death, there is evidence that he was alive almost six years later and he was acting as an ambassador for his stepson James II as late as 1454.[58]

Notes

1. *SP*, i, 16; Sutherland, *Five Euphemias*, 246–7.
2. *Ibid.*, 127, 135–9.
3. *Ibid.*, 136–40.
4. *SP*, i, 15.
5. *Scotichronicon*, vii, 367.
6. Sutherland, *Five Euphemias*, 150–1.
7. *Ibid.*, 151, 155.
8. *Scotichronicon*, vii, 325; Sutherland, *Five Euphemias* 158.
9. *Scotichronicon*, vii, 447.
10. Grant, 'Triumph of the Stewarts', 149.
11. *Dynasty: The Royal House of Stewart*, ed. Rosalind K. Marshall (National Galleries of Scotland 1990), 16; Boardman, *Early Stewart Kings*, 75, 88.
12. Sutherland, *Five Euphemias*, 165.
13. Boardman, *Early Stewart Kings*, 22.
14. *Scotichronicon* viii, 65.
15. *SP*, i, 18.
16. *Scotichronicon* viii, 3; Boardman, *Early Stewart Kings*, 57.
17. *SP*, i, 17–18.
18. *Scotichronicon*, viii, 3; Nicholson, *Later Middle Ages*, 204.
19. *SP*, i, 18.
20. *Facsimiles of National Manuscripts of Scotland* (Edinburgh 1870), ii, p.xlix.
21. Nicholson, *Later Middle Ages*, 215.
22. See Stuart Harris, *The Place Names of Edinburgh* (Edinburgh 1996), 82, 446; *Book of the Old Edinburgh Club*, xiv, 103, 114–5.
23. *Scotichronicon*, viii, 11; Nicholson, *Later Middle Ages*, 217.
24. *Scotichronicon*, viii, 13.
25. *SP*, i, 17; *APS*, i, 210–11.
26. *Scotichronicon*, viii, 65.
27. Nicholson, *Later Middle Ages*, 219; *Liber Pluscardensis*, ed. Felix J.H. Skene (Edinburgh 1877), i, 341.
28. *Scotichronicon*, viii, 37.
29. Wyntoun, *Chronicle*, vi, 396–7.
30. Boardman, *Early Stewart Kings*, 283.
31. *Scotichronicon*, viii, 65.
32. Fradenburg, *City, Marriage, Tournament*, 322 n.14.
33. *The Kingis Quair*, 83.
34. Fradenburg, *City, Marriage, Tournament*, 323 n.16; *The Kingis Quair*, 86–7.

35. Donaldson, *Scottish Kings*, 67; *SP*, i, 18; Nicholson, *Later Middle Ages*, 259; *Scotichronicon*, viii, 121.
36. *Ibid.*, 305–9.
37. Fradenburg, *City, Marriage, Tournament*, 131, 323 n.16.
38. Donaldson, *Scottish Historical Documents*, 73–4; Nicholson, *Later Middle Ages*, 259–60.
39. Nicholson, *Later Middle Ages*, 259.
40. *Ibid.*, 259–60.
41. *Scotichronicon*, viii, 221.
42. *Ibid.*, McGladdery, *James II*, 8.
43. *Scotichronicon*, viii, 305–9.
44. McGladdery, *James II*, 7.
45. Nicholson, *Later Middle Ages*, 315.
46. *Ibid.*, 317; Fradenburg, *City, Marriage, Tournament*, 134.
47. Nicholson, *Later Middle Ages*, 324; McGladdery, *James II*, 9–10.
48. *Ibid.*, 10–11; Nicholson, *Later Middle Ages*, 326; Fradenburg, *City, Marriage, Tournament*, 80.
49. Nicholson, *Later Middle Ages*, 328–9.
50. McGladdery, *James II*, 17.
51. *SP*, i, 440–1; McGladdery, *James II*, 17.
52. *Ibid.*, 17.
53. *Ibid.*, 18–19.
54. *APS* ii, 54–5; Nicholson, *Later Middle Ages*, 329–30; McGladdery, *James II*, 18–19.
55. Nicholson, *Later Middle Ages*, 34; Macdougall, *James III*, 12–13.
56. *SP*, i, 19, Macdougall, *James III*, 13.
57. *SP*, i, 441.
58. McGladdery, *James II*, 36–7, 123.

MARY OF GUELDRES

Four years after his mother's death, James II married Mary of
Gueldres. It is usually said that Charles VII of France suggested
this match, but it seems much more likely that the original idea and
the initial delicate negotiations were achieved through a network of
female connections. Queen Joan was the first cousin of Isabella of
Portugal, the wife of the wealthy and powerful Philip the Good,
3rd Duke of Burgundy. It seems most unlikely that Joan and Isabella
ever met, but they were almost certainly in touch with each other
by means of envoys and more ordinary messengers. Isabella was a
formidable woman. A leading figure at the Court of her brother,
John I of Portugal, she had married very late by medieval standards.
She had been no less than thirty-two when in 1430 she became
Duke Philip's third wife. In the years that followed, she displayed
outstanding administrative abilities, governing during her husband's
absences, negotiating treaties, directing finances and raising their
children.

Their only surviving son Charles is better known to history as
Charles the Bold. In his early years he had the title of Count of
Charolais, and it was his mother who negotiated not only his
marriage to six-year-old Princess Catherine, daughter of Charles
VII, King of France in 1439, but also the marriages of other
relatives. Philip and Isabella gathered around them at their highly
cultivated Court in Brussels a large extended family that included
nieces and nephews of them both. Mary of Gueldres was Duke
Philip's great-niece. Her father was Arnold, Duke of Gueldres,
which was a fertile province of some 5000 square kilometres in
the East Central Netherlands. Her mother, Catherine of Cleves,
was the niece of Duke Philip.[1]

When Mary of Gueldres was about twelve, Philip and Isabella had
plans to marry her to Charles, Comte de Maine, brother of René of

Anjou, in pursuance of an alliance between Anjou and Burgundy. Mary was brought to Brussels, but her father sent Duchess Isabella a message saying that he was not in a position to provide the required dowry, and so the arrangements collapsed.[2] In spite of her changed future, Mary stayed on at the Burgundian Court, in attendance on Duchess Isabella's young daughter-in-law, Princess Catherine. Her name occurs from time to time in the Duchess's accounts of expenditure: 'For the Count, the Countess [of Charolais] and Mademoiselle Mary of Gueldres . . . fur for their robes', and in 1445 there is mention of Mary's ten attendants, including her carver, Robert de Harpe.[3]

Mary must have lived very much under the influence of Isabella of Portugal, witnessing at first hand how a woman could dominate an important Court, and she would have observed the respect and friendship shared by the Duchess and her husband.[4] Isabella of Portugal was nearly fifty by this time, the early prettiness of her youthful portrait by an unknown artist[5] transformed into the long, shrewd, pleasantly ugly face seen in her likeness by Rogier van der Weyden.[6] It is tempting to speculate whether Mary herself sat for her portrait while she was in Brussels. It seems likely, but unfortunately no painting of her appears to have survived.

Isabella had not, of course, forgotten Mary's potential usefulness as a bride, and there are signs that not long after the death of Queen Joan at Dunbar Castle, soundings were being taken about a possible marriage between Mary and James II. At the end of June 1446, James II's ambassador was in Arnhem, the capital of Gueldres, and on 5 July a Scottish herald and an envoy from Burgundy went together to see 'the Maiden of Gueldres', who was apparently visiting her parents at the time.[7] Any further negotiations that month were delayed when Princess Catherine died in Brussels on 28 July, much regretted by everyone, and her funeral was held in the great Church of St Gudule, now Brussels Cathedral.[8] Catherine's household had always been part of Duchess Isabella's, and so Mary of Gueldres probably stayed on at the Burgundian Court in attendance on the Duchess herself.

The following year, Otto de Puflich, a knight of Gueldres, visited James II in Edinburgh and in July 1447 Duke Arnold summoned his leading subjects to Nimuégan, to discuss his daughter's marriage.

James's principal adviser, Bishop James Kennedy, is known to have been on the Continent at about that time. In 1448, James wrote to Charles VII of France, reminding him of the old alliance between Scotland and France against England and asking him to recommend a queen for Scotland.[9] In reply, Charles VII explained that he had no suitable close relative himself, but advised James to approach the Burgundian Court. No doubt he knew as well as Isabella of Portugal and indeed James II himself did that Mary of Gueldres was already the chosen bride.[10]

The specific details of the marriage contract still had to be agreed, and in late February 1449 a magnificent tournament was held at Stirling, where James Douglas jousted with Jacques de Lalain, eldest son of an influential Burgundian nobleman. Tournaments were still crucial to diplomatic negotiations, and no doubt business was done.[11] At the end of March, Mary's father went to Brussels and the marriage contract was sealed there on 1 April 1449. Scotland, Burgundy and Gueldres would in future assist each other against all enemies and promote each other's interests. Scotland would receive important trading privileges and Duke Philip would provide his great niece's dowry of 60,000 crowns (£30,000 Scots). In return, James would settle on his bride the enormous jointure of 10,000 gold crowns (£5,000 Scots) a year, from the lands of Strathearn and Atholl and the lordship of Methven. Mary would have the palace of Linlithgow as her residence should she be widowed.[12]

On 12 April 1449, Duke Philip required a subsidy of 400 livres to be paid by his town of Courtrai towards the marriage of the King of Scots to 'our great niece of Gueldres', and preparations began in earnest. As was her custom, Isabella of Portugal took charge of arrangements for the bride's trousseau, bearing all the costs of it, while the Duke would pay for Mary's journey to Scotland. At the beginning of June 1449 those who were to escort the bride began to assemble at Bruges, a brilliant tournament was held there as part of the celebrations, and the Burgundian household accounts suddenly begin to call Mary 'the Queen of Scotland'.

Mary would be accompanied on the voyage by two of Isabella's own ladies: an illegitimate sister of the Duke of Burgundy who was married to Anthoine de Rochebaron, and Isabelle, daughter of the Lord of Lalain and sister of Jacques, the famous jouster.

Henry Junem, Keeper of Mary's Wardrobe, Herman, Master of her Stable, and Henry Vandervelde, her former tutor, were all part of her retinue. Henric, Lord of Veere, Admiral of Holland, would provide a naval escort, with a guard of 300 men and a convoy of twelve other ships. Henric's son Jean was married to James II's sister, Princess Mary, and she too would sail with them. Great trouble had been taken in fitting out the galley in which the bride would travel, and Jean Codye was paid 24 francs 12 sols for vermilion silk for her chamber on board the vessel.[13]

The Scottish Chancellor, Sir William Crichton, and John Ralston, Bishop of Dunkeld, arrived from Scotland to 'bring home' the bride and they all set sail from Sluys at about four in the morning of 9 June 1449, having had to spend several days on the coast waiting for a favourable wind. Matthieu d'Escouchy, the Duke of Burgundy's Castellan de Peronne, was apparently in Mary's retinue, and his lively and informative chronicle gives us not only an account of the journey but the first detailed description we have of a Scottish royal wedding.[14] According to him, when Mary of Gueldres embarked on her galley, there was great weeping and lamentation, especially by Mary herself, as she said goodbye to the Duke, the Count of Charolais and the other lords and ladies who had come to see her off. The crossing took a week, and they finally dropped anchor in the estuary of the Firth of Forth, beside the Isle of May, where there was a hermitage and a chapel dedicated to St Adrian. Mary went ashore in a small boat to pray in the chapel. Returning to her galley, she sailed into Leith on 18 June.

While Mary rested in the Convent of St Anthony, people flocked from Edinburgh to see her. The leading noblemen were presented to her, and then she mounted her horse and rode in procession behind the Lord of Veere and his men to Holyrood Abbey, where she was to stay in the guest house. According to d'Escouchy, as many as ten thousand people came out to greet her, some playing musical instruments. The King himself came to see her, arriving just before midnight. She knelt before him, he raised her gently to her feet, greeted her two principal ladies with a kiss, and then spent three hours with her. Next day, all the leading lords and ladies came to see her, and James sent her a gift of horses.[15]

On 24 June 1449, James was in Stirling, ratifying his marriage contract under the Great Seal of Scotland and giving his final consent to a number of conditions. He renounced any right his future sons might have to the duchy of Gueldres and, in conventional manner, promised to return his bride's dowry should she die childless within a year of the marriage being consummated.[16] The wedding took place in Holyrood Abbey on 3 July. Mary was escorted there by the Lord of Veere, Anthoine de Rochebaron, her entire retinue and all the Scottish noblewomen. We do not have any description of what she wore, but it would have been a sumptuous outfit. James rode up in a great robe trimmed with white cloth, a sword at his side. He was nineteen years old, his features marked by a dramatic birthmark which gave him the nickname, 'James of the Fiery Face'.

At the church door, James made his bride the obligatory gift of her jointure lands before marrying her. Raising the jointure would be a problem, but thoughts of that were set aside as the King took Mary's hand and led her inside, to kneel before the high altar for their nuptial Mass. When the service was over, Mary was taken into a side chapel and dressed in violet robes trimmed with ermine for her coronation, her long hair left hanging loose. The robes were probably the rich violet crimson mantle and dress made for her at the Burgundian Court as the principal items in her trousseau.[17] James also wore ermine-trimmed violet. Afterwards, there was a lavish banquet, the King sitting at one end of the table, the Queen at the other. A painted and stuffed boar's head was brought in on a great plate, around which were arranged thirty-two banners with the arms of the King and the Scottish Lords. An attendant set fire to the stuffing, causing 'great joy' throughout the room. Even the sophisticated Burgundians were charmed with this novelty.

A nef (model ship) was then placed before the King and Queen, its superstructure, masts and rigging made of finely wrought silver. When everyone had admired that, William Sinclair, Earl of Orkney, and four knights led in a procession of thirty to fifty people carrying the main courses. The Chancellor and the other great lords served the Queen, kneeling as they did so. The Scottish ladies sat at the second table with the Burgundian ladies, opposite the Lords of Veere and Berzé. The Archbishop of St Andrews, the bishops and various other churchmen were at the third table, drinking enthusiastically from a large wooden bowl that was passed round and never seemed to run dry. The banquet lasted for four or five hours. The Burgundians were disappointed when there was no dancing afterwards, and no supper that day, but the celebrations went on for four or five more days. About a week after the wedding, the Lord of Veere and most of the other visitors prepared to leave for home. The King gave them expensive presents before they left, and the Queen wept.[18]

Although James II was now nineteen, he was still officially under the control of the Livingston family. His marriage, however, seems to have brought him the assurance to act for himself. Some have inferred that Mary of Gueldres encouraged him to turn against the Livingstons. We do not know whether this was really so, but it certainly seems likely that his strengthening bonds with Burgundy and France brought him a new confidence. He was already on good terms with the French king because their mutual antipathy towards England bound them together in spite of the fact that James's sister was unhappily married to Charles's son the Dauphin. No doubt with encouragement from Mary of Gueldres and from Duchess Isabella, the exchange of letters between James and Charles grew particularly cordial.

Buoyed up by his continental relatives by marriage, James turned against the Livingstons. He had probably never forgotten that Sir Alexander Livingston the Justiciar was the man who had humiliated his mother, Queen Joan, by keeping her prisoner in 1439, and he also needed Livingston lands if he was ever going to be able to provide the jointure he had promised his wife. The matter was pressing, for Duke Philip was paying Mary's huge dowry in instalments, and if satisfactory arrangements for the jointure were not in place, he might well delay sending the rest of the money. At the end of the summer, James acted. On 23 September, Sir Alexander Livingston, his son James, Keeper of Stirling Castle, his brother Alexander, Captain of Methven, Robert Livingston the Comptroller and two leading Livingston supporters were arrested. They were tried in Edinburgh the following January, presumably for treason, and were forfeited. The Captain of Methven and Robert were beheaded. The day after their execution, a charter was issued finalising Mary's jointure and noting that parliament had agreed to the grants to the Queen. She received not only the earldoms of Atholl and Strathearn, but various other lordships and revenues including the great customs of Linlithgow, formerly in the possession of Robert Livingston, and Methven Castle, although Menteith was later substituted for Methven.[19]

We know that Mary of Gueldres was present when parliament met that January, for she interceded on behalf of the bishops, when they complained that on their deaths their estates would be taken by the crown, preventing them from bequeathing anything to relatives and friends. Their executors would not even be able to settle their debts. They knelt in full parliament and spoke of their grievances, and when they had done, the Queen added her own pleas on their behalf. The King then ceremoniously granted their requests. James was demonstrating that he was most certainly ruling for himself, and Mary was already undertaking the traditional role of a consort. Coming from a much more sophisticated court, very wealthy and with the knowledge that the French King and the Duke and Duchess of Burgundy were personal and supportive friends, Mary was a poised and assured young woman. Moreover, she was now pregnant.

There was one sinister shadow over these otherwise highly satisfactory events. Parliament had to order measures to be taken against 'strangers' who smuggled poison into the realm. Details have not survived, but it was rumoured that one of the Queen's foreign servants had been bribed to assassinate her.[20] Possibly this alarming episode led to Mary's Burgundian attendants being sent home. Isabelle de Lalain set sail for the Continent soon afterwards, accompanied by Mary's confessor, Gerard Boot. Captured by English pirates, they were eventually set free after vigorous representations by Isabella of Portugal.[21]

No doubt pleased by Mary's pregnancy, the Duke of Burgundy paid a further 20,000 crowns of her dowry, probably to Bishop Ralston who was in Bruges for the annual Procession of the Holy Blood.[22] Mary's child was due in mid-August, but sadly the baby was born at Stirling on 19 May, three months early, and lived for only six hours. There is no record of whether she had given birth to a son or a daughter. Charles VII was among those who sent her consolatory messages, and on 1 July 1450 she replied from Edinburgh, telling him that she was now in good health and hoping that the Holy Trinity would keep him and his realm in happiness and prosperity.[23] This letter, in Latin, was written out for her by a scribe, but she signed it herself. By Christmas she was pregnant again.

The April parliament of 1451 saw the Queen interceding once more, this time on behalf of William, 8th Earl of Douglas. While he was in Rome for the papal jubilee, James II seized various Douglas lands and transmitted to Mary the earldom of Wigtown and lordship of Galloway as yet another part of her jointure. When he heard what was happening, the Earl hastily returned from Rome. Appearing in parliament, he was apparently given a reasonably cordial welcome by the King, 'at the request of the Queen and the Three Estates'. A new charter confirming Mary's existing properties and adding further grants of land and revenues was issued on 1 July.[24] The King's enmity towards Douglas continued, however, and when he stabbed the Earl during a quarrel on 20 February 1452, his courtiers rushed in and made sure that their hated rival was fatally wounded.[25]

By that time the King had his son and heir. In July 1451, a matter of weeks after she had interceded for Douglas, Mary had gone into labour. No doubt everyone was nervous after her previous experience, and the Exchequer accounts include the payment of six shillings to William Craig, who brought the shirt of St Margaret from Dunfermline to the Queen during her confinement. This relic was believed to be a help to women in childbirth, and with or without its assistance the future James III was born safely.[26] Mary went on to have three more sons, Alexander, David, who died when he was about three, and John, as well as two daughters, Mary and Margaret.[27]

Meanwhile, James continued to augment her jointure with grants of land,[28] and in May 1454 the Queen was personally present to watch her husband besiege Blackness Castle which had been seized by Sir James Crichton. Soon afterwards, the castle was passed to her.[29] She was a very wealthy woman now. The Exchequer rolls afford us a few glimpses of her expenditure. We know, for instance, that on one occasion in 1451, salmon costing £240 was bought for her use, and there were other purchases, of wine and of fur for her clothes. We know, too, that she spent considerable sums of money on charity. She was devout, and both she and Bishop Kennedy were anxious to extend the work of the Franciscan friars in Scotland, establishing a friary for them in Edinburgh.[30] Moreover, she had a hospital built just outside Edinburgh on the north side, where poor and needy people could find shelter.[31]

In the summer of 1460, James II decided to besiege Roxburgh Castle, which had been taken by the English. He had a passion for artillery, and had been assembling an impressive collection of big guns. He had been particularly pleased when the Duke of Burgundy sent him gifts of cannon, one of which was almost certainly the famous Mons Meg, still to be seen on the ramparts of Edinburgh Castle. This gun had been made for Duke Philip in 1449 by Jean Cambier at Mons, and it was sent to Scotland in May 1457 with an escort of fifty men-at-arms. By laying siege to Roxburgh, James not only hoped to win back his important fortress just north of the River Tweed, but looked forward to the opportunity of using some of his new weaponry.

His enthusiasm had disastrous consequences. On 3 August 1460 he was standing close to a cannon firing a salute, probably to greet the Earl of Huntly who had just arrived with his men, when the gun exploded and his femur was shattered by a fragment of flying metal. According to tradition, he was carried to the nearby Friary of St Peter, where he received the last rites. He died soon afterwards, presumably from loss of blood and shock. He was twenty-eight years old.[32] Some later accounts claimed that the fatal salute had been fired in honour of the Queen, who had newly arrived at the siege, but it seems more likely that she was in Edinburgh with her children when the tragic news came, for she had recently given birth to her second daughter, Margaret.

After the death of the King, the Scots decided to continue with the siege, and Mary brought her nine-year-old son James to the Scottish camp. They seem to have reached Roxburgh on 8 August, the day that the castle was captured. The new King James III was crowned in an impressive ceremony at the Abbey of Kelso on 10 August 1460, watched by his mother.[33] That autumn, Mary made plans to found a Collegiate Church of the Holy Trinity beside her hospital to the north of Edinburgh. It was to be a perpetual memorial to 'the late most illustrious prince, James, King of Scots, our most tender husband', and she intended being buried there herself. She was at pains to lay down all the rules and regulations for services and for the behaviour of the clerics, specifying, for instance, that any priest who was absent for fifteen days without permission or any who kept 'a concubine or chamberwoman' would be dismissed after three warnings.[34]

Given official custody of the young King, Mary was advised by a council of regency led by Bishop Kennedy, Bishop Durisdeer of Glasgow and the Earls of Angus, Huntly, Argyll and Orkney. According to the Auchinleck chronicler, 'The lords said that there were little good worth both spiritual and temporal that gave the keeping of the kingdom to a woman',[35] but in the months that followed, Mary amply demonstrated energy, administrative skills and a sense of duty. She had no doubt learned much in the household of Isabella of Portugal. James Lindsay of Covington, Andrew Stewart, Lord Avandale and the others whom she appointed to important public offices were of such high calibre that they would remain in their places for much of her son's reign too, giving a valuable stability to government.[36]

Bishop Kennedy, who would otherwise have expected to exert a significant influence, was on the Continent when James II was killed and, when he did come back, he and Mary had a series of disagreements. As he himself later told Charles VII, he found on his return to Scotland 'a great division in the country, caused by the Queen, whom God pardon, from which there resulted a great dissension between the said Queen and me'.[37] Their differences were mainly over foreign affairs, for the Queen intended to continue her husband's policy of playing off Yorkists and Lancastrians in the English Wars of the Roses to Scotland's advantage, whereas the Bishop favoured an alliance with the Lancastrians. Led by Henry VI, they had French support.

Mary's foreign policy was nonetheless shrewd. Although Duke Philip of Burgundy was now on bad terms with the French, Mary was willing to see Henry VI's Queen, Margaret of Anjou, when she arrived in Scotland in the early winter of 1460 seeking military assistance. They met at Lincluden Collegiate Church and their discussions, which apparently lasted for at least ten days in December, included the suggestion that Edward, Prince of Wales, should marry the Scottish Queen's elder daughter, Princess Mary. Mary of Gueldres must have been aware that the Yorkists were faltering and indeed, at the end of that month, Richard, Duke of York, was defeated and killed at Wakefield. Margaret of Anjou hurried south to win a further battle at St Albans and it must have seemed that Mary had been right in deciding to support Margaret and the Lancastrians.[38]

On 4 March 1461, however, the Duke of York's son proclaimed himself King Edward IV and won an important victory at Towton. Margaret of Anjou fled to Scotland, accompanied by her deposed husband, Henry VI, their son Prince Edward and the Dukes of Exeter and Somerset. Hoping for military assistance, she surrendered Berwick-upon-Tweed to the Scots and promised to cede Carlisle to them. However, Mary of Gueldres was too astute to support a failing cause. She allowed the fugitives to stay in Scotland for a year, but she sent an embassy to Edward IV to discuss the possibility of a truce. Duke Philip, who had discouraged her dealings with the Lancastrians, in the winter of 1460–1 sent the Sieur de la Gruythuse to her, urging her to ally Scotland with the Yorkists instead.

By March 1462 Mary had relieved herself of the embarrassing presence of the Lancastrian royal family by paying Margaret substantial sums on condition that they left the country.[39] A month later, Mary was having discussions with the Yorkist Earl of Warwick at Dumfries. She even held out the prospect of a marriage between herself and Edward IV. Talks continued that summer but, although there had been a brief reconciliation between Mary and Bishop Kennedy when she had seemed to be favouring the Lancastrian cause, he was now leading a powerful opposition of 'old lords' against the Queen and her supporters, 'the young lords'. The situation was complicated still further when Margaret of Anjou arrived back in Scotland in October 1462, a fugitive once more.[40]

It was at this time that Mary bought land at Ravenscraig, just outside Dysart, in Fife, with the intention of building a secure castle specifically designed for the use of artillery. She was already engaged in building work elsewhere, for the records show that she employed the royal carpenter for eighty days at Falkland Palace, making a new chamber, fireplace and stable for her. The castle at Ravenscraig, however, had a far less domestic purpose. Standing on the River Forth, across from Edinburgh, it could be easily reached by boat, and might well provide a refuge in troubled times. In 1462–3 Mary paid £600 to David Boys, the royal master of works, for building work done there.[41]

Margaret of Anjou was determined to continue her struggle against the Yorkists, and in July 1463 Mary of Gueldres was involved in a military campaign aimed at capturing Norham Castle. She may well have been reluctant, and had possibly been compelled to agree to the operation by Bishop Kennedy, who was becoming increasingly powerful. The attack on Norham was a complete failure, Margaret of Anjou departed for Burgundy, where she hoped to gain support from Duke Philip,[42] and that autumn Queen Mary fell seriously ill. She died some months later, at the age of thirty.[43] It is usually said that her death took place in Edinburgh on 1 December 1463, but her funeral was not held until June 1464, in Brechin Cathedral. The explanation traditionally given for this choice is that her Holy Trinity College Church was not yet ready, and so she was temporarily buried at Brechin before being moved to Edinburgh. However, it would surely have been much more convenient to bury her in Holyrood Abbey if a temporary resting place was required, so it may be that she had died somewhere in Angus, or perhaps Perthshire.

Her last resting place became the subject of much debate when the Holy Trinity Church was demolished in 1848 to make way for the railway, only the apse being moved to a new site. A female skeleton was found in a coffin in the chancel and examined by two eminent Edinburgh doctors, James Young Simpson and John Goodsir. They concluded that the skeleton belonged to a frail woman with a very small cerebellar space, making her a person of 'feeble or deficient intellect'. Various nineteenth-century male historians declared enthusiastically that this proved that the skeleton was Queen Mary's, for she had been promiscuous, having had affairs with the Lancastrian Duke of Somerset and Adam Hepburn, son of Patrick, Lord Hailes.[44]

In fact, the other anatomical details make it clear that the unfortunate invalid whose remains were examined could neither have borne healthy children nor lived the active life of Mary of

Gueldres. Moreover, James III's recent biographer has shown that there is no truth in the charges of promiscuity, which probably originated in part from friends of Bishop Kennedy trying to blacken Mary's reputation and in part from a confusion with Joan Beaufort's connection with the Hepburns in the last months of her life.[45] Far from being of feeble intellect, Mary of Gueldres was a dignified consort and a strong and effective ruler whose death was a blow to Scotland as well as a personal tragedy for her eldest son.

Notes

1. Sommé, *Isabelle de Portugal*, 479–86; Emmanuel Bourassin, *Philippe le Bon, le grand lion des Flandres* (Paris 1998).
2. Sommé, *Isabelle de Portugal*, 72.
3. Lille, Archives départementales du Nord, B1978, f.330, 334; B3410/115835; B1969, f338; B3415/116429; Sommé, *Isabelle de Portugal*, 71, 74, 342.
4. *Ibid.*, 480–3.
5. Now in the Louvre. Illustrated in Georges-Henri Dumont, *Marie de Bourgogne* (Brussels 1982), between pp. 172–3.
6. In the J. Paul Getty Museum, Los Angeles. Illustrated on cover of Sommé, *Isabelle de Portugal*.
7. McGladdery, *James II*, 44.
8. *Chronique d'Escouchy*, 111.
9. Stevenson, *Letters and Papers*, i, 303–4.
10. McGladdery, *James II*, 86–7; Dunlop, *Kennedy*, 95–6.
11. *Chronique d'Escouchy*, 148–53; McGladdery, *James II*, 42.
12. Lille, Archives du Nord, B308, 427; McGladdery, 44–5; Dunlop, *Kennedy*, 100; Macdougall, *James III*, 14.
13. Chronique d'Escouchy, i, 176 and n.4; Dunlop, *Kennedy*, 100; McGladdery, *James II*, 45; *ER*, v, pp. lxxvii, 386–7 and n.4; Margaret Scott, 'A Burgundian Visit to Scotland in 1449', in *Costume* xxi (London 1987), 16–17.
14. *Chronique d'Escouchy*, i, pp. iii–xxv.
15. *Ibid.*, 179–80.
16. McGladdery, *James II*, 46; Dunlop, *Kennedy*, 101.
17. Lille, Archives du Nord, B2004, f 335.
18. *Chronique d'Escouchy*, i, 179–83.
19. Macdougall, *James III*, 14–15; Nicholson, *Later Middle Ages*, 351; McGladdery, *James II*, 49–51.
20. Dunlop, *Kennedy*, 112–16; McGladdery, *James II*, 54.

21. Dunlop, *Kennedy*, 117; Sommé, *Isabelle de Portugal*, 77.
22. Dunlop, *Kennedy*, 110.
23. *Ibid.*, 116; Stevenson, *Letters and Papers*, i, 303.
24. Nicholson, *Later Middle Ages*, 356.
25. *SP*, iii, 178; McGladdery, *James II*, 69.
26. *ER*, v, 447, 512; *Treasurer's Accounts*, i, p.lxxiii n.; McGladdery, *James II*, 76; W. Angus, 'The date of the birth of James III', in *SHR* xxx (Edinburgh 1951) 199–202; A. I. Dunlop, notes in *Ibid.* xxix (1950), 212–3; xxx (1951), 202–4.
27. *SP*, i, 20.
28. McGladdery, *James II*, 65, 95.
29. Dunlop, *Kennedy*, 150, 186, n.4.
30. Nicholson, *Later Middle Ages*, 386.
31. Marwick, *Holy Trinity*, 35–6; Tolley, 'Hugo van der Goes's altarpiece', 215–22.
32. McGladdery, *James II*, 111; Macdougall, *James III*, 46–7.
33. McGladdery, *James II*, 112; *Treasurer's Accounts*, i, p.xxxvii; Macdougall, *James III*, 51.
34. Marwick, *Holy Trinity*, pp. xv–xvi, 5–36.
35. *The Auchinleck Chronicle*, ed. T. Thomson (Edinburgh 1877), 22; McGladdery, *James II*, 170.
36. Macdougall, *James III*, 52–4; McGladdery, *James II*, 107–8.
37. Macdougall, *James III*, 52–3.
38. *Ibid.*, 57–8, McGladdery, *James II*, 170.
39. *Ibid.*, 58–9; Nicholson, *Later Middle Ages*, 403.
40. *Ibid.*, 404.
41. *ER*, vii, 75, 78–9, 106.
42. Macdougall, *James III*, 60–1; Nicholson, *Later Middle Ages*, 399.
43. Macdougall, *James III*, 62; *SP*, i, 20; J.H. Baxter, 'The Marriage of James II', in *SHR*, xxv (1928), 72.
44. David Laing, 'Remarks on the Character of Mary of Gueldres', in *Proceedings of the Society of Antiquaries of Scotland* iv, 2 (1860–2), 572; D. Wilson, 'Notes of the Search for the Tomb of the Royal Foundress of the Collegiate Church of the Holy Trinity at Edinburgh', in *Ibid.*, 554–77.
45. Audrey Beth Fitch, 'Power through Purity: The Virgin Martyrs and Women's Salvation in Pre-Reformation Scotland', in *Women in Scotland*, 3, 23; Macdougall, *James III*, 54–7.

CHAPTER SIX

MARGARET OF DENMARK

James III was only twelve years old when his mother died. He had been devoted to her and he seems to have inherited from her his artistic sensibilities and his love of music. Moreover, her Burgundian connections as well as both his parents' friendship with Charles VII of France were to play an important part in the choice of his marriage partner, although he did not marry either a Frenchwoman or a Burgundian. Instead, his eventual bride was Princess Margaret of Denmark. The reasons for this choice had their origins a hundred years earlier. The invading Norse had long controlled the Western Isles, but in 1263 the Scots had won a triumphant victory over the Norwegian fleet at the Battle of Largs, and in the subsequent Treaty of Perth King Magnus IV of Norway ceded the Hebrides and the Isle of Man to the Scots, in return for an annual payment of 100 merks sterling and the lump sum of 4000 merks.[1] Time passed, the Scots stopped paying the annuity, and in the mid-fifteenth century the King of Denmark and Norway decided to press for the arrears.

Christian I, founder of the Oldenborg dynasty, was ebullient, energetic and determined to extend his territories. He engaged in a complicated series of financial transactions to fund this ambition and when, in 1456, he made an alliance with Charles VII of France, he asked him for assistance in extracting not only the annuity of 100 merks from Scotland but all the arrears of payment. Charles convened a meeting of the Scottish and Danish ambassadors at Bruges in 1460, soon after the death of James II, and apparently suggested that the problem could be solved by a marriage alliance. Christian and his wife Dorothea had a four-year-old daughter, Margaret. She could marry nine-year-old James III, and the question of the 100 merk annuity could be addressed in the discussions about dowry and jointure.

Nothing came of the idea at that time, probably because the Scots were insisting that all payments owed by them must be written off and that the bride's dowry should include Orkney and Shetland. Bishop Kennedy then began negotiations for an English bride for James, but there was no agreement and the Scots eventually turned their thoughts to Denmark once more. On 12 January 1468, representatives of the Scottish parliament meeting at Stirling decided to send an ambassador to Christian to raise both the question of the Norwegian payments and the marriage of James III.[2] Eight years had passed since the previous negotiations and they were no doubt fully aware that Christian's situation had changed and he was much more likely to be amenable.

In 1460 he had been at the peak of his power, ruling over Sweden as well as Norway and Denmark. Now he was facing a serious rebellion in Sweden, internal opposition in Denmark, and a severe financial crisis. His growing debts had made him dependent on the merchants of the Hanseatic League. In an attempt to strengthen his position, he had made an alliance with Burgundy, but this came under threat when the Burgundians reached an agreement with England. The English were the enemies of the Hanse. Although he was in no position to offend the Hanse, Christian was anxious to protect his accord with Burgundy. Everyone knew that, ever since the marriage of Mary of Gueldres to James II, the Scots and the Burgundians had enjoyed close and cordial relations, and so Christian calculated that the best way for him to shore up his alliance with Burgundy was to make an agreement with the Scots.[3] At eleven years old, his daughter Margaret was of a suitable age to be married.

Christian and Dorothea had three sons, but Margaret was their only daughter. They had named her after Queen Margaret I, who had ruled Denmark in her own right in the early fifteenth century. We do not have details of the Princess's upbringing, but she probably enjoyed a close relationship with her mother. Dorothea had previously been married to Christian's predecessor, but she had been widowed early on and was still only eighteen when she married Christian. A capable young woman, she helped him with his chaotic finances, paid his debts, looked after her own estates and would later be instrumental in founding the University of Copenhagen.[4] The

Scottish embassy to Denmark set out in the summer of 1468. Each of the Three Estates had granted £3000 towards the cost of the expedition. There were to be no fewer than eight ambassadors, led by Lord Chancellor Avandale and Thomas Boyd, Earl of Arran, the husband of the King's sister, Princess Mary.[5]

The terms of the contract they negotiated were to be of considerable significance for Scotland. King Christian agreed to provide Margaret with a dowry of 60,000 florins of the Rhine, agreeing that because he could not afford to pay the entire sum at once, he would hand over only 10,000 florins, pledging his lands and rights in Orkney as security for the other 50,000 florins. In fact, when the time came to pay the first instalment, he could raise only 2000 florins and so in 1469 he was forced to pledge his property in Shetland for the remaining 8000. Neither Christian nor his successors ever did manage to pay off the dowry, and so Orkney and Shetland became part of the kingdom of the Scots.[6] In return, it was agreed that James III would settle on his wife Linlithgow Palace, Doune Castle and one third of his royal revenues. This sum was the highest amount possible allowed under an ordinance made by the Scottish Parliament in 1466.[7] The marriage treaty was signed on 8 September 1468.[8]

It was too late in the year for Margaret to make the voyage to Scotland but, the following spring, James III's brother-in-law, the Earl of Arran, set out to bring her to Leith. His return was somewhat marred by the fact that when he arrived in Scotland he was given a message from his wife, warning him that his enemies had turned the King against him, and he immediately fled back to Denmark with her. However disconcerted Margaret may have been by the abrupt departure of her principal escort and her future sister-in-law, she had to continue with her programme and she presumably met James III for the first time shortly before her marriage in the Abbey of Holyrood on either 10 or 13 July 1469.[9]

A year after their marriage, James took Margaret on a progress to the north of Scotland. In July and August 1470, he and Margaret rode to Aberdeen, Fyvie, Banff and Inverness, before settling into the normal peripatetic routine of the Scottish Court, moving between Holyroodhouse, Linlithgow, Stirling and Falkland.[10] Since the death of Bishop Kennedy in 1465, James had largely been in the hands of the Boyd family but he was eighteen years old now and, like his father, he took the opportunity of his marriage to cast aside his guardians and rule for himself. It was not until 17 March 1473 that Margaret of Denmark gave birth to her first child, a son, whom they named James. Three years after that the Queen had a second son, Alexander, and three years after that their third son, John, was born.[11]

Margaret of Denmark is the earliest Queen of Scots whose portrait has survived. Her husband completed his mother's Church of the Holy Trinity in Edinburgh, and a special altarpiece was commissioned for it, probably by Edward Bonkil, appointed first provost of the church by Mary of Gueldres. Painted by the celebrated Flemish artist, Hugo van der Goes, the altarpiece had two wings. Part of The Royal Collection, they may be seen in the National Gallery of Scotland, Edinburgh. One wing shows Margaret of Denmark kneeling at a prie-dieu, a man in armour, believed to represent St George, standing protectively behind her. The matching panel shows James III kneeling in prayer with a boy, probably their eldest son, Prince James, watched over by St Andrew. On the back of the Queen's panel is a painting of Provost Bonkil kneeling in front of an angel who is playing a gilded organ. It has sometimes been suggested that the angel is a likeness of Mary of Gueldres, but this is a matter for speculation. On the reverse of the King's panel is a painting of the Holy Trinity. There was probably a large central panel, now lost.

So is the representation of Margaret of Denmark a true portrait? She has the conventional, meek expression and the customary oval face of a fifteenth-century lady, with arched eyebrows, rather small, uplifted eyes, long nose, neat mouth and slight double chin. As to her colouring, her hair is completely hidden by her headdress, but her eyebrows are of a lighter brown than those of the King and she may have shared the reddish hair given to the boy on James's panel. Neither James III nor Margaret went to Ghent, where van der Goes had his studio, and the assumption is that their pictures were painted from drawings done in Scotland. The head of James closely resembles the image of him on his coinage, and an infra-red examination of the altarpiece shows that his features were altered by the artist, as if to make them more accurate. We may therefore hope that Margaret's head also bore a recognisable likeness to the sitter. It was originally a very sensitive portrait, but unfortunately it became rubbed with the passage of time and at some stage has undergone a clumsy alteration.

There has also been some deterioration of the Queen's costume. She is seen in royal robes. Her mantle and skirt appear very dark in colour, almost black, but it is probable that the colour of the pigment has changed with the passage of time. Art historians have surmised that the skirt and the ermine-trimmed mantle were originally royal blue or azure blue, although it must be said that royal robes were usually described as being crimson violet. With her skirt, Margaret wears an ermine-trimmed jacket of tawny and gold brocade, the sleeves very tight-fitting, with deep, folded-over cuffs which look as though they may be made of fur. Her elaborate headdress consists of a wide, crown-like band set with jewels, on top of an intricate hairnet sewn with clusters of pearls and pendant pearls. A gold band can be glimpsed beneath. Round her neck is a gold collar set with diamonds and pearls, from which is suspended a heavy diamond pendant with a pendant pearl. From her shoulders and stretching in a long tab down the front opening of her jacket is a heavy band of gold set with large, rectangular rubies and diamonds, separated by pairs of pearls.[12]

Although the accuracy of the portrait is in some doubt, we know from the Lord Treasurer's accounts that the splendour of the Queen's costume was entirely correct.[13] The jointure of Mary of Gueldres had provided her husband with endless financial problems, but there were no such difficulties for Margaret of Denmark. Her revenues were collected each year by her husband's officials, and the Lord Treasurer paid her expenses. Because his accounts have been preserved, we have for the first time a glimpse of the lifestyle of a Scottish queen consort, and it so it is worth examining the entries in some detail. The Treasurer's accounts for 1473–4 show Margaret spending the enormous sum of £757:9:10, mainly on clothes, and during that period hardly a month went by without new garments being made for her. Indeed, she spent even more on clothes than her notoriously lavish husband did.

Whether or not she introduced Burgundian styles into Scotland, it is evident that Margaret was dressed in the height of fashion.

High-born ladies of the time wore long dresses called kirtles, beneath gowns, which were garments resembling indoor coats. Margaret does not wear a gown in the Trinity Altarpiece panel, for she is in ceremonial costume with a mantle or cloak instead. However, we know that during the period 1473-4 she had at least fifteen gowns. Six of them were black, two were purple and two were crimson, all regal colours. Black is often considered to have been for mourning, but it was also highly fashionable. Indeed, throughout the fifteenth and sixteenth centuries, black and white were both particularly associated with royalty. Margaret also had gowns in tawny, brown and blue, and they were made up in various materials. Five of the gowns were velvet, five were damask, two were satin and one was made of silk.

Each of the gowns took from three to five ells of fabric, a Scottish ell being approximately 36 inches. The gowns were variously lined with cloth, fur, velvet, buckram and silk, and we know a little about the trimmings. In August 1473 Margaret's new black riding gown had a velvet collar and trimmings to the sleeves. She wore it when she and James went on a pilgrimage to Whithorn after the birth of their first son. The following month, a crimson satin gown made for her was trimmed with no fewer than forty grey squirrel skins, and throughout 1474 large quantities of grey squirrel fur were being purchased to line her gowns and cloaks and make collars for her. Five new cloaks were made for her, all black, two of them lined with damask and two with the grey fur.

We have fewer details of her kirtles, but they were more voluminous and usually took six or seven ells of material. At least a dozen were made for her during the months under consideration, one black, another in crimson, one in green and one in blue. The other colours are unspecified, but the kirtles were made up in satin, damask, velvet and silk, and were usually lined with black cloth although sometimes satin was used instead. Some of her kirtles had separate satin stomachers, the long, pointed front piece of the bodice, and at least one of these was lined with ermine. On one occasion the Queen personally purchased ermine skins.

Court headdresses were elaborate, as the Trinity Panel shows. Margaret had 'turatis', presumably the sort of high, pointed headdresses often seen in illustrations of medieval ladies, and the crimson satin for one of her kirtles was also used to cover what were termed her 'dress bonnets'. In August 1473 she bought gloves from a skinner in Stirling, and among her later belongings were a large ostrich feather, which may have been for a headdress, and 'a poke of lavender'.[14] Queen Margaret's shoes were made by Hude, the royal shoemaker, and some of them apparently had cork heels. With her shoes the Queen wore black hose, and there are also purchases of white foot socks, perhaps to be worn when she went out riding.

The most impressive garments made for her at this period were the outfits probably connected with the parliament held in May 1474. Will of Rynd supplied more than seven ells of red crimson satin for her long gown, at a cost of £31:10/-, and Tom of Stanley provided a further ten ells for the same garment, charging £40. Fifteen ells of damask for a long gown for the Queen were bought from Isabel Williamson for £28:10/-. These ceremonial gowns would have had lengthy trains, hence the need for twice the normal amount of material, and they would have been worn with some of Margaret's splendid jewels.

A surviving inventory of items in her possession at Stirling at the end of her life gives us the first list of jewels belonging to a Queen of Scots.[15] Beginning with a belt of crimson ornamented with gold and braid, the inventory itemises four other gold belts before moving on to even more costly adornments. One great gold chain had sixty-one links and another had fifty-eight. A collar of chalcedony had a great pendant in the form of a filigree pomander, a second collar was made of gold enamelled roses and a third was engraved, set with sixteen rubies as well as diamonds and double pearls, and had as its main feature eight white swans, presumably enamelled.

Two great 'edges' were perhaps like the broad gold band to be seen round the Queen's shoulders in the Trinity Panel. One of the gold edges had four great pointed diamonds and twenty-eight pearls, while the other had eight rubies and thirty-six great pearls. Margaret had strings of great pearls, too, one consisting of fifty-one pearls. It is tempting to suppose that the heart of gold with a great pearl hanging from it may have been a marriage gift from the King, and another very personal jewel was the small chain which had a pendant in the shape of the letter M, set with great diamonds and a great pearl. There was a jewelled hairnet 'overset with great pearls set in fours and fours'. This may have been similar to the one we see in the Trinity Panel, where the pearls are in clusters of three. Margaret also had brooches, other pendants, including no fewer than twenty gold pendants set with rubies, and fifteen rings, set with diamonds, rubies, sapphires and turquoises, one of them 'a ring with a face', presumably a cameo, and one of them hinged, so that the toadstone with which it was set could be lifted up to reveal a little compartment underneath.

Some items had a prophylactic purpose. As well as various gold rosaries, there were a serpent's tongue and a unicorn horn set in gold. These feature frequently in fourteenth- and fifteenth-century inventories. Pilgrims to Malta visiting the reputed scene of St Paul's shipwreck picked up fossils thought to be the petrified tongues of vipers and valued as amulets. Grey or yellowish in colour and shaped like tongues, they were regarded as a sure means of detecting poison in food or drink. The unicorn horn was the horn of a narwhal, and it too was believed to be a reliable test for poison. After the early threat to poison Margaret's mother-in-law, Mary of Gueldres, these were no doubt particularly valued in the Scottish royal household.

Several items of plate also feature on Margaret's list. We know that she had a great round silver-gilt ball which could be filled with hot water so that she could warm her hands. Her silver-gilt basin for washing her hands had a cover, there was a silver-gilt cup and a lamp of silver, which was perhaps for an altar since it is mentioned next to the embroidered linen cloth in which the Host was wrapped. Finally, there were one or two miscellaneous items: a pair of mittens for hunting, the surplice of 'the robe royal', meaning perhaps the sort of jacket seen in the Trinity panel, and a covering, roof and hangings of shot purple silk, embroidered with thistles and a unicorn. This must have been similar to the dark, thistle-embroidered hangings behind Margaret in the painting. There were also three whips and two books.

Finally, there are other scattered but enlightening references in the Treasurer's accounts. We know that when the Queen went out riding, her blue velvet saddles had gilded trimmings and her stirrup irons were covered with velvet, sometimes blue and sometimes black. Caldwell, Andrew Wood and Tom Pate, servants of her chamber, wore black fustian doublets and green hose under English tawny gowns. Her six yeomen of the stables wore blue gowns, white fustian doublets and tawny hose and they had special blue livery for parliament. Her cook in 1474 was named George and in the 1480s her pantryman was Thomas Spence.

When Margaret's first son was born in 1473, he lay in a cradle lined with white beneath a rich silk canopy, and wore linen shirts, lawn baby caps and a white coat lined with miniver. By the time he was a year old, he had scarlet and blue coats and a gown of cloth of gold. Meanwhile, his mother in 1473 had a window of glass fitted in her chamber at Holyrood, and that same year eight ells of broadcloth were purchased to cover a bathing tub for her. At the same time, a 3-ell sheet of cloth was made 'to put about the Queen in the bath vat'. In 1474 eighteen shillings was given to a smith in Leith 'for a chimney to the Queen's closet'. Tantalisingly incomplete as these references are, they give us a vivid insight into Margaret's lifestyle.[16]

Her relationship with her husband is much more difficult to determine. For historians, James remains an enigmatic character. He used to be written off as a feckless monarch, ruined for all practical purposes by his artistic interests, his fondness for the company of low-born favourites and his avarice. Later writers claimed that there was a homosexual relationship between him and some of the favourites, but nearer to his own time the accusations were rather different. Robert Henryson the poet makes allusion in *The Lion and the Mouse* to his lustfulness and his sloth while Hector Boece, the early sixteenth-century historian, said that Bishop Elphinstone had to urge the King to avoid lust and content himself with his Queen, 'the chastest of women'. George Buchanan in the later sixteenth century accused James of seducing Lady Crichton, and in the poem *The Thre Prestis of Peblis* he is said to have seduced a burgess's daughter.[17]

Perhaps James felt that he had to look beyond his wife for sexual satisfaction for, according to an Italian life of Margaret of Denmark, written by Giovanni Sabadino degli Arienti some six years after her death, she 'would have no relations with her husband except for the procreation of children, behaving towards him in such a way that, when she knew conception had occurred, she declined relations until after the birth, despite his demands, curbing his unseemly desires by good sense and restraint'. The origins of the information are not known, but it appears likely that Sabadino received the details from a Scot. He himself was secretary to Count Andrea Bentivoglio in Bologna, and the Register of Bologna University mentions that one of the University regents at the relevant time was William Baillie of Scotland, who later became a royal doctor in his native land.[18]

Sabadino put forward his information as evidence of Margaret's chastity, for he was anxious to emphasise her devout nature and so, like Turgot with St Margaret, he is giving a distinctly slanted account. There was nothing unusual in a king taking mistresses, and historians have come to believe that James has been largely underestimated. He is now generally praised for his love of music and the arts. However, there is little doubt that he was a difficult character, and the persistent rumours swirling around his relationship with his wife suggest that they were not on particularly affectionate terms. What we do know suggests that Margaret always respected his position as monarch whatever she thought of his personal characteristics and behaviour.

Throughout the 1470s, James had become increasingly unpopular with his nobles, who accused him of ignoring their advice, relying on favourites, and hoarding money. He was anxious for peace with England, not least because he was eager to travel abroad, seeing himself somewhat unrealistically as an important mediator between various hostile foreign princes. The Scots were bitterly opposed to the King leaving the country. Regardless of parliament's opposition to his ambitions, he pushed ahead in the late 1470s with arrangements for a pilgrimage to the shrine of St John the Baptist at Amiens, his notion being to visit the French Court on the way and hold discussions with Louis XI about renewing the Franco-Scottish alliance. He even had a gold medallion struck in honour of St John in preparation for his journey. In the end, however, he did not have enough money to make his plans a reality.

Meanwhile, relations with England were fast deteriorating, financial problems caused James to debase the coinage drastically, arousing even more discontent, and, deeply suspicious of his own brothers, he imprisoned them both. John, Earl of Mar, died in 1479, possibly having been murdered, but Alexander, Duke of Albany, escaped from Edinburgh Castle and made his way to France. James III's half-uncles, John, Earl of Atholl, and James, Earl of Buchan, were also enthusiastically stirring up opposition to him. In May 1482, Albany crossed to England, where he became the tool of Edward IV, who had him proclaimed King of Scots.

Edward IV then dispatched his own brother Richard, Duke of Gloucester, to Scotland at the head of twenty thousand men, the largest English army for more than eighty years. James III summoned the Scottish forces to meet him at Lauder, but on 22 July he was seized, taken to Edinburgh and held prisoner in the Castle by his uncles. According to legend, his low-born favourites were hanged at Lauder Bridge. In fact, the three men who died were minor members of the royal household. Thomas Cochrane was one of the King's attendants, William Roger was an English musician and Thomas Preston probably the prosperous Edinburgh merchant of the same name.

While all this was happening, Queen Margaret was at Stirling, where it seemed that she spent most of her time with her children. There appears to be no doubt that she played an important political role during the events of 1482. This was not altogether surprising. According to Sabadino, Margaret was not only gentle, forbearing and very pious, but she was 'much more loved and revered by the people than was the King, since she possessed more aptitude than he for ruling the kingdom'. James, said Sabadino, was never willing to recognise his wife's virtues, and this caused her considerable distress. 'The more gentle and affectionate the love which she showed to her husband . . . the more anguish she received from him.'[19]

Because of a lack of information in the contemporary sources, it is not possible to know exactly what she was doing and why in those crucial months in 1482. Gloucester had been instructed to place Albany on the throne of Scotland, but when he entered the country he realised that the Scots would never accept the King's brother as their monarch and he went to Stirling, apparently to seek the Queen's advice. Perhaps he suggested to her that her eldest son could take his father's place with Albany ruling as regent[20] but, according to Bishop Lesley, the sixteenth-century historian, Margaret told him that he must besiege Edinburgh Castle and secure the release of the King.[21]

Whatever the sequence of events, Edinburgh Castle was besieged and James was set free. We have no details, but there are one or two fragments of evidence indicating that Margaret had played an instrumental part in restoring her husband to power. A royal charter issued by James III on 17 January 1483, rewarding John Dundas, one of the squires of his chamber, for having risked his life in liberating the King from Edinburgh Castle, was made 'with the consent and assent of our dearest consort, Margaret, Queen of Scots' while the Exchequer accounts of the period show that Margaret made a payment to John Stewart, Lord Darnley, for the custody of the castle.[22] James and Albany were officially reconciled, but Albany continued to plot against his brother. Until now, Margaret had apparently been acting with Gloucester and Albany, but when she received information that Albany meant to seize the King, she refused to have any more to do with her brother-in-law.[23]

Be that as it may, when Sabadino wrote his account of Margaret's life, he was in no doubt about the effect of the 1482 crisis on the royal marriage. According to him, after James's release from captivity 'he reposed more hatred than previously in the Queen, because of her consent to his arrest'. This hardly seems likely in view of the charter to John Dundas, unless it had been issued by Margaret in the King's name. Sabadino went on to claim that after the King's release, he and Margaret lived apart, she at Stirling, he in Edinburgh and elsewhere, and they never saw each other again. In fact Margaret had already been living at Stirling with the children and there is no real evidence that James did not continue to visit her there, for it is impossible to compile his itinerary for the relevant years.[24]

Margaret fell seriously ill during the summer of 1486, and she died at Stirling in July. She was buried at Cambuskenneth, and the King endowed daily masses for her soul.[25] Two years later, James III's enemies sent propaganda to Denmark claiming that she had been poisoned at the instigation of the King.[26] No credence was ever given to this story, which was very obviously untrue, but it would seem that those who invented it were doing so within the context of the rumours about James being on bad terms with his Queen. After her death, he sent a supplication to the Pope asking for her to be made a saint. Some have seen this as an indication of his guilt at having been a less than sympathetic husband, while others would argue that it was a sign of his genuine affection and regret. Quite

1 St Margaret's Chapel, Edinburgh Castle, exterior (Historic Scotland)

2 St Margaret's Chapel, Edinburgh Castle, interior (Historic Scotland)

3 Dunfermline Abbey, where St Margaret was buried (Historic Scotland)

4 Balmerino Abbey, founded by Queen Ermengarde (Historic Scotland)

5 Base of St Margaret's shrine, Dunfermline Abbey (Historic Scotland)

6 Edinburgh Castle, where Margaret of England spent her early married years (Historic Scotland)

7 Jedburgh Abbey, where Queen Yolande married Alexander III (Historic Scotland)

8 Kildrummy Castle, where Queen Elizabeth stayed on her flight north (Historic Scotland)

9 Dingwall Castle, where Queen Euphemia was brought up (Historic Scotland)

10 Dundonald Castle, Queen Euphemia's home after her marriage to
Robert the Steward (Historic Scotland)

11 Moot Hill, Scone, where Queen Euphemia was crowned. The building is of a later date (Historic Scotland)

12 Lady dictating to her secretary, as Queen Annabella did. From a medieval manuscript (The Trustees of the British Library)

13 James I, husband of Queen Joan, by an unknown artist (Scottish National Portrait Gallery)

14 James II, husband of Queen Mary of Gueldres, by an unknown artist (Scottish National Portrait Gallery)

15 The remains of the Collegiate Church of the Holy Trinity, Edinburgh, founded by Queen Mary of Gueldres (National Monuments Record of Scotland)

16 Ravenscraig Castle, built by Queen Mary of Gueldres (Historic Scotland)

17 James III, husband of Queen Margaret of Denmark, by an unknown artist (Scottish National Portrait Gallery)

18 Stirling Castle, where Queen Margaret of Denmark spent her final years
(Historic Scotland)

19 Cambuskenneth Abbey, where Queen Margaret of Denmark was buried.
Stirling Castle in the background. (Historic Scotland)

20 James IV, husband of Queen
Margaret Tudor, by Daniel Mytens
(Private Collection)

21 Archibald Douglas, 6th Earl
of Angus, engraved by Laurie
after F. Clouet (Scottish National
Portrait Gallery)

22 Queen Margaret Tudor with the Duke of Albany and possibly Harry Stewart, Lord Methven, by an unknown artist (Private Collection)

23 Eleanor of Austria, stepmother of Queen Madeleine, who grew up in her household, by Joos van Cleve (In the collection of the Duke of Buccleuch and Queensberry KT)

24 James V, husband of Queen Madeleine, by an unknown artist (Scottish National Portrait Gallery)

25 Queen Madeleine by Corneille de Lyon (Painting formerly at Blois, now destroyed)

26 Holyrood Abbey, where Queen Madeleine was buried (Historic Scotland)

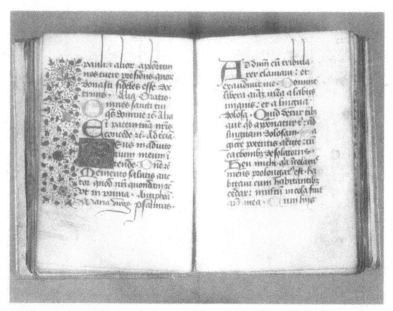

27 Queen Mary of Guise's Book of Hours (The Trustees of the National Library of Scotland)

possibly it was merely a conventional expression of piety. In spite of assertions to the contrary, James had been as devout as Margaret throughout his life, and in the later Middle Ages, queens formed the largest category of women saints.

James then contemplated marrying again. In the month of Margaret's death he made a three-year truce with England, and was soon seeking English brides not only for his two elder sons but for himself. Elizabeth Woodville, widow of Edward IV, was available, and he decided to take her for his second wife. Internal divisions within Scotland put an end to his ambitions, however, and in 1488 his nobles rose against him and confronted him at the Battle of Sauchieburn, taking Prince James with them. The King's army was defeated and he was killed as he left the battlefield. He was buried at Cambuskenneth Abbey beside his Queen.[27] Prince James, now James IV, was fifteen and began his personal rule at once, without any regent being appointed.

Notes

1. Donaldson, *Scottish Documents*, 35–6.
2. Crawford, 'The Pawning of Orkney and Shetland', 33–53; Nicholson, *Later Middle Ages*, 414.
3. Homby, 'Christian I and the pawning of Orkney', 54–63.
4. Inge Skovgaard-Petersen, 'Queenship in Medieval Denmark', in *Medieval Queenship*, 38–9; Alistair H. Thomas and Stewart P. Oakley, *Historical Dictionary of Denmark* (Oxford 1998), 85; Maclagan and Louda, *Lines of Succession*, table 17.
5. Nicholson, *Later Middle Ages*, 415.
6. *Ibid.*, 414–5; Donaldson, *Scottish Kings*, 105; Donaldson, *Scottish Historical Documents*, 85–7.
7. Nicholson, *Later Middle Ages*, 415–6; Crawford, 'The Pawning of Orkney and Shetland', 35–53; Homby, 'Christian I and the Pawning of Orkney', 54–63.
8. *Treasurer's Accounts*, i, p.xli, n.
9. *Ibid.*, i, p.xliv, nn.1 and 2.
10. *Ibid.*, i, p.xliv and n.
11. Donaldson, *Scottish Kings*, 106.
12. Colin Thompson and Lorne Campbell, *Hugo van der Goes and the Trinity Panels in Edinburgh* (Edinburgh 1974); Tolley, 'Hugo van der Goes's Altarpiece', 215–222.

13. *Treasurer's Accounts*, i, 29–39.
14. *Ibid.*, i, 85.
15. *Ibid.*, i, 79–86.
16. *Ibid.*, i, pp. cciii, 30, 34, 36, 35–6, 39–42, 56–7, 104.
17. Nicholson, *Later Middle Ages*, 235, 504.
18. S. B. Chandler, 'An Italian Life of Margaret, Queen of James III', in *SHR*, xxxii (1953), 56.
19. *Ibid.*, 55.
20. Nicholson, *Later Middle Ages*, 507.
21. Macdougall, *James III*, 116–7, 126–7, 140–83.
22. Macdougall, *James III*, 170–1.
23. Fradenburg, *City, Marriage, Tournament*, 80; Donaldson, *Scottish Kings*, 100.
24. Macdougall, *James III*, 218.
25. *ER*, ix, 408, 468; *Treasurer's Accounts*, i, pp.lxxiv n., 89–91; *RMS*, ii, nos 1164, 1434.
26. Macdougall, *James III*, 194.
27. *Ibid.*, 260–2.

CHAPTER SEVEN

MARGARET TUDOR

From the start, James IV was an effective and popular ruler. His father in his last months had sought an English wife for him, and in October 1474 he had been formally betrothed to Edward IV of England's daughter Cecilia. Nothing was done, but talk of this match persisted until 1487, when Cecilia was married to Viscount Welles.[1] The idea of a matrimonial alliance was revived when James and Henry VII signed a seven years' truce in September 1497. James was twenty-five by then and his lords were pressing him to take a wife. Henry offered his daughter Margaret, who was nine.[2] The disparity in ages meant nothing to those concerned, and although some claimed that James had secretly married his favourite mistress, Margaret Drummond, he was set on having the princess as his bride.[3]

Later English commentators were to point out that it was as if fate had intended the baby to be Queen of Scots. Born on 29 November 1489 in Westminster Palace, she was baptised on St Andrew's Day. Her christening took place in St Margaret's Church, Westminster, which was dedicated to St Margaret of Scotland. In fact, this church was probably chosen because she was named after Henry's mother, Lady Margaret Beaufort.[4] Princess Margaret was brought up in the royal nurseries at Richmond Palace with her older brother Arthur and her younger brother, the future Henry VIII. Petted and spoiled by her family, she did not receive a demanding education. She was taught to read and write, but otherwise she was instructed in the feminine accomplishments thought necessary for a princess, dancing and playing the lute.

Margaret was also initiated into public life at an early age. When she was five, she was sitting on a cloth-of-gold cushion beside her parents watching the tournaments held when Prince Henry was created Duke of York.[5] Four years later, she must have been told about the arrangements for her future. James IV wanted to marry her as soon as possible and take her back to Scotland, but family pressure was brought to bear on Henry VII to prevent him from allowing the wedding to take place right away. His mother reminded him that her own early marriage had been disastrous. She had given birth to Henry himself when she was only twelve, and as a result had been unable to have any more children.[6]

Badgered by his wife as well as his mother, Henry VII was forced to agree that it was too soon to conclude the match, but he continued with the arrangements. Since Margaret and James were within the forbidden degrees, related through the Beauforts, he obtained the necessary papal dispensation in 1500.[7] When his privy councillors expressed concerns about a Scottish king one day inheriting the throne of England as a result of the marriage, Henry brushed their objections aside with the sage remark, 'The smaller will ever follow the larger kingdom'.[8] The treaty was finally signed on 24 January 1502. Margaret would take with her a dowry of £10,000 sterling, James would settle on her lands and castles in Scotland worth £2,000 and there would be a separate treaty of perpetual peace between Scotland and England. The princess would be allowed to bring with her twenty-four English servants, and should she be widowed, she would be free to remain in Scotland or return home to England.[9] The proxy marriage took place the following day at Richmond Palace, and Margaret became Queen of Scots.[10] By the terms of the marriage treaty, she did not have to be in Scotland until 1 September 1503, by which time she had suffered two family bereavements. Her brother Prince Arthur died on 2 April 1502, and in February 1503 her mother died after the birth of a short-lived daughter.[11]

At the end of June, Margaret said goodbye to her father and grandmother, receiving from Henry VII a fine Flemish Book of Hours in which he had written, 'Remember your kind and loving father in your good prayers'.[12] She then set off for the north, riding with Thomas, Earl of Surrey, at the head of a long procession of noblemen, ladies, minstrels, trumpeters, servants and soldiers. The towns and villages honoured her along the way with elaborate pageants and church services, and people flocked to see her. Throughout what might have been an ordeal, Margaret conducted herself with complete assurance. She was a self-centred, strong-willed thirteen-year-old now, confident and full of aplomb. She was the Queen of Scots. She knew what was expected of her and she was proudly conscious of being her father's daughter. On they went, through Newark, Doncaster, York, Hexham, Durham, Newcastle and Alnwick until, more than a month after her departure, Margaret finally crossed the border into Scotland.[13]

She expected to meet James IV in Edinburgh, but when she arrived at Dalkeith Castle she was told that he was coming to see her privately and, sure enough, he arrived on 3 August, casually dressed in a velvet coat, his luxuriant auburn hair and beard, which he never cut, adding an air of romantic distinction to his appearance. He bowed, Margaret curtsied, and they talked together. Her ladies were impressed with him. They asked her eagerly afterwards what she thought of him, and she replied laconically that his beard was too long. Her comment was relayed to him and he immediately had it trimmed. Discovering that his bride shared his love of music, James performed on his lute for her and played cards with her each evening.

When they eventually made their formal entry into Edinburgh, she was riding pillion behind him. He guided her through all the ceremonial with his arm round her waist. They were married at Holyrood Abbey on 8 August 1503, both wearing rich white damask, she with her long golden red hair loose, and then she was crowned Queen of Scots. One of the earliest surviving vernacular songs celebrates her arrival with the words, 'Now fair, fairest of every fair ... Welcome to Scotland to be Queen' while the court poet William Dunbar composed a poem appropriately entitled 'The Thistle and the Rose'.[14]

At first Margaret was homesick but she soon settled down and, despite the age difference, she and James suited each other rather well. He had inherited a full measure of the Stewart intelligence and energy. Indeed, had he not been such an effective monarch, he might have been regarded as a likeable but wearing eccentric. His intellectual curiosity was boundless. He was interested in music, medicine, surgery, dentistry, alchemy, education and the law, artillery and naval warfare. He spoke Latin, French, German, Flemish, Italian, Spanish and Gaelic and allegedly sent twin babies to the Island of Inchkeith with a dumb nurse, in an experiment designed to discover what tongue they would use when they began to speak. Would it be Latin, perhaps, or Hebrew or even Gaelic?[15]

James had a powerful physique, great stamina, a kind heart and an enduring liking for women, accumulating mistresses and illegitimate children. Margaret was fully capable of holding her own with him, and if he did go on seeing other women, that was only to be expected. He was endlessly indulgent to her, he made sure that his courtiers treated her with respect, and she knew that her father would make sure that all was well with her. According to the English chronicler who described her journey to Scotland, James and Margaret slept together the night after their Holyrood marriage. This may or may not be true, but their first child was not born until 1507 and Margaret almost died afterwards. James was convinced that she was saved by his desperate pilgrimage on foot to his favourite shrine at Whithorn. Four more babies followed in the next five years. During at least one later confinement, the Queen had St Margaret's shirt brought to her from Dunfermline to help her delivery, but even with this spiritual assistance only her fourth child, Prince James, survived infancy.[16]

As long as Margaret's father was alive, Scotland and England were at peace, but in 1509 Henry VII died, her brother Henry VIII came to the English throne, and the situation changed. Young and ambitious, Henry soon decided to attack France. Anne of Brittany, Louis XII's Queen, wrote to James IV imploring him to remember the Auld Alliance and advance into England. He decided that he could not refuse. Margaret was furious. She was pregnant, she reminded him. He could not possibly leave her at such a time, but he brushed aside her protests. It was probably she who arranged for a ghostly figure to appear before him in the church at Linlithgow to warn him not to invade England but he paid no attention to that either, made his will and marched south to his death at the Battle of Flodden on 9 September 1513.[17]

Margaret was never one to keep her feelings to herself, but even as her screams of despair echoed through the royal chambers at Linlithgow Palace, she knew what she must do. James had said in his will that she was to be the official guardian of their children, and she set off for Stirling Castle with her son, who was crowned as James V in the Chapel Royal there on 21 September. Whoever had custody of a child king controlled the country, and Margaret intended to rule as regent for him. This was what her late husband intended, she told everyone. The Scots, of course, viewed the matter rather differently. After their disastrous defeat, the last person they wanted ruling over them was an English queen regent,[18] and many of them agreed that the obvious candidate for the regency was John, Duke of Albany, James IV's cousin and heir to the throne. He had been born and brought up in France, but it was time for him to come home.[19]

In February 1514 the Scots agreed to a truce with England, but they ignored Margaret's urgings that what was needed was a perpetual peace, and she began to realise the difficulties of her position. The respect accorded to her when James was there to protect her had ebbed away, she was excluded from much of what was going on because she was a woman, and she was held back still further by her pregnancy. She needed another husband, she believed, and when Lord Drummond of Stobhall introduced his grandson, Archibald Douglas, 6th Earl of Angus, to the Council in March 1514, she decided that she had found him.

A widower of nineteen, Angus was young, strong and handsome. On 8 April 1514 Margaret gave birth safely to James IV's posthumous son, Alexander, Duke of Ross, and that summer her relationship with Angus flourished. No one told her that he was already betrothed to Lady Jane Stewart of Traquair. Angus was deeply in love with Jane, but his grandfather convinced him that the entire Douglas family would benefit if he married the Queen Regent. After all, he could keep Jane as his mistress. Margaret was still in her official year of mourning for James IV, but she did not let that deter her. She married Angus secretly on 14 August 1514 at Kinnoull Church, near Perth, an ecclesiastical nephew of Lord Drummond performing the ceremony.

Inevitably, news of the wedding leaked out and the Scottish nobles were furious. The Douglas family had already made themselves far too powerful, and Angus's rivals could not bear to think of him being raised to this new position of eminence. 'We have shown heretofore our willingness to honour the Queen contrary to the ancient custom of this kingdom', Lord Home told his fellow councillors angrily. 'We have suffered and obeyed her authority the whiles she herself kept her right by keeping her widowhood', he went on. 'Now she has quit it by marrying, why should we not choose another to succeed in the place she has voluntarily left? Our old laws do not permit that a woman should govern in the most peaceable times, far less now when such evils do threaten.' Agreeing that Margaret had forfeited her position by remarrying, the council deposed her as regent, ordered Angus to appear before them and sent the Lord Lyon to France to tell Albany that he had been elected to rule the country instead.[20]

Albany had no desire to leave the French Court where, as the husband of his own cousin, Anne de la Tour, a very wealthy heiress, he enjoyed a lavish lifestyle. However, his friend King Francis I saw the invitation as a useful opportunity. Queen Margaret provided a direct line of communication to Henry VIII. With Albany in Scotland as a counterpoise to her, he himself would be kept informed of exactly what was going on there. Albany accordingly sailed north in May 1515 and made his way to Edinburgh. Perhaps to her surprise, Margaret found that she rather liked him. A sturdy man with a broad face, a long, straight nose and a short, square-cut beard, he might speak little English but he was a polished courtier who treated her with not only courtesy but with the deference she always expected and was now so rarely receiving.[21]

There were, of course, problems. Not only did Albany turn against her husband's relatives, the Douglas faction, imprisoning Angus's uncle Gavin Douglas and his grandfather, Lord Drummond, but he told Margaret that she would have to hand over her sons to the care of eight noblemen, four appointed by her, the other four by himself. Margaret tried to resist. She stood at the entrance to Edinburgh Castle with the boys, ordered the portcullis to be slammed down and then shouted through it, refusing to hand her children over, while Angus lurked nervously in the background.[22] After further argument, she took the boys and fled to Stirling Castle, pursued by Albany with an army of seven thousand men and the famous Flemish cannon, Mons Meg. When she saw that she was about to be besieged, Margaret gave way and handed over her sons.[23]

Angus retreated to his own lands and Margaret began to regret that she had ever stayed on in Scotland after James IV's death. Lord Dacre, her brother's representative in the north of England, was constantly sending messages to tell her that Henry VIII would like her to bring her boys to the English Court. So far she had refused, but now that she no longer had her children with her, the prospect of going south was extremely tempting.[24] By this time she was pregnant with Angus's child, and on 1 September she announced that she was going to Linlithgow for her confinement.[25] Once there, she pretended to be ill and the gallant Albany allowed her husband to go to her. She and Angus then stole out of the Palace by night and rode for his castle of Tantallon, on the east coast. When Albany heard what had happened, he set off in pursuit, causing Margaret to flee precipitately, leaving her jewels and some of her clothing behind her.

Margaret and Angus rode desperately to the Border, only to discover that they were not allowed to enter England without a safe conduct from Henry VIII. She therefore sought refuge in Coldstream Priory until Henry's official invitation came. By that time, her pregnancy was far advanced. Lord Dacre sent an escort to bring her to his own comfortably furnished castle at Morpeth and she set off on 5 October, thinking that the baby was not due for another fortnight. However, her labour pains began on the way and she screamed hysterically that she could go no further. Her alarmed companions hurried her to Harbottle Castle, the grim fortress where Lord Dacre was living. Disconcerted by this turn of events, he refused to allow any Scot to enter his Border stronghold, and even Angus had to retreat in disarray.

After a labour lasting forty-eight hours, Margaret gave birth to a daughter, whom she named after herself. She was dreadfully ill for days afterwards, suffering such pains in her right hip and leg that she screamed out in agony whenever she was helped to sit up in bed. Lord Dacre callously complained that her stay was both 'uneaseful and costly' but she obviously could not be moved.[26] From her symptoms, it seems likely that she was suffering from deep vein thrombosis, and it is surprising that she survived. It was more than three weeks before she was able to travel, very slowly, towards Morpeth, where Angus came to visit her. She was still there when she heard at the end of the year that her little son, Alexander, had died at Stirling Castle. Lord Dacre hinted that Albany had probably murdered the child, but Margaret sensibly retorted that if the Duke had been trying to get the throne for himself, then he would have killed James V, not poor little Alexander.[27]

Albany had in fact been corresponding with Margaret in an attempt to persuade her to return to Scotland, but Lord Dacre intercepted and doctored their letters, with the result that Margaret took umbrage and decided that she could not possibly go back.[28] On 8 September, after a frightful scene when she learned that Angus had refused to accompany her south, she set off for London in a litter with her baby daughter.[29] She had not seen Henry VIII for thirteen years, and they had a glad reunion. Where was her husband, he enquired, and when she told him that Angus had refused to come with her, he growled, 'Done like a Scot!' For the next year Margaret happily occupied her place at the centre of the English Court, revelling in tournaments and entertainments held in her honour.[30] Henry obligingly paid all her expenses, and the Duke of Albany was persuaded to send south the items she had left behind on her flight from Tantallon: her chapel furniture, velvet and satin sleeves, five silk hats, and her jewels. There was a gold collar enamelled with red and white roses, 'the King of France's great diamond set upon a red hat of silk', rosaries, brooches, a bird of gold and a silver pomander.[31]

Her stay in London was a very pleasant interlude, but it could not last forever. By the spring of 1517 Henry was telling her that she must go back to Scotland, and Albany wrote to her too, urging her to return. His wife had been seriously ill and he was anxious to go to France to visit her. Margaret should act as regent in his absence. Privately, he told the English herald 'he had had so much trouble he wished he had broken both his legs before he set foot in Scotland'.[32] Taking her little daughter with her, Margaret left London on 18 May 1517 and travelled north at the head of the usual impressive retinue. She was eager to see James V again. When she arrived at Berwick, she found the Earl of Angus waiting with the welcoming party.[33] She gave him a frosty reception, but she was soon suggesting that he should rule jointly with her as co-regent, a notion swiftly rebuffed by the entire council. It was decided that the Earl of Arran should take charge, as Deputy Governor to Albany.[34]

By 1519, Margaret was in dire financial straits, forced to dismiss her servants and pawn her jewels. Only a personal loan from the King's Comptroller, Robert Barton, saved her from personal destitution and, to add to her problems, she was having difficulty in gaining access to her son, for the Scottish lords were afraid that she might spirit him over the Border. Declaring 'I had rather be dead than live among them',[35] she wrote to Henry VIII announcing that she wanted to separate from Angus and return to England. Henry would not hear of it. Margaret and Angus should be ruling Scotland together, in the English interest, for it was known that Albany was not simply visiting his sick wife. He was busy negotiating the Treaty of Rouen, renewing Scotland's alliance with France.[36] Unabashed, Margaret went on pleading to be allowed to go back to England, and when Henry refused to listen she enraged him still further by telling him that she did not merely wish to separate from Angus. She wanted to divorce him. 'He loves me not,' she said.[37] She had not only found out about his continuing affair with Lady Jane Stewart but she had discovered that the pair were living on rents from her own Border properties. Still virtuously married to his first wife, Catherine of Aragon, Henry adopted a high moral tone and sent a series of messengers to Margaret, telling her how shocked he was that she could consider dishonouring him and their family by even contemplating divorce.

Henry was obviously going to be no help, but by the spring of 1519 Margaret discovered that Albany now had considerable influence in Rome. His wife's sister had married Lorenzo de Medici, the Pope's nephew. She therefore lost no time in enlisting Albany's assistance, and when he found out, Henry was angrier with her than ever.[38] The Scottish lords were by this time begging Albany to return. They liked him, and he had given the country a stability it sadly lacked. He arrived back on 18 November 1521 to a warm welcome from the Queen. She was delighted when he promptly turned against the Douglases, arresting Angus and his brother on a charge of treason, but she was horrified when they were sentenced to death. She hastily interceded for them, and they were banished to France instead. During one of their violent quarrels, Angus had snatched their little daughter from her, and he took her away with him. After a stay in the north of England, the child was eventually brought up at court with Henry VIII's daughter Princess Mary, and Margaret never saw her again.

Angus was now appointed resident Scottish ambassador in Paris, much to Henry VIII's annoyance. Events were not at all going according to plan. Instead of ruling Scotland with Angus, Margaret was acting with Albany in the French interest. As so often happened, when men were confronted with a female ruler they lost no time in accusing her of immoral behaviour, and Lord Dacre was soon telling Cardinal Wolsey, 'There is marvellous great intelligence between Queen Margaret and the Duke of Albany, as well of the day as much of the night. They are over tender . . .' Henry sent his sister another scorching letter, expressing horror at her shameless behaviour. He also warned the Scottish privy council that Albany was helping Margaret to get a divorce because he wanted to marry her himself. Margaret wept bitter tears, but she managed a dignified response, telling Dacre, 'You should not give so lightly credit to evil tales of me as you do when you know the truth'. She was suing for divorce because Angus had seized her lands. For his part, Albany 'swore by the sacrament . . . and prayed he might break his neck if ever he minded to marry her. He had enough of one wife', he said, and expressed astonishment that the King could think so ill of his own sister.[39]

Rule by Albany and Margaret might have been the remedy for Scotland's internal problems, but of course Henry was never going to tolerate it, for that would have led to a perpetual threat on his northern border. When Albany returned to France to collect men and ammunition for Scotland, Margaret found herself financially dependent on Henry once more. He was willing to supply her with some funds, although he would not allow her to travel south. If she offended him, he would cut off her money, and so when Albany came back she relayed details of his military plans to her brother, while at the same time plying the Duke with apparently cordial letters. As her former friend the Prioress of Coldstream warned Lord Surrey, 'She is right fickle'.[40]

Albany was finding life in Scotland increasingly stressful. He had a quick temper and was known for snatching his bonnet from his head and throwing it into the fire when something annoyed him. Surrey told Cardinal Wolsey that, according to Lord Dacre, 'at his last being in Scotland, the Regent did burn above a dozen bonnets after that manner'.[41] Hostilities with England had broken out again, and when the Scots refused to follow Albany across the Border to besiege Wark Castle, it was the last straw. He decided to return to France and urged Margaret to negotiate a peace with England so that he could get away. His wife died that winter and Margaret was all sympathy, but he had had enough. On 31 May 1524 he left Scotland for good, and Margaret occupied the position of regent once more.

Any satisfaction she experienced was soon overshadowed when she heard that Angus had left France, was in London and Henry VIII intended to send him back to Scotland to lead the pro-English party. Wolsey remarked on 1 August that although Henry and he considered the Queen of Scots to be a convenient instrument, 'it is no folly for a good archer to have two strings to his bow, specially whereas one is made of threads wrought by a woman's fingers'.[42] By this time they were all thoroughly exasperated at Margaret's unreliability, and she was highly indignant when she heard that Lord Dacre had been telling some Scots 'that he marvels that they will let any woman have authority and specially ME'.[43] She was beginning an affair with the head carver in James V's household, Henry Stewart, the son of Andrew Stewart, Lord Avandale, and the last person she wanted to see was her husband. Henry dispatched Archdeacon Magnus to rebuke her, but he could only report that he found her 'entirely perverse'.[44]

Angus arrived in Edinburgh with his men that November, and Margaret ordered the cannon of Holyrood to be turned on them.[45] When the Archdeacon protested that she must not attack her lawful husband, she told him to go home and not meddle with Scottish affairs.[46] In the event, her guns killed four innocent bystanders, and although Angus and his men thought it prudent to retreat to Tantallon, they were soon back with a large force. Margaret was compelled to see her husband and agree to yet another reconciliation,[47] but she continued her relationship with Henry Stewart, and the following summer Magnus discovered that she was actively pursuing a divorce, on the bizarre grounds that James IV had not really been killed at Flodden but had still been alive, unknown to her, when she married Angus.[48] Henry VIII made vigorous efforts to prevent the Pope from granting the divorce, Angus's power was growing by the day, and by 1526 Margaret's regency had collapsed.

It was now arranged that groups of nobles would take it in turn to look after James V, but when it was time for Angus to give up the boy, he refused. Both Margaret and the young king were deeply upset, for despite her erratic behaviour he was devoted to her. Angus ignored their protests. Making himself Chancellor and giving his own relatives all the leading appointments in James's household, he more or less held the young King prisoner for the next two years.[49] The one cheering event for Margaret in an impossible situation came when, in February 1527, Pope Clement VII granted her desired divorce on the grounds of Angus's pre-contract with Lady Jane Stewart. It took nine months before she heard the news, but as soon as she realised that she was free, Margaret secretly married Henry Stewart.[50]

By this time, James V was sixteen, old enough to take matters into his own hands, and in June 1528 he managed to free himself and ride to his mother at Stirling. He forbade any of the Douglas faction to return to Court on pain of treason and three months later parliament passed the death sentence on his hated stepfather. Angus and his brother fled to England and James, who had disliked his mother's third marriage, nevertheless granted Henry Stewart the title of Lord Methven.[51] A vigorous monarch with strong views of his own, James V no longer relied on his mother for guidance, and although she saw herself as an important intermediary between her brother and her son, relations between Henry VIII and James V deteriorated rapidly. Henry wanted James not only to give up the alliance with France but to break with Rome, as he himself had now done. James refused to recognise his uncle's 'new constitution of religion', and when he realised that Margaret was reporting everything he planned, he quarrelled bitterly with her, even threatening to throw her into prison.[52] Her letters to Henry VIII became increasingly full of complaints about her son's cruelty as well as about Lord Methven's misdeeds.

Like everyone else, James was beginning to find Margaret incredibly exasperating. Set on his own policies, he went to France to collect the French bride promised to him in the Treaty of Rouen, and was appalled to discover on his return that his mother was busy divorcing Lord Methven so that she could marry the Earl of Angus all over again. James immediately put a stop to the divorce and

Margaret was forced to return to Methven, although by now he had a second family in the form of a long-term mistress and their children. Eventually, under the influence of James's second wife, Mary of Guise, it seems that Margaret reconciled herself to the notion of staying with Lord Methven and even turned to religion for consolation.

On Friday 20 November 1541 Margaret suffered a stroke at Methven Castle. Her condition deteriorated and she sent for her son. James was at Falkland. Strangely, in this extremity, her thoughts were all for the Earl of Angus. Weeping, she asked God's mercy for having offended him and told her friars that they were to kneel before the King and beg him to be good and gracious to her former husband. All her belongings were to be given to her daughter. Margaret died before James could reach Methven. Their past differences forgotten, he gave her a magnificent funeral in the Carthusian monastery in Perth, accompanying her body there from Methven Castle and attending the service in person. She was buried in the vault of James I and Joan Beaufort. When Henry VIII heard the news, he sent a messenger to see if she really was dead and to ask whether she had left a will.[53] Often derided for her emotional behaviour and her tangled marital career, Queen Margaret's pragmatic nature, her determination and her valiant efforts at self-preservation deserve greater recognition, and her career demonstrates all too clearly the difficulties encountered by any woman attempting to assert her authority over ruthless nobles and councillors.[54]

Notes

1. Macdougall, *James III*, 167, 169, 186, 220.
2. J.J.Scarisbrick, *Henry VII* (London 1968), 3.
3. R.L.Mackie, *King James IV of Scotland* (Edinburgh 1958), 100–1; Macdougall, *James IV*, 113–4.
4. Strickland, *Queens of Scotland*, i, 2–4.
5. *Ibid.*, i, 5–8.
6. Perry, *Sisters*, 10–11.
7. *Ibid.*,15.
8. Strickland, *Queens of Scotland*, i, 9.

9. Nicholson, *Later Middle Ages*, 554; Strickland, *Queens of Scotland*, i, 10.

10. Hill Buchanan, *Margaret Tudor*, 12–13.

11. *Ibid.*, 13–14; Perry, *Sisters*, 21–2.

12. *The Thistle and the Rose* (Stirling Castle exhibition souvenir guide, 2002), 13.

13. Strickland, *Queens of Scotland*, i, 26–40.

14. Helena M. Shire, *Song, Dance and Poetry at the Court of Scotland under King James VI* (Cambridge 1969), 2–3; *The Poems of William Dunbar*, ed. John Small (Scottish Text Society 1893), ii, 183–9.

15. Pitscottie, *Historie*, i, 237; P. Hume Brown, *Early Travellers in Scotland* (Edinburgh 1978), 39–40.

16. *SP*, i 21; Hill Buchanan, 54–7; *Treasurer's Accounts*, ii, 44–7; Denis McKay, '"The four heid pilgrimages of Scotland"', in *The Innes Review*, xix, i (Glasgow 1968), 77.

17. Hill Buchanan, 59–71; Macdougall, *James IV*, 263–76; Gordon Donaldson, *The Auld Alliance* (Edinburgh 1985), 17; Nicholson, *Later Middle Ages*, 605–6.

18. Macdougall, *James IV*, 273–6; Hill Buchanan, 82–3; Lynch, *New History*, 162.

19. Donaldson and Morpeth, *Who's Who*, 56; M.W.Stuart, *The Scot who was a Frenchman* (Edinburgh 1940); Caroline Bingham, *James V, King of Scots* (London 1971), 30.

20. Strickland, *Queens of Scotland*, i, 92–7; Hill Buchanan, 86–92; Perry, *Sisters*, 76–9; John Finlay, 'Women and Legal Representation in Early Sixteenth-Century Scotland', in *Women in Scotland*, ed. Ewan and Meikle, 167–8.

21. Strickland, *Queens of Scotland*, i, 100–104; Perry, *Sisters*, 120–1; Hill Buchanan, 94–5.

22. *L and P Henry VIII*, ii , part 1, 205–6.

23. *Ibid.*, ii, part 1, 207–10.

24. *Ibid.*, ii, part 1, 13, 16; Strickland, *Queens of Scotland*, i, 107–9; Hill Buchanan, 96–100; Perry, *Sisters*, 121–3.

25. *L and P Henry VIII*, ii, part 1, 225.

26. *Ibid.*, 277, 309.

27. *Ibid.*, 271, 277.

28. *Ibid.*, 273–4, 309.

29. Strickland, *Queens of Scotland*, i, 110–20; Hill Buchanan, 109–30; Perry, *Sisters*, 124–33.

30. Strickland, *Queens of Scotland*, i, 121–32; Hill Buchanan, 132–44; Perry, *Sisters*, 133–41.

31. Strickland, *Queens of Scotland*, i, 124–6.

32. Hill Buchanan, 148.

33. Strickland, *Queens of Scotland*, i, 134–6.

34. Perry, *Sisters*, 142–4.
35. *L and P Henry VIII*, iii, part 1, 1024.
36. *Ibid.*, iii, part 2, 1427; Donaldson, *Scottish Historical Documents*, 98–100; Perry, *Sisters*, 144; Hill Buchanan, 147–58; Strickland, *Queens of Scotland*, i, 137–9.
37. Perry, *Sisters*, 147.
38. Strickland, *Queens of Scotland*, i, 139–44; Hill Buchanan, 159–66.
39. Hill Buchanan, 171–3.
40. *Ibid.*, 187.
41. Strickland, *Queens of Scotland*, i, 169.
42. *L and P Henry VIII*, iv, part 1, 239.
43. Strickland, *Queens of Scotland*, i, 178.
44. *L and P Henry VIII*, iv part 1, 335–440 *passim*.
45. *Ibid.*, 381–2.
46. *Ibid.*, 364.
47. *Ibid.*, 381–2; Strickland, *Queens of Scotland*, i, 181–90.
48. Strickland, *Queens of Scotland*, i, 204.
49. Hill Buchanan, 214–5, 226–7.
50. Strickland, *Queens of Scotland*, i, 212; Hill Buchanan, 227–32.
51. Strickland, *Queens of Scotland*, i, 209–12, 215–6; Perry, *Sisters*, 171–4.
52. Strickland, *Queens of Scotland*, i, 227–8.
53. *Ibid.*, i, 243–4.
54. Louise O. Fradenburg, 'Troubled Times: Margaret Tudor and the Historians', in *The Rose and the Thistle: Essays on the Culture of Late Medieval and Renaissance Scotland*, ed. Sally Mapstone and Juliette Wood (East Linton 1998), 38–58; I am grateful to Christine Claxton for allowing me to read her as yet unpublished article 'Vegetables are good (or bad?) for you: the surviving images of Margaret Tudor, Queen of Scotland'.

CHAPTER EIGHT

MADELEINE OF FRANCE

James V's marriage negotiations were long and varied, for in the shifting sands of European politics he found himself in a uniquely influential position. Because of their rivalries, he was able to play off his uncle Henry VIII, the Holy Roman Emperor Charles V and Francis I of France in a manner quite surprising for the king of a much smaller country. Throughout all the machinations and manoeuvrings, however, he always had at the back of his mind the French king's daughter. Ignoring Henry VIII's efforts to make him end the Auld Alliance and break with Rome, he turned instead to the Treaty of Rouen which the Duke of Albany had negotiated in 1517.[1] Francis I was married to his sweet-natured cousin Claude, and although she had tuberculosis she had seven children in as many years. Madeleine was the eldest surviving daughter.

The Princess was born at ten o'clock at night on 10 August 1520[2] and christened soon afterwards, with the Venetian ambassador as her principal godparent.[3] She spent her earliest years in the royal nurseries with her two elder brothers, the Dauphin Francis and Henry. The Lady Governess in charge of the children's household was Madame de Brissac, an aunt of the celebrated French historian, Brantôme. A charming early portrait of Madeleine by Jean Clouet shows a plump, pretty baby clutching a rattle decorated with bells and a bear's-tooth teether.[4] When she was four, her life changed. On 20 July 1524 her mother died at Blois, soon after the birth of another daughter, Marguerite.[5] Madeleine and the baby were taken to live in the household of an aunt, their father's much loved sister, Marguerite de Valois, Duchess of Alençon, a famous poet and intellectual.[6]

The little princesses had hardly settled down with her when the following year brought further disaster. Their father was captured by Charles V's forces at the Battle of Pavia. His strong-minded mother, Louise of Savoy, ruled as regent until his release in 1526, but the family disruption did not end there, for Madeleine's two older brothers were then sent to Spain as hostages in his place.[7] Madeleine and Marguerite went on living with their aunt after Marguerite de Valois married Henry, King of Navarre, in 1527, but three years later their father married again. His new wife, Charles V's sister, Eleanor of Austria, a kind-hearted widow of thirty-two, took them into her own household and looked after them affectionately.[8]

By the time Madeleine was entering her teens, James V was urging Francis to implement the Treaty of Rouen by allowing him to marry her. Each time he raised the subject, the French king replied that his daughter was too young and delicate for the matter to be considered.[9] That did not have the desired effect, and so, at the end of 1534, Francis instead offered him Marie de Bourbon, daughter of the Duke of Vendôme. James was not enthusiastic. He wanted a royal princess, but Francis assured him that he would in future treat Marie as if she were his own daughter, and he would make sure that she had a dowry of 100,000 crowns.

The Duke of Albany led the negotiations and the marriage contract was signed on 6 March 1536 in the little town of Crémieu in the Dauphiné.[10] Francis I ratified the treaty three days later, but James was not in such a hurry. He was strongly tempted to marry his favourite mistress, Margaret Erskine, instead. He decided to seek permission from the Pope, but Paul III was horrified and sent a swift refusal, reminding James that Margaret was already married to someone else.[11] The King of Scots then turned his attention back to Marie de Bourbon and decided that he must see her for himself.

After an abortive first attempt when he was driven back by storms,[12] he set off again at the beginning of September 1536. Sailing from Kirkcaldy to Dieppe, he arrived on 10 September and rode for St Quentin in Picardy, where the Duke of Vendôme had his Court. The story of what happened next has been much embroidered by historians, but it seems that James was in disguise and intended to pass himself off as the squire of one of his own attendants, John Tennant, Keeper of his Wardrobe. He had forgotten, however, that during the negotiations for Marie, his portrait had been sent to her. When he entered the ducal hall, she recognised him at once, and made him a deep curtsey, greeting him as King of Scots. James stayed for eight days at St Quentin,[13] but although he was entertained lavishly, he decided that he was not going to marry Marie after all. She was, it was later claimed, lame and misshapen, but it may well have been that the ducal court simply did not measure up to James's regal standards.

Whatever the reason, he left for the south of France, where Francis was engaged in his latest military campaign. Still incognito, he paused in Paris. It was the first time that a Scottish king had been in France since his great-great-grandfather James I had been taken there as a prisoner. James V was under no such restraint, and he was very excited by everything he saw. He dashed from one merchant to the next, buying lengths of cloth of gold and crimson velvet, jewellery and anything else that took his fancy.[14] At home in Scotland, he often passed himself off successfully as 'the Gude Man o' Ballengeich' when he rode about the country on his amorous exploits, but the sophisticated French soon saw through his disguise. As John Penven sardonically informed Sir George Douglas, James was 'running up and down the streets of Paris, buying any trifle himself, he thinking no man knows him'. However, 'any carter pointed with their finger saying, "Yonder goes le Roi d'Ecosse"'.[15]

When Francis I learned that James was in France, he sent him a message inviting him to come to Lyons. The two kings met at Chapelle, near Saint-Symphonen de Lay, on the road to Roanne. Francis gave the visitor a warm welcome and James asked to be treated as his son. This remark had a particular resonance, for the Dauphin had died two months earlier, plunging the court into mourning. Francis roused himself from his grief and honoured James by assigning to him the dead man's household. Many of the French hoped that James had come to offer military assistance, but of course it was something rather different that was on the Scottish king's mind, and he lost no time in telling Francis that he could not marry Marie de Bourbon. Instead, he reminded him that the Treaty of Rouen had promised him a princess.

This posed a major problem for Francis. He had assured Henry VIII that he would never marry one of his daughters to the King of Scots, and some of his own courtiers, including the influential Cardinal of Lorraine, were opposed to the match. The Cardinal wanted Madeleine for his own nephew Francis, son of the Duke of Lorraine, and was busily spreading rumours that James had committed himself to Margaret Erskine and was not free to marry anyone else. Apart from that, there was the embarrassing fact that Francis had actually ratified the draft marriage treaty between James and Marie. What was he to tell her family? Assuring James smoothly that they would go to visit his daughters, Francis played for time and made elaborate and long-drawn-out preparations for the trip. He also sought the approval of the Pope for a Scottish marriage, tried to persuade Henry VIII to withdraw his objections, and pondered how he could compensate Marie de Bourbon and her family for the loss of such a prestigious husband.

Happily, a solution occurred to him. Marie could marry the Cardinal of Lorraine's nephew instead. Although the Cardinal and his relatives promptly rejected the idea, Francis felt that his helpful suggestion exonerated him from any further responsibility, and when he learned that Henry VIII was deeply preoccupied with a rising in the north of England, he felt that it was safe to proceed. He and James set out at last for Amboise, where his daughters were staying with the Queen. As there was still no word yet from the Pope, Francis insisted on stopping at Châtellerault for three weeks, making the excuse that James must have the opportunity of enjoying the hunting there. When papal approval finally arrived, the royal party moved on and James met the princesses at last. Francis had told him that he might choose whomever he preferred, and without hesitation James selected Madeleine.

His intended bride was sixteen now, six years younger than James himself, charming, witty and vivacious, but she had contracted tuberculosis and she was suffering from severe bouts of fever. Indeed, she was too weak to ride and had to travel in a chariot when the Court moved from place to place. A portrait of her by Corneille de Lyon shows a thin, sallow, rather wistful girl.[16] James and Madeleine apparently fell passionately in love with each other as soon as they met, but of course there were other considerations too.[17] James was keenly aware that Madeleine, as the older sister, had the higher status, and for her part, according to Brantôme, she had always said that her greatest ambition was to be a queen. Her family and friends tried to dissuade her from marrying James, pointing out that she would have to go and stay in 'a barbarous country with a brutal people', but she replied, 'At least I should be Queen as long as I live, and that is what I have always wanted'.[18]

Madeleine's doctors warned that she could not survive the Scottish climate, but James brushed their opinion aside. In a way it is surprising that he was willing to ignore her perilous state of health, for one of the prime objects of the marriage would be to provide him with heirs, but then Madeleine's illness came and went, and everyone was always hoping that she would recover completely. She herself was adamant that she would go with him and, faced with her determination, Francis finally gave way. The Court moved on from Amboise and the marriage contract was signed at Blois on 26 November 1536.[19] Madeleine would bring with her a dowry of 100,000 gold crowns, a French crown being worth slightly more than a pound Scots,[20] and a further 30,000 francs a year was settled on James himself. In return, he gave Madeleine the earldoms of Strathearn and Fife, Falkland Palace and other lands as her jointure.

That same evening, the betrothal ceremony took place before a small gathering of guests. James had purchased the spousing ring set with a great table diamond in Paris, paying 1,100 crowns for it. The French royal family were there, of course, the King and Queen of Navarre, the Cardinal of Lorraine, the Venetian ambassador and the English ambassadors, Sir John Wallop and Stephen Gardiner. Henry VIII was not going to be able to complain that he had known nothing about the marriage treaty.[21] Afterwards, the Court travelled to Fontainebleau, where Francis planned to spend the winter. Accompanied by his future brothers-in-law, the Dauphin Henry and the Duke of Orléans, James decided to see some more of Paris before he settled down, and he and the Princes engaged in a round of parties and entertainments in the company of attractive young women.

After that, the King of Scots withdrew to the Abbey of Cluny for a religious retreat which the French soon complained was lasting too long.[22] James had inherited the Stewarts' religious intensity but, apart from that, he was probably exhausted after the excitement of his marriage negotiations. His high-spirited moods always did alternate with periods of lethargy and black depression. While he was in the seclusion of Cluny, he received a less than sincere letter from his uncle Henry VIII, congratulating him on his impending marriage and hoping that God would grant him children. Soon afterwards he was ready to emerge into public life once more. There was now great activity as plans went ahead for his formal entry into Paris and the actual wedding ceremony. A special wooden gallery was being erected, from Cardinal du Bellay's episcopal palace, where James would spend his last night as a single man, to the nearby Cathedral of Notre Dame where the marriage would take place on a special platform just outside the Cathedral. Scaffolding was being put up so that a huge number of spectators could watch, poets were composing celebratory verses and the invited guests were fussing about what they would wear to all the ceremonies.[23]

There was much pleasurable gossip, too, about the bride and groom. Henry VIII's ambassadors had already told him that James 'is a man of the fewest words that may be. The Ambassador of Venice was with him and spake a long matter unto him and neither by himself nor any other he answered him one word. He spake not to us very many. His wife shall temper him well, for she can speak, and if she spake as little as he, the house should be very quiet'.[24] At long last, Sunday 31 December 1536 came, and the members of the Paris Parlement assembled soon after noon in new scarlet robes to ride in solemn procession over the bridge of Notre Dame and out to St Anthony in the Fields, where James and his nobles were waiting, the King of Scots in a sumptuous crimson velvet and gold doublet slashed with cloth of gold, fringed with gold and lined with red taffeta.

James listened to the President of the Parlement's complimentary address, embraced him, but typically made no speech in reply. He and Francis I then rode side by side into Paris. The streets were hung with tapestries and packed with people as they made their way to Notre Dame for prayers before a lavish, celebratory supper.[25] Accounts of all these activities scarcely mention the bride, until the moment when she walked with her father up the steps and on to the platform hung with cloth of gold at ten o'clock on the morning of her wedding day, 1 January 1537. All the French royal family and nobility, including Marie de Bourbon's father, were there as were David Beaton, Sir David Lindsay and the other Scots who had accompanied James to France.

Louis, Cardinal de Bourbon, Marie de Bourbon's uncle, married the young couple, Francis ordered gold and silver coins to be scattered among the crowd, and James and Madeleine went down the steps and into the Cathedral for the nuptial mass. At the banquet afterwards, James apparently announced that he had ordered a special dessert, and had covered cups brought in, containing, so he said, the fruits of his own country. The lids were removed with a flourish to reveal gold dust and pieces of gold from the mines at Crawfordmuir. These were distributed among the guests, no doubt in an attempt to prove that Scotland was not such a wretched place after all. There was another banquet that evening, in the great hall of the Louvre, with dancing and masques.[26]

It was not possible to set sail for Scotland in the dead of winter, and so further, leisurely celebrations followed. As well as lavishing gifts of jewellery upon Madeleine, her father gave the young couple four sets of rich tapestry hangings, four sets of cloth-of-gold hangings, four of coarser arras, three very rich cloths of state and three rich beds. To these valuable presents he added a large cupboard of silver-gilt plate, a second cupboard of ungilded plate, sixteen fine tablecloths and twenty Persian carpets, probably for tables rather than for floors.[27] At long last everything was packed up and ready, Francis departed to rejoin his army, and James and Madeleine set off for the coast.

Until now, Madeleine had been remarkably well, but at Rouen she fell ill with such a violent fever that it was feared that she would die. The royal party had to spend a month there until she had recovered. They moved on at last, and by 7 May, Madeleine was able to write from Montvilliers to the French Chancellor on behalf of two of her servants who were both involved in a lawsuit. Jean de St Aubin, her maître d'hôtel, and Charles de Marconnay, one of her valets, were going with her to Scotland, and they were anxious to have everything settled before they set sail. On the same day, 33 ells of yellow and red satin (the Scottish royal colours) were purchased for the uniforms of the four trumpeters, four

drummers and three fifes who were also accompanying the Queen
of Scots to her new life. Madame de Montreuil, her governess,
was in her retinue, as were eight other ladies and the Bishop of
Limoges.[28]

On 11 May, Madeleine, James and all their attendants embarked
at Dieppe. Storms delayed them for another two or three days, and
when they finally did set sail the gales were so fierce that they had to
anchor one night off Scarborough until the wind moderated.[29] After
a voyage lasting four days, they sailed into Leith on 19 May 1537.
When she landed, Queen Madeleine knelt down and kissed the
ground, in gratitude to God for having brought them safely ashore.
James then escorted her to Holyroodhouse. Warned in advance by
the gloomy French courtiers that Scotland was very different from
France, Madeleine told one of her pages, the poet Ronsard, that it
was 'just as she had been previously told', and he said that he also
heard her exclaim ruefully, 'Alas, I would be a queen!'[30]

Everyone was worried about her health, but the Scots were
delighted with their new Queen, admiring her spirit and hoping
that she was on the way to recovery. The Bishop of Limoges,
writing to tell Francis I of their safe arrival, remarked, 'they have
hopes of the cure of this princess, thanks to the care of her old
doctor, Maître Patrix'.[31] Madame de Montreuil, however, would
remark that Madeleine 'had no good days after she came to Scotland,
but was always sickly with a catarrh which descended into her
stomach'.[32] James wrote urgently to his father-in-law, asking him
to send over the famous physician, Monsieur Francisco, and held
a conference of his own doctors about his wife's health. On their
advice, Madeleine seems to have made a short stay at Balmerino
Abbey in Fife, where the air was very healthy, but as soon as she
began to improve she insisted on returning to Edinburgh because
she wanted to be with her husband.

Meanwhile, preparations were being made for her formal entry
into Edinburgh and her coronation. There would be processions,
pageants and the fountains would flow with wine. Madeleine wrote
to her father's Grand Master of the Household, urging him to
remind Francis about the pearls he had promised her and asking
for a rosary to be sent with her royal robe, as it had none. The fur
trimming of the robe must be beautiful, she said.[33] She was feeling

so much better that she believed that she had almost completely recovered. 'Sire,' she wrote to her father on 8 June, 'Since the King of Scotland requested you to send Master Francisco the physician, there is a great amendment, thanks to God, for all my sufferings are abated, so that if he come now, he can only be allowed to contribute to my perfect cure.'[34] In fact, her disease was only in remission and on 7 July she died peacefully in her husband's arms.

Sir David Lindsay was among the poets who composed elegies for Madeleine. His 'Deploration of the Death of Queen Magdalene' rages against Venus and Cupid, amongst others, for taking away this young Princess. They in their Court 'never had sic two/So leal [loyal] lovers, without dissimulance/As James the Fifth and Magdalene of France'. The happy preparations made for her entry into Edinburgh were abruptly cancelled, garments of joy laid aside and replaced by mourning, 'Our "Alleluia!" has turned into "Alas!"' On the very day of her death, James wrote to Francis to tell him what had happened, saying that if it were not for the fact that he was relying on the French King to remain 'his good father', he would be in even greater pain. Sincere as his grief might be, James' thoughts were already turning to his next wife.[35]

Madeleine was buried in Holyrood Abbey and, soon afterwards, David Beaton set off to persuade Francis I that he must send Princess Marguerite to take her sister's place.[36] Several of Madeleine's attendants travelled to France with him, but most of her household remained in Scotland to await the new bride. Five years later some of her belongings were still in Edinburgh Castle. There were her gowns of black velvet, black taffeta and cloth of gold, her crimson velvet and cloth-of-gold nightgowns (dressing gowns), her silver-gilt altar vessels and the two little gold cups and the agate cup with the gold basin and laver which, the inventory poignantly records, had been used by Queen Madeleine 'when she was a bairn'.[37]

Notes

1. Donaldson, *Scottish Kings*, 155–9; text partially printed in Donaldson, *Scottish Historical Documents*, 99–100.
2. Strickland, i, *Queens of Scotland*, 273; Retha M. Warnicke, *The Rise and Fall of Anne Boleyn* (Cambridge 1989), 22.
3. Strickland, *Queens of Scotland* i, 273.
4. Reproduced in Etienne Jollet, *Jean et François Clouet* (Paris 1997), 76.
5. MacLagan and Louda, *Lines of Succession*, Table 67; Bouyer, *Dictionnaire*, 267–9; Strickland, *Queens of Scotland*, i, 272.
6. *Ibid.*, i, 273–9; Bouyer, *Dictionnaire*, 248–9; Bertière, *Reines de France*, 154–66, 173–4, 186–90; Eric Ives, *Anne Boleyn* (Oxford 1986), 40.
7. *Papiers d'état*, ed. Teulet, i, 66.
8. Bouyer, *Dictionnaire*, 251; Strickland, *Queens of Scotland*, i, 278–82.
9. Bapst, *Mariages*, 33–175; Donaldson, *Scottish Kings*, 155–9.
10. *Mémoires de Martinet Guillaume du Bellay*, ed. V-L. Bourrilly and F. Vindry (Paris 1908–19), iii, 338–9; Bentley Cranch and Marshall, 'Iconography and Literature', 275; Bapst, *Mariages*, 233–72.
11. Bapst, *Mariages*, 279.
12. *Ibid.*, 283–5.
13. *Ibid.*, 287–9; Cameron, *James V*, 131.
14. Bapst, *Mariages*, 291; Rosalind K. Marshall, '"To be the Kingis Grace ane Dowblett"': the Costume of James V, King of Scots', in *Costume: The Journal of the Costume Society* (London 1994), 18–20; Rosalind K. Marshall, 'The Jewellery of James V, King of Scots', in *Jewellery Studies*, 7 (London 1996), 83–4.
15. Bapst, *Mariages*, 291 and 291n.
16. This painting was stolen from the Musée des Beaux Arts in Blois on 19 July 1996 and subsequently destroyed; Anne Dubois de Groër, *Corneille de la Haye dit Corneille de Lyon* (Paris 1996), 111–2.
17. Strickland, *Queens of Scotland*, i, 293–5.
18. Bapst, *Mariages*, 302; see also A.H. Millar, 'Scotland described for Queen Magdalene: a curious volume', in *SHR*, i (1904), 27–38.
19. Bapst, *Mariages*, 304; Margaret Sanderson, *Cardinal of Scotland* (Edinburgh 1986), 64.
20. Cameron, *James V*, 281, n.47.
21. Bapst, *Mariages*, 304 and 304n; Strickland, *Queens of Scotland*, i, 301.
22. Bapst, *Mariages*, 305.
23. *Papiers d'état*, ed. Teulet, i, 122–3; *L and P Henry VIII*, xi, no. 1352; Bentley Cranch and Marshall, 'Iconography and Literature', 273–4.

24. Bapst, *Mariages*, 307.
25. Strickland, *Queens of Scotland*, i, 304, 278.
26. *Ibid.*, i, 303–12; Bapst, *Mariages*, 308; Bentley Cranch and Marshall, 'Iconography and Literature', 279.
27. *Historical Works of Sir James Balfour*, i, 266–7.
28. Strickland, *Queens of Scotland*, i, 315–16.
29. *Ibid.*, i, 315–18; Bapst, *Mariages*, 309–10.
30. Strickland, *Queens of Scotland*, i, 326.
31. *Ibid.*, i, 318–19.
32. *Ibid.*, i, 327.
33. *Ibid.*, i, 318.
34. *Ibid.*, i, 322–5.
35. *Sir David Lyndsay: Selected Poems*, ed. Janet Hadley Williams (Glasgow 2000), 101–8; Bentley Cranch and Marshall, 'Iconography and Literature', 282.
36. *Ibid.*, 283.
37. *A Collection of Inventories and other Records of the Royal Wardrobe and Jewelhouse; and of the Artillery and Munitioun in some of the Royal Castles 1488–1606* (Edinburgh 1815), 100–101, 63, 58.

CHAPTER NINE

MARY OF GUISE

It was all very well for James V to assume that Princess Marguerite was his for the asking, but Francis I had other ideas. Busy as he was with his military campaigns against Charles V, he could not risk Henry VIII taking offence and invading France. In any case, he had no intention of exposing his sole surviving daughter to the rigours of the Scottish climate, and so he offered Mary of Guise instead. The eldest daughter of his friend Claud, Duke of Guise, a famous military hero, Mary had an impeccable pedigree, for she was descended from the earlier French king, St Louis. Moreover, she was herself recently widowed. She and James could console one another.[1]

Born on 20 November 1515 at Bar-le-Duc, Mary was the eldest of twelve children. She was brought up at Joinville, an elegant, turreted castle set amidst apple, plum, orange, lemon and pomegranate orchards on a vine-covered hill above the River Marne in Lorraine. Her parents' household had more than a hundred servants, with fine singers and the famous composer Clément Jannequin supplying the music in the ornate castle chapel.[2] It was a luxurious and cultured environment. Religion meant a great deal to the Guise family, and as soon as she was old enough her parents sent Mary to Claud's mother, Philippa of Gueldres, who had recently retired to a nunnery of Poor Clares at Pont-à-Mousson. By planning a career in the Church for Mary and his other daughters, Claud was not only showing his devotion to religion. He would save himself the expense of providing them with large dowries.

In the nunnery, Mary experienced a very different way of life from the one she had known. Like the other nuns, her grandmother slept on a straw mattress on bare boards, wore simple clothes of the coarsest material, ate the plainest food, cooked, weeded the garden and worked in the laundry. Mary may not have shared in all these austerities, but she would certainly have been expected to help her grandmother, and in return she received an education designed to fit her to become an abbess.[3] It was presumably at this time that Philippa gave her the Book of Hours which survives to this day in the National Library of Scotland bearing Mary's signature and including in its litany the name of St Clare.

Claud's elder brother, Anthony, Duke of Lorraine, the head of the family, had other ideas. Visiting his mother when Mary was about fourteen, he decided that his tall, well-built, charming niece was far too eligible to be shut away from the world. At this time the King's two elder sons were still single and Duke Anthony may have harboured hopes of a very prestigious marriage alliance. At any rate, he convinced his reluctant mother that he should take Mary away to his own palace at Nancy, where he and his wife would prepare her to be launched into society.[4] On 5 March 1531 Francis I's new Queen, Eleanor of Austria, was crowned at St Denis and immediately after the ceremony Duke Anthony presented Mary to the King and Queen. A few days later, in a mantle of purple velvet and a surcoat of ermine heavily encrusted with jewels, she rode in procession with Eleanor's ladies when the Queen made her formal entry into Paris.

For the next three years, Mary spent most of her time at the centre of one of the most civilised and elegant courts in Europe, enjoying the friendship of the King's daughters, Madeleine and Marguerite, and earning great praise not only for her wit but for her modest, circumspect behaviour. She did not, in the end, marry a royal prince, but she was betrothed to Louis, Duke of Longueville, Grand Chamberlain of France. He was a year or two older than she and owned extensive estates in Normandy and the Loire Valley, with castles at Rouen, Amiens and Châteaudun. When Mary's father refused to give more than 80,000 livres as her dowry, the King came to the rescue, supplying the additional 40,000 livres. Louis settled on her the lands and castle of Châteaudun.[5]

They were married on 4 August 1534 in the chapel royal of the Palace of the Louvre, before the royal family and the entire Court. Afterwards, there were 'jousts and tournaments for sixteen days, in great triumph'.[6] They then settled into a pleasant routine, spending a great deal of time at Court but, in the summer months, travelling round their estates, making a ceremonial entry into each of the towns they visited. Wherever they went, Mary made a point of visiting the sick and the poor, providing for orphans and others in need of financial assistance. This was the traditional role for a great lady, but she seems to have been particularly energetic and concerned, and she no doubt expected to spend the rest of her life in this way, at the same time raising a large family.[7]

Her first child was born on 30 October 1535 at Amiens Castle, a son named Francis, after the King.[8] A year later, she and Louis must have been at Court when James V arrived to claim a French bride, and they certainly attended his marriage to Mary's friend Princess Madeleine on 1 January 1537.[9] Mary was pregnant again, and late that spring she left Paris and crossed the great plain of Beaune to stay at her castle of Châteaudun rather than travelling through Normandy with Louis. The castle had belonged to his ancestor Jean, Count of Dunois, the friend of Joan of Arc, and it was a fine place, with an elegant, late Gothic chapel next to the original twelfth-century sturdy round tower. Mary's apartments were in a delicately ornate Gothic wing built by her father-in-law. Its spacious chambers have huge fireplaces and long rows of windows looking out over the castle's terraced gardens at one side and the gorge of the Loire on the other.

Louis intended to join his wife, but he was delayed, and sent her an apologetic letter telling her that he was ill. He had a headache and a rash, he said, and his doctors had diagnosed chicken pox. He would, they had told him, be better soon. 'I shall say no more', he concluded, 'praying God to give you always whatever you desire . . . your good husband and friend, Louis.' A few days later, on 9 June 1537, he died at Rouen. Mary kept his letter for the rest of her life.[10] Later that summer, she received word that her friend Queen Madeleine had died in Scotland on 7 July. On 4 August 1537 her second son, Louis, was born at Châteaudun. A few weeks later, she received a letter from Francis I telling that she was to become the wife of James V, King of Scots as soon as possible. She was appalled, but she dared not oppose him and her distress intensified when the marriage plans were rushed forward with unseemly haste. David Beaton, the Scottish envoy, had heard rumours that the Dauphin Henry was in love with Mary and meant to put away his wife,

Catherine de Medici, so that he could marry her instead. To add to the complications, when Henry VIII heard about James's plans he promptly tried to counter them by announcing that he intended to marry Mary himself.[11]

As if this were not troublesome enough, Mary learned that her father intended giving no money at all as her dowry. The 115,000 livres the Scots were demanding would have to come from the Longueville lands, with an additional sum supplied by the King. Mary opposed this vehemently, for it meant that when she died, the French properties which rightfully belonged to her son the little Duke would pass to James V instead. Before any of this could be settled, her baby son Louis died at the age of four months.[12] After strenuous efforts by Mary, her mother and their friend Marguerite, Queen of Navarre, Francis finally agreed to provide 70,000 livres and told Claud that he would have to supply the other 80,000 livres himself.

In return, James promised to settle Falkland Palace on Mary, along with the castles of Stirling, Dingwall and Threave, the earldoms of Strathearn, Ross, Orkney and Fife, and the lordships of Galloway, Ardmannach and the Isles. The contract was signed at Lyons at the end of March, James V sent to the Pope for a dispensation because he and Mary were both descended from the Dukes of Gueldres,[13] and in April a large contingent of Scots arrived at Châteaudun for the betrothal ceremony. James was not coming in person this time to collect his bride and so, on 9 May 1538, it was Lord Maxwell who placed on Mary's finger a diamond spousing ring which had cost a fraction of the one James had given Madeleine.[14]

On 10 June 1538, Mary sailed from Le Havre, leaving her small son to be brought up by her mother at Joinville. The parting was very painful, but she knew that his future lay in France, for he was Hereditary Grand Chamberlain. Sailing with the same three royal galleys that had taken Madeleine to Scotland the previous year, Mary arrived at Balcomie Castle in Fife on Trinity Sunday. The following morning, James V escorted her to St Andrews, where they were married in the Cathedral. After forty days of celebrations, they set off on a tour of the new Queen's jointure lands, Mary delighting everyone with her tactful, enthusiastic comments about what she saw. Linlithgow Palace, she said, was as fine as any castle in France. Finally, she made her formal entry into Edinburgh on St Margaret's Day, 16 November 1538.[15]

Eagerly reading regular reports from her mother about her small son, Mary took up her new role. She and James spoke French together and she began learning Scots. She won over her difficult mother-in-law, Margaret Tudor, and was kind to James's various illegitimate children, taking his small daughter Lady Jane Stewart into her own household. She sent to France for masons to help with James's ambitious building plans, miners to mine the gold at Crawfordmuir and seedlings for their gardens. Her husband's letters to her are almost deferential in tone. With her tall, statuesque figure and her regal manner she already had a formidable presence, and he was well aware that she had the full support of the French king. In his worsening relationship with England, that was more important than ever.[16]

Mary and her family were anxious that she should have a child as soon as possible, for they were afraid that James might repudiate her if she did not give him a son. It was noticeable that he had not yet arranged her coronation. However, when she had been in Scotland for just over a year, she found that she was pregnant. Delighted, James appointed the coronation to take place at Holyrood Abbey on 22 February 1540,[17] and on 22 May Mary gave birth to the desired boy, amidst great rejoicing. Only two months after the arrival of Prince James, she conceived again and Prince Robert was born at Stirling on 24 April 1541. After only a week, however, the celebrations were brutally cut short by a dreadful tragedy. Prince James was being brought up with his own household at St Andrews and he suddenly fell ill and died there. A few hours later, the new baby died at Stirling. The Princes were buried together in the Abbey of Holyrood, in the same vault as Queen Madeleine, and Margaret Tudor wrote to tell Henry VIII that the King and Queen were both in great distress.[18]

Mary was tormented by rumours that her children had been poisoned, and although James V tried to console her, his own confidence was shattered. If he had distrusted his courtiers before, his suspicion of them now bordered on paranoia. From childhood he had been unable to rely on any of those around him and he was convinced that his nobles were plotting his death. Worse still, he began to imagine that Mary was unfaithful to him. Four brief letters written by him in French to Mary after Margaret Tudor's death in November 1541 give some hint of friction between them. He had gone to Methven to sort out his mother's affairs, but people had apparently been hinting that he was staying away from his Queen on purpose. Although he denied this, the rumours that he had a mistress persisted.[19]

By the summer of 1542, Mary was pregnant again, but there was little cause for rejoicing. Henry VIII had been trying to prove that he was Scotland's overlord, and when that failed, he decided to send his forces north. James marched towards the Borders with his own army, but suffered a crushing defeat at the Battle of Solway Moss. He was not himself present at the battle, but this latest disaster brought him to the verge of nervous collapse. 'His mind near gone through dolour and care', he rode to Tantallon Castle in East Lothian where it was said that he kept a mistress. After a brief visit to Linlithgow, he moved on to Falkland, where he took to his bed with a high fever. On 8 December 1542, Mary gave birth to their third child, a daughter. James V died six days later and the baby, Mary, became Queen of Scots.[20]

Lord Lisle, the English commander, quickly sent a message to Henry VIII telling him that he 'thought it should not be to your Majesty's honour that we, your soldiers, should make war or invade upon a dead body or upon a widow or on a young suckling his daughter' but everyone knew that this was merely an interlude in the hostilities.[21] The country was confronted with the worst crisis that it had known for centuries. Mary might have expected to become regent for her daughter but, lying in childbed at Linlithgow, she could do nothing to assert her rights and the Scottish nobility were determined that they were not going to be ruled by a woman again. Pushing aside Cardinal David Beaton, who wanted to be regent himself, they appointed James, 2nd Earl of Arran, head of the powerful House of Hamilton and heir to the throne, to be Lord Governor. That done, the king was buried in the Abbey of Holyrood beside his first wife and his two infant sons.[22]

Seizing his opportunity, Henry VIII announced that he wanted to marry his only son, Prince Edward, to Mary, Queen of Scots,

Arran quickly agreed and the Treaties of Greenwich were signed on 1 July 1543. As soon as she was eleven, the little Queen was to be taken to England for her wedding. But Arran was a notoriously weak and vacillating young man, and Cardinal Beaton, who was a much more forceful personality, went to work on him. In December the Scottish parliament declared the Treaties of Greenwich null and void and on 15 December 1543 Scotland's alliance with France was solemnly renewed.[23]

Henry VIII's reaction was swift and predicable. He sent Edward, Earl of Hertford, north with an army, the first of the English invasions known as 'The Rough Wooing'. Hertford had been ordered to sack Holyroodhouse, and when he desecrated the Abbey where James V and her two sons were buried, Mary of Guise was particularly upset. Blaming Arran for the entire débâcle, she tried to wrest the regency from him but he managed to cling on to power and she was unable to remove him. In the end it was agreed that he would remain Lord Governor but she would be the principal member of a special council set up to advise him.

Although Francis I sent forces to assist the Scots against the English, 'The Rough Wooing' continued, and in May 1546 Cardinal Beaton was murdered by a band of Protestants in revenge for having burned at the stake George Wishart, a leading Protestant. Henry VIII had long been trying to destabilise the Scottish government by encouraging the spread of Protestantism, and now more and more Scots were adopting the reformed religion and turning to England for assistance instead of France. In January 1547 Henry VIII died, to be followed four months later by Francis I. Mary of Guise's old friend the Dauphin now became Henry II, while England was ruled by the Earl of Hertford as Lord Protector for Henry's nine-year-old son, Edward VI. 'The Rough Wooing' continued and on 10 September the Scots were routed at Pinkie Cleugh, near Edinburgh.

Informed of the disaster, Henry II decided that the time had come to end England's aspirations in Scotland once and for all. He would send the Scots more help, on condition that they marry Mary, Queen of Scots to his son, the Dauphin Francis.[24] Mary of Guise could hardly bear to part with the child, but when she heard on 21 February 1548 that yet another English army was on its way north, she hurriedly took her daughter to Dumbarton Castle on the west coast, ready to be whisked away to France. The English did not stay in Scotland for long but, as well as causing the usual destruction in the Borders, they captured Haddington, the wealthy and strategically placed market town some twenty miles east of Edinburgh.[25]

Mary of Guise persuaded Arran to begin the siege of Haddington and, at last, in June, a French fleet arrived. Mary sent the reinforcements to Haddington and rode along the High Street of Edinburgh, rooting out deserters from the Scottish army. She urged them not to forget their honour and assured them that she had always said that no nation on earth could equal their courage. On 7 July 1548, she was one of the signatories of the Treaty of Haddington by which it was agreed that her daughter would be the Dauphin's bride. She spent the next two days touring the Scottish and French camps, and on the evening of Monday 9 July narrowly escaped death when the English cannon fired on her as she was about to climb the tower of St Mary's Church, just outside Haddington, for a better view of the siege. More than sixteen of her retinue fell wounded and dying around her and, although unharmed, she fainted from shock. After she had arranged the funerals of the dead, she hurried to Dumbarton to see her daughter set sail for France.[26]

The Earl of Arran had been bribed by Henry II to agree to the Treaty of Haddington, and he now had a new French title: Duke of Châtelherault. The combined French and Scottish efforts to take Haddington met with little success, however, and it was not until September 1549 that the English garrison, weakened by sickness and short of supplies, finally left. When the French and the English signed the Treaty of Boulogne on 24 March 1550, agreeing a peace in which Scotland was included, the threat of an English invasion was at last removed and Mary of Guise decided to visit France. In part this was because she was desperate to see her children again, but there was another pressing reason. She was determined to persuade Henry II that Châtelherault should be removed from his position as Lord Governor so that she could rule as regent herself. Henry had to be consulted, for when his son married her daughter, the Dauphin would become King of Scots.

Taking with her a large retinue of troublesome Scottish nobles whom she did not dare leave behind, Mary arrived in France in September 1550 to find Henry II waiting at Rouen with her children. Francis, the baby son she had left behind, was almost fifteen now, and little Mary was nearly eight. After a rapturous reception, Mary of Guise travelled with the Court to Chartres and then Blois, and visited her own castle of Châteaudun in February 1551. There were disquieting rumours that Henry II meant to replace Arran with a Frenchman so that Mary of Guise could stay in France with her children, but she made sure that Henry knew that she had no intention of doing that.[27] She had always treated Francis I with the greatest deference, but Henry was an old friend and she could speak more freely to him. The English ambassador, afraid that she would persuade the French king to renew his war with England, declared sourly that her 'service in Scotland is so highly taken here as she is in this Court made a goddess'.[28]

Mary dared not leave the Scots to their own devices for too long, and in April she began to prepare for her voyage north. However, she was deeply shaken when a plot to poison Mary, Queen of Scots was discovered at the end of the month and she postponed her departure. 'The Dowager of Scotland makes all this Court weary of her, from high to low, such an importunate beggar is she for herself and her chosen friends,' Sir John Mason reported, adding, 'The King would fain be rid of her'.[29] In fact, Mary continued to be treated as an honoured guest, accompanying Henry when he visited Tours, Angers and Nantes and then made a progress through Brittany that summer. When the Court moved on to Fontainebleau, she took her Scottish retinue to Joinville, to see her childhood home, and stayed there until the beginning of September.[30]

With the approach of autumn, she knew that she would have to leave, for galleys could not sail in rough weather. She began to travel towards the coast, but at Amiens her son Francis was taken ill, and although she nursed him herself, he died in her arms.[31] She bore his loss with characteristic fortitude, saw to all the arrangements for his funeral and then sailed from Dieppe in mid-October, not to Scotland but to Rye on the English coast. She had decided to visit Edward VI and then complete her journey overland. Her visit was brief and ceremonial in nature, with processions, entertainments and a banquet at which she sat next to the young King under the same cloth of state. No doubt she was eager to assess the various English statesmen for herself, and she was possibly curious to see this boy who had so nearly married her daughter. She left London on 6 November and was back in Scotland in time for Christmas.[32]

She now set about bribing the Duke of Châtelherault to resign as governor, offering financial inducements and gifts of property to his relatives and promising him the position of Lieutenant General of Scotland, an office he would be allowed to pass on to his eldest son. Her letters to her brothers at this time make it clear that she shared the general French view that Scotland was an infant nation which would have to be led carefully into the modern world. Finally convinced, Châtelherault signed a personal contract with Mary on 19 February 1554, accepting all these benefits and agreeing that he would formally hand over the government of the country to her. When parliament opened on 12 April, he solemnly resigned and Henry II's representative, the Sieur d'Oysel, placed the Scottish crown on Mary's head and handed her the sceptre and the sword of state.[33]

When parliament met in June, much of the legislation was concerned with the administration of justice as Mary tried to restore law and order after the long years of warfare and chaos. A committee was set up to fix weights and measures, game laws were re-enacted in an effort to improve the food supply, and laws to prevent trees being cut down were repeated. Later that summer she travelled to Dumfries to supervise the trial of Border thieves, and the following year she held justice ayres throughout the country.[34] It was an uphill task. Apart from resenting a woman ruler, the Scots were becoming increasingly alarmed that they were being taken over by France and they resisted almost everything she proposed. 'God knows, brother, what a life I lead,' she told Charles, Cardinal of Lorraine. 'It is no small thing to bring a young nation to a state of perfection . . . .Happy is he who has least to do with worldly affairs. I can safely say that for twenty years past I have not had one year of rest, and I think that if I were to say not one month I should not be far wrong, for a troubled spirit is the greatest trial of all.'[35]

For the previous ten years Mary had been afraid that Henry II might not keep his promise to marry the Dauphin to Mary, Queen of Scots, but to her relief the ceremony finally took place on 24 April

1558. She was not there, of course, for she dared not leave Scotland. Protestant tracts and English translations of the Bible were pouring in and an alarming number of the nobility were converting to the reformed faith for reasons that had little to do with religion. In August 1558 there was a riot when the image of St Giles was attacked as it was carried in procession through the streets in the presence of Mary herself, and the Protestants were demanding the right to hold services in English and take both wine and bread at communion instead of only the bread given at the Catholic mass. On 17 November 1558, Catholic Mary I of England died and was succeeded by Protestant Elizabeth I, giving the Scottish Protestants a potentially powerful new ally.[36]

When the Protestant preacher John Knox arrived back from exile the following spring and there were riots after he preached an inflammatory sermon in Perth, Mary marched there with an army but, outnumbered, had to withdraw. The stress was beginning to affect her usually robust health, and when the Protestant Lords of the Congregation assembled their forces at St Andrews she did not have the strength to move against them in person. After a confrontation in Fife, the Congregation occupied Edinburgh, pulling down images in friaries and abbeys, burning prayer books and removing chalices. Mary commanded them to leave the capital, but she had no way of enforcing her orders and was forced to sign an agreement with them on 23 July 1559 at Leith Links. In return for freedom of worship, the Congregation would leave Edinburgh and obey the authority of Mary, Queen of Scots and the Dauphin.[37]

A few days later, Mary received word that her old friend Henry II had died after being wounded in a tournament. Her son-in-law the Dauphin was now King Francis II and her daughter was Queen of France as well as Queen of Scots.[38] At the end of August, the Duke of Châtelherault changed sides and joined the Congregation. 'Our troubles and affairs increase here by the hour,' Mary told one of her brothers, 'and I am reduced to such need that I shall be forced to retire with all the French to Leith, very poorly furnished with money and with little in the way of food and other supplies.'

She wrote to Francis II as well, begging him to send an army and money as soon as he could.[39] She was by this time seriously ill with what seems to have been chronic heart disease but she managed to slip away to Leith just before the Protestant army marched back to Edinburgh and took the town once more. On 21 October the Lords of the Congregation announced that her regency was suspended. Instead, the country would be ruled by a council led by Châtelherault. However, when they tried to attack Leith, d'Oysel drove them off and they were forced to withdraw to Linlithgow.

Mary returned to Holyroodhouse the next morning. She was so ill that there were rumours of her death, and the French wanted to replace her with her youngest brother, René, Marquis d'Elboeuf. She refused to retire to France, however, and by sheer force of will she was up and about again by Christmas, holding a council meeting. Even her enemies were forced to praise her as 'a woman with a man's courage',[40] but on 22 January 1560 an English fleet sailed into the estuary of the Firth of Forth. Elizabeth I had sent help to the Protestants and Mary's few remaining supporters began to drift away. On 27 February 1560 the Lords of the Congregation signed the Treaty of Berwick with the English, promising to resist any annexation of their country to France in return for Elizabeth's protection. The French were still sending vague promises of assistance to Mary, but no men or money came and in March 1560 an English army entered Scotland. By 29 March they were just outside Edinburgh, and Mary took refuge in Edinburgh Castle.

Playing for time, she negotiated with the English commander, and when the French envoy, the Bishop of Valence, arrived to try to mediate, he found her 'in want especially of health and of everything else except greatness of spirit and good understanding, for she is quite undaunted by these troubles'.[41] Her condition was deteriorating rapidly, however, and although she went on determinedly fortifying the castle and trying to contact d'Oysel, who was besieged in Leith, by June 1 she could no longer eat and found it easier to pass the night sitting in a chair rather than lying down. Realising that she was dying, she sent for the Lords and asked them to forgive her if she had ever offended any of them. When they left, many of them were in tears. Her stepson Lord James Stewart and the Earl of Argyll were with her when she died, at about half an hour after midnight on 11 June 1560.[42]

On 6 July, the Scots, the French and the English signed the Treaty of Edinburgh, agreeing that all foreign troops should withdraw from Scotland except for small French garrisons at Inchkeith and Dunbar. Mary, Queen of Scots would stop quartering the English arms with the French and the Scots, and a council of state, chosen jointly by her and by the Scottish parliament, would govern the country in her absence. On 15 July the French began to embark for home, the English moved away from Leith and the local people started dismantling the fortifications. When parliament met in August, its members passed a series of acts making Scotland an officially Protestant country.

Mary of Guise's body lay in its lead coffin in the little Chapel of St Margaret on the highest point of the rock of Edinburgh Castle for many months. The Protestants refused to allow her a Catholic burial at Holyrood, and it was not until 16 March 1561 that the coffin was finally taken at midnight to a ship in Leith harbour and transported to Rheims. She was buried in the Abbey Church of St Pierre-les-Dames, where her youngest sister was abbess, and a splendid monument with her bronze effigy in royal robes was erected over her tomb.[43] Although her regency had ended in failure, Mary of Guise had not only succeeded in preserving the throne for her daughter. She had ruled Scotland more effectively than any woman had done before.

Notes

1. *L and P Henry VIII*, ii, 150.
2. René de Bouillé, *Histoire des Ducs de Guise* (Paris 1849), i, 41, 54, 97n, 220–3; Pimodan, *Mère des Guises*, 14, 23–4, 32–6, 96–8; H. Forneron, *Les Ducs de Guise et Leur Epoque* (Paris 1877), i, 42; H. Noel Williams, *The Brood of False Lorraine* (London n.d.), 5–6.
3. Micheline de Fontette, *Les Réligieuses à l'âge classique du Droit Canon* (Paris 1967), 129–51; C. Merigot, *La Vie de la Serenissime Philippe de Gueldres* (Paris 1627); Pimodan, *Mère des Guises*, 28–9; Coste, *Eloges*, ii, 535.
4. *Ibid.*, ii, 536; d'Espence, Oraison, 26–9.
5. Pimodan, *Mère des Guises* 59–60; Strickland, *Queens of Scotland*, i, 342–5; *The Letters of James V*, ed. Denys Hay (Scottish History Society 1954), 340–1; Paris, Archives Nationales, KK907, f.3 (discharge for the third instalment of Mary's dowry, 1537).

6. *Le Journal d'un bourgeois de Paris*, ed. V-L. Bourrilly (Paris 1910), 19–23.
7. d'Espence, *Oraison*, 33–7; Coste, *Eloges*, ii, 536–7.
8. Strickland, *Queens of Scotland*, i, 345.
9. Desmond Seward, *Prince of the Renaissance* (London 1973), 51–9.
10. *Balcarres Papers*, i, 5.
11. *L and P Henry VIII*, ii, 150, 291–2, 336–7, 348, 421–2, 449.
12. Pimodan, *Mère des Guises*, 65.
13. *L and P Henry VIII*, ii, 150, 291–2, 336–7, 348, 421–2, 449, 453, 540–1; *Balcarres Papers*, i, 3–5; *Papiers d'état*, ed. Teulet, 14.
14. *Inventaire Chronologique des Documents relatifs à l'histoire d'Ecosse*, ed. A. Teulet (Abbotsford Club 1839), 88; Bibliothèque Nationale, f.fr. 5467, f.66; *Treasurer's Accounts*, vii, 56.
15. Pitscottie, *Historie*, i, 377–81; Lesley, *History of Scotland*, ii, 241; *Diurnal of Occurrents*, 22.
16. *Treasurer's Accounts*, vii, 130–1, 136–8, 149, 173, 182, 184, 204–5, 252; NLS, *Balcarres Papers*, iv, 45; *Balcarres Papers*, i, 18–19, 20, 25, 27, 33, 34, 38; E. Marianne H. McKerlie, *Mary of Guise-Lorraine, Queen of Scotland* (London 1931), 48.
17. *Treasurer's Accounts*, vii, 177–8; *Diurnal of Occurrents*, 23.
18. *Treasurer's Accounts*, vii, 312, 319–20, 333, 396–7, 403–4, 433, 442, 445, 495; Pitscottie, *Historie*, i, 382, 394; *Balcarres Papers*, i, 51–2, 60–1; *Diurnal of Occurrents*, 24; Lesley, *History*, ii, 246; *Hamilton Papers*, i, 73.
19. *Ibid.*, i, 74; NLS, *Balcarres Papers*, 29.2.1/4–6; Marshall, *Mary of Guise, Queen of Scots*, 38–44.
20. Donaldson, *James V to James VII*, 60; Lesley, *History*, ii, 258–9; *Hamilton Papers*, i, 329, 333, 334–7, 336–58; Pitscottie, *Historie*, i, 407–8; ii, 3–4; *CSP Spanish*, vi (2), 189–90, 192–3, 222–3.
21. *Hamilton Papers*, i, 358.
22. Pitscottie, *Historie*, i 407–8; *Hamilton Papers*, i, 336–58; *CSP Spanish*, vi (2), 189–90.
23. *Hamilton Papers*, i, 342, 358, 370, 387–91, 397–8, 405, 448, 450–3, 461, 462–8, 526, 554–94, 597; ii, 12–20; *The State Papers and Letters of Sir Ralph Sadler*, ed. Arthur Clifford (Edinburgh 1809), i, 84–8, 93–270; Donaldson, *Scottish Historical Documents*, 110–11.
24. *Hamilton Papers*, ii, 89–90, 137–42, 186–8, 220–1, 241, 250–1, 276–7, 294, 323, 337, 325–7, 361–80, 409–10, 415, 433–5, 486, 537–8, 552–65; *Balcarres Papers*, i, 31, 33–4, 38–40, 57–8, 67–70, 82–3, 89–92, 95–7, 104–5, 106–8, 108–11, 129–30, 136–8, 151–2, 174–81; *Two Missions*, ed. Dickinson, 19; Jules de la Brosse, *Histoire d'un Capitaine Bourbonnais au XVIe siècle, Jacques de la Brosse 1485–1562, ses Missions en Ecosse* (Paris 1929); *CSP Scot.*, i, 17–18, 54, 58; Marcus Merriman, *The Rough Wooings* (East Linton 2000).

25. Marshall, *Ruin and Restoration*, 13–19.
26. *CSP Scot.*, i, 85, 115–22; *CSP Foreign Series 1547–53*, 20; *Diurnal of Occurrents*, 46–7; *Histoire de la guerre d'Ecosse; pendant les campagnes 1548 et 1549 par Jean de Beaugué* (Maitland Club 1830), 11–13, 37–9, 51; Donaldson, *Scottish Historical Documents*, 113–4; Marshall, *Ruin and Restoration*, 13–20.
27. *CSP Foreign 1547–53*, 57–8, 68; Lesley, *History*, ii, 335–7; Donaldson, *James V to James VII*, 80.
28. *CSP Foreign 1547–53*, 75.
29. *Ibid.*, 102–3.
30. *Ibid.*, 102–3; NLS, Balcarres Papers, 29.2.5, ff.142–51.
31. *Ibid.*, 29.2.5; Pimodan, *Mère des Guises*, 143.
32. *The Journal of King Edward's Reign, written in his own hand* (Clarendon Historical Society 1884), 50–2; Pimodan, *Mère des Guises*, 143; Lesley, *History*, ii, 339–41.
33. L'Abbé de Vertot, *Ambassades de MM. De Noailles en Angleterre* (Leyden 1763), ii, 140–1, 209–12; iii, 156–60; *Diurnal of Occurrents*, 51; Pitscottie, *Historie*, 113–16.
34. Marshall, *Mary of Guise*, 199–206; *Papal Negotiations with Mary, Queen of Scots 1561–7* (Scottish History Society 1901), 4–8; *Balcarres Papers*, i, 388–9.
35. Pollen, *Papal Negotiations*, 425–9.
36. Knox, *History*, i, 124–9; *Diurnal of Occurrents*, 267; Pitscottie, *Historie*, ii, 119–20; Leslie, *History*, ii, 371–2; *CSP Foreign 1558–9*, 14, 21, 78–9.
37. Knox, *History*, i, 161–3; *CSP Scot.*, i, 212–13, 215, 220–1, 233; *CSP Foreign 1558–9*, 282, 410; Pitscottie, *History*, ii, 145–59; *Papiers d'état*, ed. Teulet, i, 310–11; 316–9, 325–7, 331–2.
38. *Ibid.*, i, 333.
39. Archives of the Ministry of Foreign Affairs, Paris, Angl. Reg, xv, 40–1.
40. *CSP Foreign 1559–60*, 45–7, 99–100, 146–7, 152–3, 163; *CSP Scot.*, i, 255, 269; Donaldson, *James V to James VII*, 97; *Balcarres Papers*, 79–80; *Papiers d'état*, ed. Teulet, i, 381–92.
41. *Ibid.*, i, 574.
42. *CSP Foreign 1559–60*, 295, 313, 324, 327–8, 332n, 353–5, 380–1, 385–7, 430–1, 444, 459–61, 480–1, 499–502, 475–6, 513–4, 560–1, 585–6, 604–5; *1560–1*, 116–26; *Diurnal of Occurrents*, 55, 57, 59, 277; *Papiers d'état*, ed. Teulet, i, 408–13; *Two Missions*, 63–5, 89–91, 93, 95, 101–5, 121, 125–33, 141–9, 171–5; Archives of the Ministry of Foreign Affairs, Paris, Angl. Reg., xv, 82–3, 86–106, 112–14; Knox, *History*, i, 319; Pitscottie, *Historie*, ii, 167–8, 171.
43. *Two Missions*, 178–9; *CSP Foreign 1560–1*, 133, 143–4, 156; *Treasurer's Accounts*, xi, 24; *Diurnal of Occurrents*, 64; Knox, *History*, i, 359; d'Espence, *Oraison*; Archives Nationales, Memo 3B, f.91. The monument was destroyed during the French Revolution.

CHAPTER TEN

MARY, QUEEN OF SCOTS

'Queen of Scots' was the title used by female monarchs and consorts of Scotland before 1603, but for most of us these words mean only one person, Mary Stuart, the daughter of James V and Mary of Guise.[1] Thousands of people who have no particular interest in history can recount the general outlines of Mary's career and are ready to argue about her character, her motives and whether or not she deserved her ultimate fate. Short of the discovery of the missing Casket Letters, for instance, it seems unlikely that we will ever have the definitive answer to our questions about her guilt or innocence, but it is useful to set her in the context of the other Scottish queens regnant and consort, since the problems she confronted were not exclusively hers but were theirs too.

One of the most extraordinary features of Mary's extraordinary life is that she was recognised as Queen at six days old by Scottish nobles who regarded any female ruler as being not merely undesirable but unnatural. The Bible said that women should be subservient to men, and that was what everyone believed. So why did the Scots so readily accept a female infant as their monarch?[2] There was a precedent, of course, for the Maid of Norway had inherited Alexander III's throne. She had not lived long enough to rule, but everyone knew how her untimely death had plunged the country into chaos and led to Edward I's dangerous threat to Scotland's independence. Even a woman's rule was preferable to that sort of situation, and the nobles no doubt looked forward to profiting yet again from a royal minority. Indeed, some ambitious lord had only to marry his son to the little Queen and not only would the happy bridegroom receive the title of king but all his relatives would stand to enjoy an amazing increase of power, wealth and status.

In December 1542, however, all thoughts of self-interest for once had to be set aside, for this was a time of great crisis. The English were poised to invade the country after the disaster at Solway Moss and James V's tiny daughter was the symbol of Scotland's continuing independence. No one knew better than Mary of Guise how vulnerable her child's position was. James, 2nd Earl of Arran, now ruling as Lord Governor, was a weak and vacillating young man, but he was also a slippery expert in the art of self-preservation and he was heir to the throne. If anything happened to Mary, Queen of Scots, he would be king. Mary of Guise was terrified that he would either have her daughter killed or sent to England. He had surrounded Linlithgow Palace with his men, ostensibly to guard the little Queen, but Mary of Guise felt like a prisoner and was determined to move to the greater safety of Stirling.[3] For his part, Henry VIII was busily putting it about that the infant Mary, Queen of Scots was unlikely to live.[4] Had she died, he would have stepped in as king-maker, just as Edward I of England had done after the death of the Maid. Actually, the baby was thriving, and when Henry's envoy, Sir Ralph Sadler, saw her in March 1543, he had to admit that she was 'as goodly a child as I have seen, of her age'. Mary of Guise remarked to him that her daughter would be as tall as she was herself and she, Sadler said, was 'of the largest size of women'.[5]

On 1 July 1543 Arran signed the Treaties of Greenwich, agreeing to the little Queen's marriage to Prince Edward, on 26 July he consented to Mary of Guise moving to Stirling Castle with her daughter and on 9 December Mary, Queen of Scots was crowned in the Chapel Royal at Stirling.[6] She was nine months old. Two months after that, Arran repudiated the Treaties of Greenwich and Henry VIII began his Rough Wooing.[7] Against this background of turmoil, Mary, Queen of Scots spent her earliest years at Stirling, cared for by her nurse, Jean Sinclair, and later by her Lady Governess who was also her aunt, Lady Fleming, an illegitimate half-sister of James V.[8]

It was not surprising that Mary and her mother shared an intensely close emotional bond, and they were never apart until the disaster at Pinkie. With real fears that the enemy would besiege Stirling Castle, Mary of Guise sent her daughter to the little island of Inchmahome, on the Lake of Menteith, where she remained hidden for more than a week until it was judged safe enough for her to go back to Stirling.[9] When the situation deteriorated still further, Henry II's proposal that Mary, Queen of Scots should live in France and marry his son seemed to be the only way forward. The child would be safe, she would have a glorious future as Queen of France as well as Queen of Scots, and Henry would send the military assistance that the Scots so desperately needed. The Treaty of Haddington was duly signed.[10]

Mary of Guise wept as she watched her daughter embark for France, and when contrary winds delayed the departure, she could not bear to wait on the shore and returned to Edinburgh to immerse herself in the continuing military crisis. Mary, Queen of Scots set sail at last on 7 August 1548. Her large retinue included not only her official guardians Lord Erskine and Lord Livingston but her governess, Lady Fleming, and a number of her other relatives. We are accustomed to thinking of Mary as an only child, which of course she was, but as well as her half-sister Lady Jane Stewart and her half-brother, the Duke of Longueville, waiting for her in France, she had various other half-brothers, her father's illegitimate children. Three of them travelled with her, Lord James, Lord Robert and Lord John Stewart. There were also the famous Four Maries, high-born girls of about her own age who would be her Maries or maids of honour and were all coincidentally called Mary: Mary Seton, Mary Beton, Mary Fleming and Mary Livingston.

Sailing through fierce storms down the west coast of England, they arrived near the little village of Roscoff in Brittany on 13 August 1548. Henry II was away campaigning in Italy but Mary was taken to the medieval castle of Carrières, near St Germain, where the French royal children were staying, and there she met her future husband for the first time. The contrast between the two children was painful. Mary at almost six was tall and sturdy. Four-year-old Francis was very small for his age, adenoidal, with pale, puffy features and bad breath. Mary, however, had been taught that Francis was the partner God had chosen for her, and she accepted him without question.[11] When Henry II arrived back on 9 November he was very impressed with her. His one complaint was that she did not speak French, and he used this as a pretext for sending away her Scottish retinue. Even the Four Maries were whisked off to a convent at Poissy, but Lady

Fleming stayed on as Lady Governess at Mary of Guise's insistence until she disgraced herself by having an affair with Henry, gave birth to his child and was sent home in disgrace.[12]

Mary, Queen of Scots settled down in the French royal children's household, sharing a bedchamber with Princess Elizabeth, and whenever Henry II visited the children he liked to converse with her, amused by her charmingly adult manner. She was now receiving the highly academic education thought suitable for a Renaissance monarch's children. She learned Latin, Italian, Spanish and Greek as well as having lessons in dancing, singing and playing the lute. Like her mother's family, she loved music[13] and, like them, she grew very tall. She was self-conscious about her height when she was ten, and her new French governess, the Dame de Paroys, complained that she stooped instead of holding herself erect. However, by the time she was in her teens, she was much praised for her beauty and dignity as well as her intelligence. There was every reason to suppose that she would continue to flourish in her sheltered position at the centre of a highly sophisticated Court.[14]

Meanwhile, her mother and her French relatives agonised over whether Henry would go through with the marriage planned for her. The Guises had plenty of enemies at Court who had no desire to see them raised up still further by having their niece marry the Dauphin. However, the marriage was central to Henry's foreign policy, and by 1557 he was ready to proceed with the negotiations for the contract. By its terms, Mary, Queen of Scots promised to preserve her country's ancient freedoms and privileges while Henry agreed that, if Francis died, she could either stay in France or return to Scotland. She was betrothed to the Dauphin in the Great Hall of the Louvre on 19 April 1558.[15] Unknown to the Scots, she had also signed a secret agreement on the instructions of Henry II. If she died without children, not only would her kingdom pass to him instead of to the Earl of Arran but he would also inherit her right to the English crown.[16]

Mary was married at the Cathedral of Notre Dame in Paris on 24 April 1558.[17] That winter, Elizabeth I succeeded to the English throne. Roman Catholics throughout Europe considered her illegitimate, the bastard daughter of Henry VIII and Anne Boleyn, and Henry II promptly announced that the rightful monarchs of

England were his son and daughter-in-law. Mary, Queen of Scots was, after all, the entirely legitimate great-grand-daughter of Henry VII of England and, as her husband, Francis was King of Scots. Soon Mary's royal canopy, banners and silver plate appeared with the arms of England quartered with those of Scotland and France. This was an outright challenge to Elizabeth, but in June 1559, before he could pursue his policy any further, Henry was fatally injured while taking part in a tournament, and the fifteen-year-old Dauphin and sixteen-year-old Mary became King and Queen of France.[18] Francis II was considered to be old enough not to require a regent to rule for him, but in reality he was still unready for his new responsibilities, and heavily reliant on his mother, Catherine de Medici, and the government of the country was really in the hands of Mary's uncles. The following June, Mary of Guise died, her enemies triumphed and Scotland became an officially Protestant country. The Auld Alliance with France was over, and the auld enemy, England, had become the new friend.

Mary, Queen of Scots had 'loved her mother incredibly', wrote Giovanni Michiel, the Venetian ambassador in France, describing her agonies of grief when she heard the news.[19] Just as she began to recover a little, her husband came home from hunting one day complaining of a violent pain in his ear. Mary and his mother nursed him devotedly, but he died of an abscess on the brain on 5 December 1560. His brother, Charles IX, succeeded to the throne of France, Catherine de Medici gladly took on the position of Regent and Mary, Queen of Scots was relegated to the secondary role of Queen Dowager.[20] Mary had been genuinely fond of her inadequate young husband and, already shaken by her mother's death, she seemed inconsolable at her loss. 'At work or at rest, he is always near me,' she wrote in a poem expressing her grief.[21] Her hard-headed Guise uncles did not waste their time mourning and, within a fortnight of Francis' death, they were arranging meetings between Mary and ambassadors, bishops and diplomats. With Catherine de Medici now in charge, the Guises had been displaced and they needed a new source of power. Mary must take another husband as soon as possible.

There would be many suitors for someone as eligible as Mary, a queen in her own right and now known to be not only

28 Queen Mary of Guise by Corneille de Lyon (Scottish National Portrait Gallery)

29 St Andrews Cathedral, where Queen Mary of Guise married James V (Historic Scotland)

30 The Palace of Holyroodhouse, drawn by an English spy in 1544 (Edinburgh City Libraries)

31 Linlithgow Palace, showing the window of the room where Mary, Queen of Scots was born (Historic Scotland)

32 Mary, Queen of Scots, aged about sixteen, by François Clouet
(Bibliothèque Nationale, Paris)

33 Francis II of France, first husband of Mary, Queen of Scots, attributed to the workshop of Limousin (Scottish National Portrait Gallery)

34 Henry Stewart, Lord Darnley, second husband of Mary, Queen of Scots, by an unknown artist (Scottish National Portrait Gallery)

35 James Hepburn, 4th Earl of Bothwell, third husband of Mary, Queen of Scots, by an unknown miniaturist (Scottish National Portrait Gallery)

36 The execution of Mary, Queen of Scots, by an unknown Dutch artist (Scottish National Portrait Gallery)

37 Queen Anne of Denmark, 1595, attributed to Adriaen Vanson (Scottish National Portrait Gallery)

38 James VI and I, husband of Queen Anne of Denmark, 1595, attributed to Adriaen Vanson (Scottish National Portrait Gallery)

39 Dunfermline Palace, Queen Anne of Denmark's favourite Scottish residence, with the abbey in the background. (Historic Scotland)

40 Prince Henry Frederick, Queen Anne of Denmark's eldest son (The Earl of Mar and Kellie)

41 Charles I, shortly before he married Queen Henrietta Maria, by Daniel Mytens (The Earl of Mar and Kellie)

42 Queen Henrietta Maria, engraved after a painting by Daniel Mytens (Scottish National Portrait Gallery)

43 Queen Catherine of Braganza, by an unknown artist (Scottish National Portrait Gallery)

44 Charles II, husband of Queen Catherine of Braganza, engraved by R. White after Sir Godfrey Kneller (Scottish National Portrait Gallery)

45 Queen Mary of Modena by Willem Wissing (Scottish National Portrait Gallery)

46 James VII and II, at about the time of his marriage to Queen Mary of Modena, by an unknown sculptor (Scottish National Portrait Gallery)

47 James VII and II's wedding suit (The Board of Trustees of the Victoria & Albert Museum)

48 Prince James Francis Edward, Queen Mary of Modena's only surviving son, by Nicholas de Largillière (Scottish National Portrait Gallery)

49 Princess Louise, Queen Mary of Modena's only surviving daughter, by a follower of Largillière (Scottish National Portrait Gallery)

50 William II and III, husband of Queen Mary II, after Sir Godfrey Kneller (Scottish National Portrait Gallery)

51 Queen Mary II, after Willem Wissing (Scottish National Portrait Gallery)

52 Queen Anne as a child, by an unknown artist (The Royal Collection 2003, Her Majesty Queen Elizabeth II)

53 Anne Hyde, Duchess of York, mother of Queen Mary II and Queen Anne, by Sir Peter Lely (Scottish National Portrait Gallery)

54 Queen Anne as a young woman, by Willem Wissing and J. van der Vaardt (Scottish National Portrait Gallery)

55 Prince George of Denmark, Queen Anne's husband, engraved by
J. Houbraken after Sir Godfrey Kneller (Scottish National Portrait
Gallery)

56 William, Duke of Gloucester, Queen Anne's longest surviving son,
engraved by J. Houbraken after Sir Godfrey Kneller (Scottish National
Portrait Gallery)

personally attractive but to possess other qualities too. Nicholas Throckmorton, the English envoy in Paris, remarked on 31 December 1560, 'During her husband's lifetime there was no great account made of her, for that, being under band of marriage and subjection to her husband (who carried the burden and care of all her matters) there was offered no great occasion to know what was in her'.[22] Since the death of Francis, however, she had demonstrated great wisdom and judgment as well as modesty. Unfortunately for Mary and the Guise family, these advantages did not secure the husband they were hoping to attract. They had decided on Don Carlos, the son and heir of Philip II of Spain. He was hardly a robust physical specimen, but one day he was expected to inherit his father's extensive territories and, as a queen and the widow of a king, Mary was inclined to settle for no one of a lesser rank. However, Philip rebuffed the proposal, for he had recently married Mary's childhood companion, Elizabeth, the daughter of Henry II, and so he had no need of a further French alliance.[23]

Mary was bitterly disappointed, and when her half-brother Lord James Stewart arrived in France a few weeks later to invite her to come back to Scotland, she decided to accept. Ignoring the warnings of her friends, who told her that she, a Roman Catholic monarch, could only hope to return to her newly Protestant kingdom if she went at the head of an army, she sailed into Leith in her great white galley at about nine o'clock in the morning of 19 August 1561.[24] Despite all the dire prognostications, the Scots welcomed her enthusiastically. Their rightful monarch had come home again, she was young and she was charming. One of the most interesting comments on Mary in her youth comes from George Buchanan, the neo-classical poet and scholar who knew her well. His remark is all the more interesting because he made it much later, when he had become one of her most bitter enemies. Describing her earlier years, he wrote, 'She was graced with surpassing loveliness of form, the vigour of maturing youth and fine qualities of mind, which a court education had increased', but 'her natural goodness would be weakened by an earnest desire to please'.[25] In other circumstances, this predominantly feminine characteristic would have been regarded as a virtue, but for an inexperienced monarch trying to assert her authority in an intensely competitive masculine society, it was to have fatal consequences.

At first, Mary, ruled with considerable success, taking her responsibilities seriously, sitting at privy council meetings stitching away at her needlework as she listened to the arguments of her statesmen eddying around her. She was content to be guided by Lord James and by her secretary of state, William Maitland of Lethington, both of whom urged on her friendship with England. Dutifully, she tried to establish amicable relations with Elizabeth, plying her cousin with engaging letters and little gifts. Trained from her earliest days to believe that the throne of England was rightfully hers, she nevertheless seems to have been willing to settle for being recognised as Elizabeth's successor, but of course that recognition was something that Elizabeth could not give. As soon as she nominated a successor, there was the very real danger that discontented subjects in her own realm would try to depose her in favour of the official heir – all the more so if that heir were Roman Catholic. In the end, Mary's much-desired meeting with Elizabeth never did take place, for the English queen did not share her enthusiasm for a personal encounter. Mary still had not ratified the Treaty of Edinburgh, and in any event Elizabeth did not wish to risk being overshadowed by this rival whom everyone praised so irritatingly for her beauty and her accomplishments.[26]

Mary was deeply disappointed that her efforts at diplomacy had failed, and she found even more difficult the demanding business of confrontation with those she regarded as troublemakers. Gentle by nature, intelligent and fond of irony, she had inherited her father's highly-strung sensitivity rather than her mother's tough-mindedness. Even so, she was always willing to do what she thought was expected of her. Soon after her arrival in Edinburgh she summoned the leading Protestant preacher John Knox to an audience and taxed him with stirring up her subjects against her mother. She was then astonished by his violent assertions that it was the duty of subjects to disobey an ungodly Catholic monarch. Brought up with a strictly hierarchical view of the world and the belief that God had chosen her to rule, she could only wish that she had eminent theologians with her from the Sorbonne to answer his arguments in a way that she could not.[27] In fact, as long as the lords kept their promise that she herself could worship as she pleased, Mary intended to pursue the line taken by Catherine de Medici and the *politiques* in France. Civil war was to be avoided at all costs and so, to avoid anarchy, she would for the time being tolerate Protestantism.[28]

Not long after Elizabeth finally cancelled their rendezvous, Mary allowed herself to be persuaded by Lord James, now Earl of Moray, to turn against his rival, the powerful Catholic nobleman, George, 4th Earl of Huntly. Full of excitement, she rode north in the autumn of 1562, telling the Highland chiefs who came to present their respects that she was sorry she was not a man, for then she could have lain all night in the fields or walked in the streets with a helmet and sword. Huntly, defeated at Corrichie, died of a stroke on the battlefield. Mary managed to sit through his subsequent trial in Edinburgh, watching his corpse, propped up in its coffin, being solemnly convicted of treason, but when she was forced to witness the bungled execution of one of his sons, she was appalled and had to be carried away, weeping hysterically.[29]

By this time, there was enormous pressure on her to take a second husband and provide an heir. It must have seemed to her that a new partner would be an enormous asset in helping her both to assert her authority and to take on those tasks which she found so physically draining. However, as long as wives were legally subservient to their husbands, matrimony would remain a highly controversial and indeed a dangerous area for a queen in her own right. Whoever married Mary would have the title King of Scots, and his influence on her and on the life of the country could be incalculable. Elizabeth I knew this all too well, for she had seen at first hand the effect of her sister Mary I's marriage to Philip of Spain on Protestant England and so she deliberately remained single. Mary of Guise had similarly refused to remarry, but they both possessed unusual resolve and a willingness to sacrifice their own emotions to the political role in which they had been cast. Other less politically motivated women felt differently, and for Joan Beaufort, Margaret Tudor and Mary, Queen of Scots, all struggling for survival, the thought of a strong, supportive partner was irresistible.

Mary tried again to secure Don Carlos as a husband, but by now a serious accident and subsequent brain damage had rendered him incapable of marrying anyone. Elizabeth allowed Lord Darnley to go to Scotland in February 1565 in an effort to distract Mary from thoughts of a foreign husband.[30] Mary had met him twice before, when his mother had sent him to France with congratulations when Francis II became king and later with commiserations when Francis died. Darnley had matured since then. He was nineteen now, and very tall, taller indeed than Mary herself, which she found most unusual. He was also handsome in an effeminate way. Seeing him in London, Mary's envoy had dismissed him as 'more like a woman than a man ... beardless and lady-faced'[31] but he had a polite, engaging manner and his proud mother, Lady Lennox, was never done singing his praises to Mary and to everyone else. Indeed, she did not let anyone forget that her son had a strong claim to the English throne through her, for she was none other than Lady Margaret Douglas, the long-lost daughter of Queen Margaret Tudor by the Earl of Angus. Likewise, Darnley had a good claim to the Scottish throne through his father, Matthew, 4th Earl of Lennox.

Darnley was not a prince, but it must have seemed to Mary that he had everything else to recommend him, both personally and dynastically. By marrying him she would even manage to please Queen Elizabeth, who had dangled him before her in the first place. If that was what Mary believed, she was soon disillusioned. Elizabeth had intended Darnley as a distraction, nothing more, and when rumours drifted down to her that Mary had been tenderly nursing him when he fell ill and had fallen in love with him, she was affronted. The ungrateful youth had obviously forgotten where his true loyalty lay. The last thing Elizabeth wanted was for someone with a claim to her throne to marry the Queen of Scots, and so she summoned Darnley back to London at once. He refused to go, and he and Mary were married on 29 July 1565.[32]

At first, they were happy together, although no one else was pleased with the match and the Earl of Moray rose in open rebellion against them. Confident with her new husband riding at her side in his fine gilded armour, Mary led her army against Moray, pursuing him across Scotland and back in the Chaseabout Raid until he and his friends fled across the Border. All too soon, however, Darnley showed his inadequacy for his new role. Instead of being a helpful, trusted consort, he was spoiled and immature, took no interest in affairs of state and increasingly spent his time hunting and drinking by day and engaging in bisexual adventures by night. Mary's enemies encouraged his insecurities, hinting that she was having an affair with her Italian secretary, David Riccio, and telling him that, if the Queen really loved him, she would grant him the crown matrimonial, which would allow him to rule as king should anything happen to her. She was wise enough to refuse his demands, and so of course he grew more resentful than ever.

Matters came to a head in the early weeks of 1566. The Earl of Moray and his associates, having fled to England after the Chaseabout Raid, dared not return north, but they knew that when the Scottish parliament met in March they would be condemned and forfeited for treason. Determined to prevent that from happening, they concocted a desperate plan, drawing Darnley in as some sort of safeguard of their own future. Mary, Queen of Scots was pregnant now, and his false friends put into Darnley's head the idea that the child was not his but the little Italian's.

Mary opened parliament as planned. Less than a week later, on the evening of 9 March, she was sitting at supper with some of her household in a small room off her bedchamber in Holyroodhouse. Suddenly, to their surprise, Darnley appeared and, in uncharacteristically cheerful mood, sat down beside Mary, put his arm round her and began to chat to her pleasantly. Moments later, the convivial atmosphere was shattered. A band of armed men burst in, Lord Ruthven, their leader, demanding that the Queen hand over her secretary. Terrified, Riccio cowered behind her, clutching the pleats of her gown, but one of the conspirators held a pistol to Mary's side and the secretary was dragged away, screaming for justice, to die beneath fifty-six dagger blows.[33]

Any remaining fondness Mary may have had for her husband died that night with Riccio, but in spite of the horror of the events in the supper chamber she devised a plan to escape from the palace, taking Darnley with her. When the conspirators heard of his defection, they scattered and she was able to instal herself safely in Edinburgh Castle. There she made her will, sent for St Margaret's relics and, on 19 June 1566, gave birth to a son, the future James VI. His birth did nothing to improve her relationship with Darnley, and by the autumn she was thinking of divorcing him. This was difficult because any annulment of her marriage would make Prince James illegitimate. She had a lengthy conference with her lords at Craigmillar Castle and they indicated that they were prepared to find a way to solve her problem. Even the upright Moray would be prepared to 'look through his fingers' at any arrangement that would eliminate King Henry without endangering the Prince's position. Mary expressed alarm at the thought, but in the end it is probable that she, too, indicated a willingness to go along with whatever was done.[34]

Darnley fell ill with smallpox (or possibly syphilis) after the christening of their son, which he had refused to attend. When he was convalescent in Glasgow, Mary visited him there in the early days of 1567. He seemed miserable, contrite and she brought him east to a house at Kirk o' Field, just beside the Edinburgh city wall, where the Old College of Edinburgh University now stands. On the night of Sunday, 9 February 1567, the house was blown up in a massive gunpowder explosion, and Darnley's body was found in a garden nearby. He and his servant had been asphyxiated or strangled, presumably while trying to escape. Mary was taken to see his embalmed body lying in state at Holyroodhouse. Usually her emotions were near the surface and she wept easily, but she stood for a long time looking at him in utter silence.[35]

Had Mary deliberately lured her husband to his death because she was having a passionate affair with James Hepburn, 4th Earl of Bothwell, a married man? That is what most people thought. Her French friends sent her urgent warnings that she must have nothing more to do with Bothwell, but she ignored them. She sought out his company, spent time with him, and left her baby son in his care when she went to East Lothian for the sake of her health. When she came back, she was seen in public with him, consulted him about affairs of state, gave him valuable gifts and flew to his defence when people accused him of Darnley's murder. She took no action to prosecute those responsible, and when Darnley's father did initiate his trial, she made it plain that she supported Bothwell. He was acquitted.

On 20 April 1567, Mary went to Stirling to visit her son. On the way back, Bothwell intercepted her and took her to Dunbar Castle where he allegedly raped her. Sir James Melville had been with her entourage, was with her at Dunbar and reported that Bothwell had indeed 'ravished her' and lain with her against her will.[36] Few people believed, however, that Mary had not been party to the plan. Had she really been raped she could have had Bothwell arrested and executed but as it was, she still did not utter any real criticism of him. Two days later, Lady Bothwell began proceedings for a Protestant divorce on the grounds that her husband had committed adultery with one of her servants, and the following day Bothwell applied to the Roman Catholic authorities for an annulment of his marriage. Lady Bothwell was granted her divorce on 3 May, on 8 May Bothwell got his annulment and on 15 May he and Mary were married.

Mary's Dominican confessor solemnly swore to the Spanish ambassador in London that until the prospect of her marriage to Bothwell, he had never seen a woman of greater virtue, courage and uprightness, and he insisted that she had been completely innocent of any part in Darnley's murder.[37] It is perhaps not without significance that when Darnley was killed, his distraught mother commissioned a painting of him lying in state, surrounded by placards and inscriptions calling for vengeance against Mary, Queen of Scots, and yet in later years the two women were reconciled. Knowing the strength of Lady Lennox's maternal feelings, it is difficult to believe that she could have returned to friendly terms with her niece had she truly gone on believing her responsible for Darnley's violent death. However, lacking any conclusive evidence, we can only speculate about what really happened. What is certain is that the Bothwell marriage brought disaster.

The Protestant lords rose against Mary in rebellion. The Queen's marriage was their pretext, but it is possible that some of them were anxious to be rid of her before she had her twenty-fifth birthday in December, for that was the traditional moment when she would be able to revoke any charters or grants made during her minority. They might lose substantial amounts of property. On 15 June they confronted her with an army at Carberry Hill. She surrendered, sending Bothwell away to seek help. He was arrested in Scandinavia by the friends of one of his discarded mistresses, and kept prisoner in Denmark until his death in 1578.

Ignominiously brought back to Edinburgh from Carberry, the Queen was imprisoned in Lochleven Castle where she miscarried twins. On 24 July, as she lay recovering from the miscarriage, weak from loss of blood, Lord Lindsay came to her and forced her to sign papers abdicating in favour of her thirteen-month-old son. Five days later, James VI was crowned at Stirling. Mary escaped from Lochleven on 2 May in 1568 and gathered an army, but she was defeated at Langside, near Glasgow, on 13 May. Believing that Elizabeth I would support a sister queen in distress, she fled across the Solway to England, and nineteen years of captivity. It was at this point that Moray and Morton produced the notorious Casket Letters, alleging that these proved her guilty of Darnley's murder. The letters are now known only in the form of copies. They are generally believed to be forgeries or at least concoctions made in part from someone else's writings, interleaved with her own, and so they cannot be taken as conclusive evidence.

From the start of her imprisonment, Mary said plainly, 'If I shall be holden here perforce, you may be sure then, being as a desperate person, I will use any attempts that may serve my purpose, either by myself or my friends', and she never gave up her efforts to regain her freedom.[38] One plan after another to restore her collapsed, she was involved in many Roman Catholic plots and, in the end, Elizabeth's agent Sir Francis Walsingham deliberately ensnared her in a scheme to assassinate the English Queen. Protesting that the court had no jurisdiction over her, Mary was tried for treason and found guilty. She was executed at Fotheringhay Castle on 8 February 1587, going to her death with dignity and the assertion that she died for her Roman Catholic faith.[39]

Notes

1. Stewart was, of course, the family name but, when Mary went to France, the French used the spelling 'Stuart' and that version persisted for her and for her successors.
2. *Cf.* Sarah Hanley, 'The Monarchic State in Early Modern France: Marital Regime Government and Male Right', in *Politics, Ideology and the Law in Early Modern Europe*, ed. Adrianna E. Bakos (University of Rochester Press 1994), 107–26; Sarah Hanley, 'Identity Politics

and Rulership in France: Female Political Place and the Fraudulent Salic Law in Christine de Pizan and Jean de Montreuil', in *Changing Identities in Early Modern France*, ed. Michael Wolfe (Durham and London 1996), 78–94.

3. *Ibid.*, i, 448.
4. *Ibid.*, i, 323, 328, 340, 342, 346, 348.
5. *The State Papers and Letters of Sir Ralph Sadler*, ed. Arthur Clifford (Edinburgh 1809), i, 84–8.
6. *Hamilton Papers*, ii, 33, 38, 39; *Historical Works of Sir James Balfour*, i, 275, 279.
7. Donaldson, *Scottish Historical Documents*, 110–11; Marcus Merriman, *The Rough Wooings: Mary, Queen of Scots 1542–51* (East Linton 2000).
8. *Balcarres Papers*, ii, 6, 32.
9. *Historical Works of Sir James Balfour*, i, 288; W. Fraser, *The Lennox* (Edinburgh 1874), ii, 431–2; W. Fraser, *Red Book of Menteith* (Edinburgh 1880), 331–3.
10. Donaldson, *Scottish Historical Documents*, 113–4.
11. *Diurnal of Occurrents*, 47; Hay Fleming, *Mary, Queen of Scots*, 198, n. 96–7.
12. Alphonse de Ruble, *La première jeunesse de Marie Stuart* (Paris 1891), 31; Fraser, *Mary, Queen of Scots*, 53–4.
13. Hay Fleming, *Mary, Queen of Scots*, 202–205, nn. 20–22.
14. *Balcarres Papers*, ii, 58, 124, 138, 163, 198, 201, 204, 210, 236.
15. *Discours du Grand et Magnifique Triumphe* (Paris and Rouen 1558); *CSP Venetian*, vi part 3, 1265, 1366, 1487.
16. *APS*, ii, 508–19; Archives Nationales, Paris, AEII 646, marriage contract of Mary and the Dauphin.
17. *CSP Venetian*, vi part 3, 1486–7.
18. *Ibid.*, vii, 106 and n.
19. *Ibid.*, vii, 227–8, 234.
20. *Ibid.*, vii, 268–9, 274–6, 278; *Foreign Calendar, Elizabeth* iii, 408n., 420–4.
21. Fraser, *Mary, Queen of Scots*, 108.
22. *CSP Foreign, Elizabeth*, iii, 472–3.
23. *CSP Foreign*, iii, 491–2; iv, 76, 82–3, 97.
24. *CSP Foreign, Elizabeth*, iv, 260–1, 263; v, 14; *Diurnal of Occurrents*, 66.
25. George Buchanan, *The Tyrannous reign of Mary Stewart*, ed. W. A. Gatherer (Edinburgh 1958), 50.
26. *CSP Foreign, Elizabeth*, iii, 573; Fraser, *Mary, Queen of Scots*, 165–79.
27. Knox, *History of the Reformation*, ii, 13–20; Marshall, *John Knox*, 164–70.

28. J.W.Allen, *A History of Political Thought in the Sixteenth Century* (London 1928), 292–6.
29. *Diurnal of Occurrents*, 74; Hay Fleming, *Mary, Queen of Scots*, 305–6, nn. 28 and 29.
30. *CSP Foreign*, v, 12–14; Caroline Bingham, *Darnley: A Life of Henry Stuart, Lord Darnley, Consort of Mary, Queen of Scots* (London 1995), 86–7.
31. *Melville, Memoirs*, ed. Francis Steuart (London 1929), 92.
32. *Diurnal of Occurrents*, 80; Hay Fleming, *Mary, Queen of Scots* 105, 348, n. 114; Caroline Bingham, *Darnley* (London 1995), 39–107.
33. Hay Fleming, *Mary, Queen of Scots*, 387–90, n. 49 conveniently summarises the various accounts of the murder.
34. James Anderson, *Collections relating to Mary, Queen of Scots* (Edinburgh 1727–8), iv, part ii, 188–93.
35. Knox, *History*, ii, 202.
36. *Melville, Memoirs*, 149.
37. Andrew Lang, *The Mystery of Mary Stuart* (London 1901), 210.
38. *CSP Scot.*, ii, 516.
39. P. J. Holmes, 'Mary Stewart in England', in *The Innes Review*, xxxviii, 195–218; Fraser, *Mary, Queen of Scots*, 536–42; Jayne E. Lewis, *Mary, Queen of Scots: Romance and Nation* (London 1998), 50–9.

CHAPTER ELEVEN

ANNE OF DENMARK

With his father murdered when he was an infant and his mother a prisoner in England, James VI was brought up to be Scotland's first Protestant monarch. He was cared for by the Earl and Countess of Mar, and his tutors, George Buchanan and Peter Young, gave him an unremittingly academic education. Mary, Queen of Scots wrote letters to him and sent him gifts, but these were kept from him and he was encouraged to hate her. He did not, but he had no real relationship with her. For more than thirty years the most important woman in his life was Elizabeth I. He had a burning desire to be recognised as her heir, he was always anxious to avoid offending her, and her views would have to be taken into account when he chose a wife.

During his early adolescence there was a great deal of speculation about James's likely bride, with talk of French, Spanish and Swedish princesses.[1] From the start, however, a Danish match seemed the most likely, because of existing links between the two countries, the wealth of Denmark and the suitability of the Danish royal family. They were Lutherans and Elizabeth I would not object to that. Fortunately the restless, energetic King Frederick II and his young wife Sophie of Mecklenburg had available daughters. In Denmark the children of royalty and the aristocracy were often brought up by their grandparents, and so the first two girls, Elizabeth and Anne, were sent to Sophie's parents, the Duke and Duchess of Mecklenberg, who lived at Güstrow, a small town in northern Germany.

Duke Ulric was known to his admiring contemporaries as 'the German Nestor', after the wise and experienced Greek monarch of classical times, and his household provided a kindly atmosphere for his small granddaughters. Anne had been born on 12 December 1574 at Skanderborg Castle in Jutland, and, when she was two, her mother gave birth to a son, the future Christian IV. He was taken to join his sisters at Güstrow only a week after his christening but, two years after that, the Danish Council were seized with the thought that it was hardly desirable for the heir to the throne to be raised in a foreign country, and all three children were brought back to Denmark to be reunited with their parents. Queen Sophie, fair-haired, attractive, and devout, was interested in science and astronomy but she was also a careful housewife and an affectionate mother, and she created a loving environment for her children. Two more sons and two more daughters arrived after little Christian.[2]

Denmark was a prosperous country and Anne was brought up in luxurious and cultured surroundings. She and her sisters attracted many suitors,[3] but James VI stood out among them, for Frederick II believed that the existence of a bachelor King of Scots would provide him with the ideal opportunity to negotiate the return of Orkney and Shetland. In 1585, he therefore sent diplomats to the Scottish Court, to discuss the Orkney and Shetland question and let the Scots know that James could choose either Princess Elizabeth or Princess Anne for his wife. Nothing came of these initial approaches, but not long afterwards James sent to Denmark for portraits of the princesses and their parents. Both girls were personable. Like her mother, Anne had fair hair and a thin, oval face, with her father's long, aquiline nose. By all accounts, she was tall and well-made.[4]

During 1587, the negotiations gathered pace, only to be interrupted by the death of Anne's father in 1588. The Danes had the reputation of being the heaviest drinkers in Europe, and the clergyman officiating at Frederick's funeral remarked regretfully that 'had the King drunk a little less, he might have lived many a day yet'.[5] Afterwards, the Danish councillors wanted Queen Sophie to go and live in the country with her daughters while they themselves ruled on behalf of her young son, Christian IV, but she refused. At twenty-eight she was hardly ready to retire from the world, and she was certainly not going to be separated from her eldest boy. With energy and decision she fought their plans and won. The Danish Council agreed that she could remain in Copenhagen, not merely to look after her children but to rule as Regent, and the whole family rejoiced.

That settled, the Scottish proposal could be considered once more. Sophie's eldest daughter, Elizabeth, was by now betrothed to a German duke, but Anne would suit King James perfectly. Encouraging messages were conveyed to Scotland and George, 5th Earl Marischal set off with an official embassy to Denmark in the summer of 1589. It was he who placed the betrothal ring on Anne's finger on 20 August, presented her with jewels worth £12,600 Scots from her bridegroom at the banquet that followed, and then symbolically climbed on to the royal bed with her.[6] The terms of the marriage contract had been finalised by now and they were fairly conventional, although in return for Anne's dowry of 75,000 thalers (£170,000 Scots) the Danes insisted that James should settle on her lands worth twice that amount. The Scots therefore agreed that she should have the palaces of Linlithgow and Falkland although, as the Danes suspected, these were not sufficient to provide the agreed sum. Anne would have freedom to worship according to Lutheran rites in Calvinist Scotland, and should her husband die first, she would be allowed to go back to her native land at any time during the first three years of her widowhood. No mention was made of Orkney and Shetland, which remained part of Scotland.[7]

Her farewells finally said, Anne sailed from Copenhagen on 5 September 1590 but a gale blew up, her ship sprang a leak and after a series of false starts and long, harrowing days tossed on the stormy seas, her fleet was forced back again to shelter in the Norwegian Sound. Weak from dreadful sea-sickness and thoroughly unnerved, Anne was escorted to Oslo, where she lodged in the Old Bishop's Palace. No one seemed to know quite what to do next, but in the end she was just about to set off for home again, by land, when a startling piece of news arrived.[8] Contrary to all expectation, the King of Scots had resolved to collect his bride in person, and he was even now in Norway and travelling towards her.

After a formal correspondence with Anne, James had decided that he was passionately in love with her. He had no experience of women, of course, but he had read poetry and classical mythology and he fancied himself as a romantic hero. Seized with the notion of rescuing his beloved, he swept aside all opposition, gave a terse answer to his lords when they demurred at the prospect of their monarch leaving the country and pointed out that his own grandfather, James V, had gone abroad to fetch his bride. Why should he not do the same? He would, he promised, be home again within twenty days. He sailed from Leith on 22 October 1589, accompanied by his Chancellor, Sir John Maitland of Thirlestane, and five other special ambassadors. Bad weather caused delays in his journey, too, but at about four o'clock on the afternoon of 19 November he rode triumphantly into Oslo, accompanied by Axel Gylderstierne, the Danish Governor of Norway.[9]

Neither the Scottish nor the Danish account of events gives any indication of Anne's feelings when she heard of the imminent arrival of her bridegroom, but she was standing in the Great Hall on the first floor of the Old Bishop's Palace waiting for him when he appeared, 'a tall, slim gentleman with lean cheeks', wearing a red velvet coat sewn with gold stars beneath a black velvet cloak lined with sable.[10] So eager was he to see her that he had not even paused to take off his boots. She recoiled when he made to greet her with a kiss 'after the Scots fashion' but he said a few quiet words to her.[11] He did not speak German, which was her first language, and she spoke neither English nor Latin, the language of diplomacy, but she had been learning French and so they were able to converse without an interpreter. When he explained that he was not being overly amorous but merely polite in wanting to kiss her, Anne allowed him to do so, and after that they seemed to get on famously.

The following morning James was at the Palace at nine o'clock, this time arrayed in blue velvet sewn with gold, and he and Anne spent the entire day together. The intention had been that they would marry in Scotland, but James decided that after her recent experiences he could not possibly inflict a winter voyage on his bride, and so their wedding took place in the Great Hall of the Old Bishop's Palace on 23 November 1598. David Lindsay, the King's chaplain, preached a sermon in French, for Anne's benefit, outlining the reasons for marriage and reminding the bride and groom that 'the man shall watch for his wife diligently, and, since he is her head, he shall see for her with his eyes, hear for her with his ears and answer for her with his tongue'. For her part, the wife should 'obey her husband in all things, and always have in mind the axiom that God pronounced after the Fall, which is that she is commanded to be submissive for eternity'.[12]

Anne's mother had invited them to spend the winter with her, and so on 7 January 1590 they set off across the ice in black velvet, gold-embroidered, horse-drawn sleighs sent for their use by Queen Sophie. Ten days later, Anne was introducing her husband to the relatives she had thought she would never see again. James then rushed about with characteristic Stewart curiosity, sightseeing, hunting, discussing predestination with Niels Hemmingsen, the leading Danish theologian, and furthering his knowledge of astronomy with the celebrated Tycho Brahe, while Anne enjoyed the pleasing companionship of her family. They stayed in Denmark long enough to attend the wedding of Anne's sister Elizabeth to Duke Henrik of Brunswick on 19 April, but two days after that, Anne and James set sail for Scotland.[13]

Landing at Leith, they spent a few days there, ostensibly to recover from the voyage but in reality to allow time for the final preparations to be made at Holyroodhouse. When the new Queen of Scots finally entered Edinburgh, the citizens had their first sight of her, dressed in white, sitting in her own carriage drawn by eight brown horses. Once installed in her apartments, she prepared for her coronation on Sunday 17 May, the first Protestant coronation of a Scottish Queen. Robert Bruce, the unyieldingly Presbyterian Edinburgh minister, performed the ceremony. He had been reluctant to include the traditional anointing, but rather than let a bishop officiate, he had agreed in the end.

The Countess of Mar unfastened the Queen's kirtle and Bruce poured a little of the sacred oil on to Anne's shoulder and right arm. He then crowned her and gave her the sceptre, telling her that in this way 'we acknowledge your majesty as our most gracious lady and queen of Scotland', and pledging their obedience to her 'in all that concerns the honour of God, the comfort of His Church and the welfare of your majesty'. David Lindsay repeated the words in French for her, and Anne then swore an oath on the Bible, promising to love and honour God and 'advance and support religion with true and reliable ceremonies', repudiating 'all popish superstition and false teaching'.[14]

Anne and James now settled down to the customary peripatetic royal life together. He would always remain fond of 'his Annie', as he liked to call her, but he had many other demands on his attention and, whether or not he was truly bisexual, he always preferred the company of men. Women, to him as to many of his contemporaries, were lesser creatures not to be taken seriously. When he and she were together, he very likely bored her with his endless talk of politics, religion, and the shocking news that the recent storms had been raised by witches in an effort to prevent him from marrying. Anne was passionate about the visual arts, but he had no appreciation of paintings. He liked to treat his courtiers with irritatingly couthy jocularity. Anne loved formal ceremonial and pageantry. He was gregarious while she preferred her own company. Someone who met her during her first summer in Scotland remarked that the Queen 'carries a marvellous gravity which, with her partial solitariness, contrary to the humour of our people, hath banished all our ladies clean from her'.[15] She was probably homesick.

Anne did try hard to do what was expected of her, dutifully learning to speak Scots, but whenever she expressed any strong opinions about what was going on, James attributed her views to tiresome wilfulness, and when they quarrelled and she had a tantrum, he would send one of his ministers to calm her down instead of going to her himself. Like many men, he evidently felt at a loss when dealing with an emotional female. One of their most bitter arguments was over Lord Chancellor Thirlestane, whom Anne had two reasons to dislike. He refused to give up the lordship of Musselburgh which was rightfully part of the abbey and lands of Dunfermline, James's wedding gift to her, and she found out that he had all along opposed her marriage, wishing James to marry a Frenchwoman instead. After eighteen months she and Thirlestane were still at loggerheads, but when she was able to tell James that she was pregnant, he ordered the Chancellor to hand over the disputed property at once and banished him from the Court.

Anne's pregnancy came to a successful conclusion when her first son was born at Stirling Castle in 1594. He was named Henry Frederick, after his grandfathers. The King was triumphant, there was great rejoicing throughout the country, and the usually parsimonious Elizabeth I sent a handsome gold font for the christening. However, the baby's arrival led to an epic battle between his parents. From the start, Anne had the strongest possible maternal feelings.

She probably thought that she now had someone of her own in this foreign land, and she certainly expected to replicate the happy family atmosphere that had prevailed in her mother's household.

James had other ideas. Traditionally, royal children in Scotland were brought up in their own household, well away from their parents, for reasons of safety as much as anything else, and James was obsessive about security. His enemies must be given no chance of wiping out both the King and his heir, nor must they have the opportunity of using the baby Prince against him, as had been done when he himself was made King after his mother's forced abdication. He therefore announced that the child would be sent to Stirling to be brought up by his trusted friend Lord Mar and Mar's mother, the formidable dowager who had raised James himself.

When she heard the news, Anne was aghast. She stormed, raged and sobbed, but all to no purpose. Her husband remained adamant. She had conceived again very soon after Henry's birth, and now she was so agitated that she miscarried. Although concerned, James gave strict instructions that no one, not even the Queen, was to remove the Prince from Stirling Castle without his express orders.[16] He told Anne that she was perfectly free to visit the baby, but she loathed Lady Mar, and after one particularly trying encounter she refused to go back to Stirling even if it meant never seeing her child again.

James thought she was hysterical, but he allowed their first and second daughters, Elizabeth and Margaret, to be cared for by Lord and Lady Livingston at Linlithgow rather than sending them to Stirling,[17] and two subsequent sons, the future Charles I, born in 1600, and the short-lived Robert, born two years later, were allowed to stay at Dunfermline, Anne's favourite residence. Despite the arrival of these younger children and her frequent protestations that, naturally, she would obey the King, Anne did not give up the battle to have Prince Henry with her. No doubt she had vivid memories of her own mother's successful struggle for possession of Christian IV. Her tug of war with Mar and his mother was to be a continuing source of court gossip, and as late as the summer of 1602 it was reported that the Queen's 'broils' with Mar were worse than ever although it now seemed likely that she would get the better of him.[18]

Anne had always been devout, and in her domestic troubles she turned to religion for comfort but that, too, led to difficulties. She had brought with her a German Lutheran chaplain, Johan Sering. He conducted services for her, but he felt increasingly isolated and before very long he converted to Calvinism. This left Anne in a very difficult position. She did not like Calvinism herself, and some of her friends were Roman Catholic, like Lord and Lady Livingston and Henrietta Stuart, Countess of Huntly. Perhaps encouraged by them, she began in 1600 to take instruction from a priest and secretly entered the Catholic Church. There would have been a great crisis had her conversion become known. It was only forty years since the Scottish Reformation, and Anne had deliberately violated her coronation oath. James knew what she had done, but he did not prevent her from attending Mass although he did insist that she kept her conversion strictly secret. However, a Roman Catholic wife might prevent English Catholics from rebelling against him when in due course he inherited Queen Elizabeth's throne.[19]

Apart from her religion, Anne diverted her thoughts from the problem of Prince Henry by spending money lavishly. She was interested in architecture, and her own residence of Dunfermline became the focus of her attention. Perched on the edge of Pittencrieff Glen, it was built round an irregularly shaped courtyard, with the main wing to the south-west. James seems to have ordered repairs to it when he gave it to Anne as her wedding gift, and although subsequent building work is very poorly documented, it is almost certain that it was she herself who was responsible for rebuilding and enlarging the part known as The Queen's House, close to the west front and linked to the other wings by a gallery. She also seems to have laid out the attractive gardens praised by later visitors.[20]

It is not known when Anne became, like her brother Christian IV, an avid collector of pictures, but her interest in jewellery was well-known from the start. She was intrigued by jewellery design and of course she accumulated an impressive array of gems from various sources. There were her own jewels that she brought from Denmark, there were the jewels James had sent her when they were betrothed, including an amethyst in the shape of a heart, and there was the purple box bearing the letter A in diamonds on the lid and containing jewels worth 20,000 crowns presented to her when she made her formal entry into Edinburgh. She had a Danish jeweller in her retinue, but when he complained that his pay was in arrears and made off with some of her gems,[21] Anne began to employ George Heriot, the Edinburgh goldsmith, instead.[22] They were to have a long association, and as well as purchasing gold and jewelled items from him, the Queen borrowed vast sums of money from him. Like those of her husband, her finances were always chaotic and her household expenses rose alarmingly after her first years in Scotland.[23]

The King and Queen's financial difficulties were about to be solved, however, for on 24 March 1603 Queen Elizabeth I died and James VI at long last inherited her throne. He set off joyfully for the south almost as soon as he heard the news, leaving Anne to follow him at a more sedate pace, for she was pregnant. As soon as he had gone, she hurried to Stirling Castle, intending to collect Prince Henry and take him with her. She knew that Mar had accompanied James to England, but she had reckoned without her old adversary, the Dowager. Lady Mar flatly refused to hand over the Prince without an official warrant from the King.[24] Anne and she had a furious quarrel, and the Queen miscarried and lay dangerously ill for some days. Lord Fyvie, who looked after her children at Dunfermline, wrote to urge the King to act sympathetically, for 'physic and medicine requireth a greater place with Her Majesty at present than lectures on economics or politics'.[25] Unfortunately, James's solution was to send Mar back to Scotland to escort Anne and the Prince south.

When Mar arrived, Anne declined to see him, would not even allow him to hand over the Prince to her and sent her husband an angry letter accusing him of preferring the Earl to herself. James retorted, 'I ever preferred you to all my bairns, much more than to any subject', but he added fuel to the flames by defending Mar. Anne demanded that Mar make a public apology to her, he refused, and in the end James arranged for the Duke of Lennox to deliver Prince Henry to the Council, who would then pass him on to the Queen.[26] Something of James's general attitude towards Anne may be seen in an undated letter he sent her, probably at about this time. 'Thank God I carry that love and respect unto you which by the law of God and nature I ought to do to my wife and mother of my children,' he told her, 'but not for that ye are a King's daughter, for whether you were a King's or a cook's daughter ye must be alike to me, being once my wife. For the respect of your honourable birth and descent I married you, but the love and respect I now bear you is for that you are my married wife and so partaker of my honour, as of all other fortunes.'[27]

Anne set off triumphantly for England on 2 June 1603, accompanied by Prince Henry. Princess Elizabeth followed a few days later, when she had recovered from a sudden illness, Margaret and Robert were dead by now, and delicate little Charles would have to stay at Dunfermline with Lord Fyvie until he was strong enough to stand the long journey south.[28] Anne was the last Queen of Scots to have her home in Scotland, but when she left it she never returned. She and the children were reunited with King James at Windsor. Delighted with himself, James swept up little Princess Elizabeth into his arms and commented to the surrounding courtiers, 'She is not an ill-favoured wench and may outshine her mother one of these days', no doubt another of his tiresome jokes. Perhaps catching sight of Anne's expression, Lord Southampton quickly interposed, 'If she equals Her Majesty some years hence, it will be more, I will be bold to say, than any other princess upon earth will do'. Queen Elizabeth I's courtiers were well practised in flattery.[29]

Anne's new life began with gratifying ceremony. On 2 July 1603, she attended Prince Henry's installation as a Knight of the Garter at Windsor and on 25 July she and James were crowned at Westminster, Anne walking in procession to the Abbey in a robe of crimson velvet, her hair hanging loose on to her shoulders, a plain gold coronet on her head. Her failure to take communion aroused a great deal of gossip about her possible Catholicism, but although that persisted, she never did admit to having converted. That would have damaged James's position.

After the coronation, he and she made a progress through the south of England. Anne loved the theatre, and she must have enjoyed her stay at Wilton House where she not only saw a performance of Shakespeare's *As You Like It* but made the acquaintance of the famous poet, Ben Jonson. When the Court returned to London, Somerset House, Hatfield and the Palaces of Nonsuch and Pontefract were settled on her as her English jointure, with Somerset House becoming her principal residence.[30] In 1609 she was employing the famous French garden designer Solomon de Caus to build a huge fountain there in the form of Mount Parnassus surmounted by Apollo and the Muses, and he also reorganised her garden at Greenwich.[31]

Now that they were in the south, Anne and James drifted further apart. They continued to live together at first and their sixth child was born on 8 April 1605 and named Mary, for James's mother, Mary, Queen of Scots. The following year, Anne gave birth to another daughter who was called Sophia, after her own mother, but the baby lived for a few hours only and little Mary died of a fever the following year. After that, Queen Anne decided to have no more children. From her seven confinements and at least three miscarriages, only two of her sons and one daughter were still alive. She and James kept separate Courts after that and lived largely separate lives. Their letters to each other are like those of old and affectionate friends but Anne was perfectly happy when her husband developed close and indeed intimate relationships with a series of male favourites. She was on surprisingly cordial terms with George Villiers, Duke of Buckingham.

James's preoccupation with his favourites left Anne free to pursue her own interests. She has often been written off by historians as a stupid woman, partly on the basis of a comment by Lady Arabella Stuart, the King's intellectual cousin, to the effect that the Queen and her ladies wasted their time in childish little games,[32] and partly because she distanced herself from politics. However, now that she had greatly increased financial resources, she became an important patron of the arts. Employing Inigo Jones as her stage designer and Ben Jonson to write the text, she was responsible for the most innovative court masques ever seen in Britain. The first theme she chose was one in which the performers appeared with blackened arms and faces. Inigo Jones provided elaborate costumes and wonderful scenery, and Anne herself took part, riding in a giant shell on artificial waves. *The Masque of Blackness* was performed in the Banqueting House at Whitehall for her Twelfth Night celebrations for 1605, and it was followed by others, all equally lavish and expensive.[33]

At these performances, Anne wore dazzling jewellery with her specially designed costumes. George Heriot had come south with her, and her commissions from him during her English years show that her preference was for jewels with naturalistic designs: brooches in the form of pansies, lilies, honeysuckle, butterflies and a parrot, hair ornaments shaped like a crossbow (a reference to her love of hunting) and her brother's cipher, C4. She was also fond of unusual earrings. A full-length portrait of her out hunting shows her sporting a shoelace suspended from a gold ring in one ear.[34] She began to patronise portraitists like Marcus Gheeraerdts, the Italian Constantino de Servi and the miniaturist Isaac Oliver, and she collected still lifes, mythological and religious pictures and objets d'art. Four scenes of Christ's Passion hung in her bedchamber at Somerset House, and in her apartments at Oatlands she placed the Trinity Altarpiece, which the King must have brought from Edinburgh. Lord Salisbury remarked drily on one occasion that she preferred pictures to people.[35]

Many of the courtiers did find Anne's reserve chilling, and failed to recognise that she had strong feelings beneath her self-contained exterior. One recent historian has remarked perceptively that her letters to her Danish relatives suggest 'melancholy and a continuing sense of exile'.[36] In an emotionally sterile marriage, she may well have felt a deep nostalgia for the happy days of her childhood. She had schooled herself never to show anything but respect for the King and she seemed to be fond of him, perhaps in a sisterly way, but their personal relationship brought her no fulfilment. She was close to her children, however, particularly her sons, and there is no doubt that it was from her that both Henry and Charles inherited their love of the arts.

Anne never entirely recovered from the greatest tragedy of her life, the premature death of Henry from typhus in 1612. For days afterwards she shut herself away in a darkened room at Somerset House, weeping uncontrollably, and although James was also grief-stricken, they were unable to comfort one another. She was cheered when her brother Christian IV paid her a visit in 1614. It was his second trip to England, for he had been before to see her, after the deaths of her two small daughters. Her health was declining, however, and she was often described as suffering from 'the gout', which in seventeenth-century terminology could mean anything from rheumatism to tuberculosis. She did not accompany King James on his one return visit to Scotland in 1617, and when her son Charles, now Prince of Wales, put on his first masque at Twelfth Night that year, she was too ill to attend. She suffered a haemorrhage of the lungs the following autumn, and had another in December.

Alarmed, James visited her no fewer than three times at Hampton Court but he did not stay with her, of course, and it was left to Prince Charles and her faithful Danish maid of honour, Anne Kaas, to attend her deathbed along with the doctors and the ecclesiastics. She could not have a Roman Catholic priest with her, even at the end, for the King had sent the Archbishop of Canterbury and the Bishop of London to her. She finally died in the early morning of 1 March 1619. Her funeral took place at Westminster Abbey on 13 May, Prince Charles walking behind the coffin and the Duke of Lennox and the Marquis of Hamilton escorting the chief mourner, the Countess of Arundel. King James, who hated funerals, stayed away.[37]

Notes

1. Stevenson, *Last Royal Wedding*, 2–3.
2. Maclagan and Louda, *Lines of Succession*, Table 19; Williams, *Anne of Denmark*, 1–9.
3. Stevenson, *Last Royal Wedding*, 2–3.
4. *Ibid.*, 4–8.
5. Williams, *Anne of Denmark*, 6.
6. Stevenson, *Last Royal Wedding*, 12–22, 85; Williams, *Anne of Denmark*, 7–9.
7. Stevenson, *Last Royal Wedding*, 36, 84.
8. *Ibid.*, 36, 86–9.
9. *RPC*, iv, 423–30; *Papers Relative to the Marriage of King James the Sixth of Scotland with the Princess Anne of Denmark* (Bannatyne Club 1828), ed. J.T. Gibson Craig, 12–16; Stevenson, *Last Royal Wedding*, 25–33.
10. *Ibid.*, 91.
11. Moysie, *Memoirs*, 9.
12. Stevenson, *Last Royal Wedding*, 94.
13. *Ibid.*, 38–57.
14. Moysie, *Memoirs*, 159; Stevenson, *Last Royal Wedding*, 101–7.
15. *Illustrations of British History* (London 1791), iii, 2.
16. Maureen M. Meikle, 'A meddlesome princess: Anna of Denmark and Scottish court politics, 1589–1603', in *The Reign of James VI*, ed. Julian Goodare and Michael Lynch (East Linton 2000), 132–5.
17. *Register of the Privy Council of Scotland*, v, ed. David Masson (Edinburgh

1882), 327n., 343, 558; M.A. Everett Green, *Elizabeth, Electress Palatine and Queen of Bohemia* (London 1855), 2–4; Rosalind K. Marshall, *The Winter Queen* (Edinburgh 1998), 19–20.

18. *CSP Scottish*, xiii, part 1, 640–1, 661, 667, 783, 863–4, 920, 945, 948, 1001, 1003, 1007–8, 1013, 1026, 1028.

19. *CSP Scottish*, xiii, part 1, 448, 558, 850, 941, 1017, 1029n., 1150–2.

20. John G. Dunbar, *Scottish Royal Palaces* (East Linton 1999), 90–1; Deborah Howard, *Scottish Architecture: Reformation to Restoration 1560–1660* (Edinburgh 1995), 26–30.

21. Williams, *Anne of Denmark*, 32, 67.

22. Maureen M. Meikle, '"Holde her at the Oeconomicke rule of the House": Anna of Denmark and Scottish Court Finances, 1589–1603', in *Women in Scotland*, 107–8; Bruce Lenman, 'Jacobean Goldsmiths and Jewellers as Credit-Creators: The Cases of James Mossman, James Cockie and George Heriot', in *SHR*, lxxiv, 2, no. 198 (October 1995), 166–71.

23. Meikle, in *Women in Scotland*, 109.

24. Williams, *Anne of Denmark*, 70; Strong, *Henry, Prince of Wales*, 10.

25. *CSP Venetian*, 1603–7, x, 40; Williams, *Anne of Denmark*, 70–1.

26. *Ibid.*, 71; John Nichols, *The Progresses, Processions and Festivities of King James I, his Royal Consort and Family* (London 1828), i, 153–4; *HMC Report 60, Mar and Kellie*, ii, 51.

27. 'Two unpublished letters of James VI', in *SHR*, xvi, 141–3.

28. Carola Oman, *Elizabeth of Bohemia* (London 1938), 14.

29. Williams, *Anne of Denmark*, 81.

30. *Ibid.*, 82–91.

31. Strong, *Henry, Prince of Wales*, 106.

32. David N. Durant, *Arbella Stuart: A Rival to the Queen* (London 1978), 132–3.

33. Orgel and Strong, *Inigo Jones*, 6–7, 42–3, 85–9, 131, 191.

34. Diana Scarisbrick, 'Anne of Denmark's Jewellery: The Old and the New', in *Apollo* (April 1986), 228–36; Diana Scarisbrick, *Anne of Denmark's Jewellery Inventory* (Devonshire 1991), reprinted from *Archaeologia*, cix (1991). The full-length portrait is in the Royal Collection.

35. Oliver Millar, *The Queen's Pictures* (London 1977), 22–4; Strong, *Henry, Prince of Wales*, 187–8; Timothy Wilks, 'Rivalries among the Designers at Prince Henry's Court, 1610–12', in *The Court Historian*, vi (May 2001), 58–61.

36. Stevenson, *Last Royal Wedding*, 75.

37. *Funeral Effigies of Westminster Abbey*, 9–11, 21–5, 60, 63–6, 155, plate vii; Jennifer Woodward, *The Theatre of Death* (Woodbridge 1997), 166–74; G.P.V. Akrigg, *Jacobean Pageant: The Court of King James I* (London 1962), 268–9.

CHAPTER TWELVE

HENRIETTA MARIA AND CATHERINE OF BRAGANZA

After the death of Anne of Denmark, James VI did not remarry and the business of finding wives for his successors would be conducted in a very different context from such negotiations in the past. Scotland did still have its own parliament in the century after 1603, but the Court was now permanently established in London and the question of a consort was a matter of English, not Scottish, foreign policy. Indeed, the next two women who became Queens of Scotland never did visit that country although they obviously knew the Scottish noblemen who flocked south each year to seek honours and appointments from the King and they had Scotswomen or at least the wives of Scottish peers as their attendants.

James VI liked to think of himself as the peacemaker of Europe and, having married his daughter Elizabeth to the Protestant Elector Palatine, he intended to keep the balance by finding a Roman Catholic wife for his sole surviving son, Prince Charles. For a long time he favoured the King of Spain's daughter as the most suitable choice, and in 1623 he sent Charles off with the Duke of Buckingham to woo the Infanta Maria in person. Unfortunately for him, she did not reciprocate his interest, screaming that she would rather enter a nunnery than marry him. Charles was forced to retreat home again without his intended bride and his father's thoughts turned to the French royal family.[1] Long before, James had planned to marry Prince Henry to a French princess. That scheme had died with Henry, but now it could be revived, and he learned through diplomatic channels that there was an available princess.

Henrietta Maria was the youngest daughter of Henry IV of France, the Protestant who had famously converted to Catholicism with the words, 'Paris is worth a Mass'. He was dead by now, stabbed to death by a deranged monk as he rode in his coach through his capital when Henrietta was still little more than a baby. France was being ruled by his formidable widow, Marie de Medici, on behalf of their young son, Louis XIII. Ambitious for all her children, Marie was gratified when James approached her about a possible match, and the marriage treaty was signed in Paris on 10 November 1624. The Pope had to grant a dispensation for the marriage, but he expressed horror at the notion of Henrietta marrying a heretic. However, James VI died in March 1625 and a few days later the desired dispensation arrived, with a message for Henrietta telling her that she must try to convert her husband so that all his subjects would return to the Roman Catholic Church.[2]

The marriage contract was signed on 28 April 1625, Henrietta attending the betrothal ceremony in a diamond-strewn robe of cloth-of-gold and silver sewn all over with gold fleurs-de-lys. She would have a dowry of 800,000 crowns and she would be allowed to have a chapel of her own in each of her residences and bring with her to England a Roman Catholic bishop and twenty-eight priests. When her children were born, she would be responsible for their education until they were twelve. Charles, for his part, settled suitable jointure lands on her.[3] Henrietta was married at Notre Dame on 1 May 1625, standing at the very place where Mary, Queen of Scots had married the Dauphin nearly seventy years earlier. She again wore her dress encrusted with gold fleurs-de-lys, a small crown with a huge pendant pearl perched on her dark curls. The Duke of Chevreuse represented Charles. It was unusual to have a Frenchman stand proxy for a British bridegroom, but the Duke was related to Charles through the Guise family, and as a Roman Catholic he could participate in the subsequent nuptial Mass.[4]

Henrietta set out for England on 9 June 1625. She was fifteen years old, with large and beautiful eyes, a white skin and excellent if protruding teeth. She was also tiny, less than five feet tall, but that did not matter, for she was well-shaped and, after all, Charles himself was only five feet four. Henrietta was also vivacious, loving, stubborn and undoubtedly spoiled. She had a good crossing from Boulogne and arrived safely at Dover Castle, where Charles came to meet her the next day. Henrietta had seen a miniature of him some months earlier and she had fallen in love with it, imagining him to be a dashing, romantic figure. She was bitterly disappointed when she saw the reality: a short, slight, melancholy man with a reserved manner.

For his part, Charles was touched by her ingenuousness, but his sympathy ebbed away in the days that followed when he discovered that she was used to having her own way, and was perfectly ready to fly into a tantrum when she was crossed. Henrietta found him remote and unfeeling, and when she discovered how much he relied on his father's favourite, the Duke of Buckingham, for support and advice, she grew bitterly resentful. Her devotion to her religion complicated matters further, and the situation worsened when she refused to be crowned because the Protestant Archbishop of Canterbury was to place the crown on her head. She offended many by staying away from the opening of parliament too, and the growing rift between her husband and herself was made worse by a whole series of petty quarrels stirred up, she believed, by Buckingham, who felt threatened by her presence.[5]

Henrietta began to think that she could do nothing right. She had often performed in Court entertainments in France and, eager to continue Anne of Denmark's tradition of Court masques, she presented a play in the hall of Somerset House, which was now her personal residence. The King and his courtiers sat entranced as an artificial moon rose through high clouds, a thunderstorm broke out and a story of innocent, courtly love unfolded. Inigo Jones had provided the sets, the Queen's ladies were in exquisite costumes, and Henrietta herself, clad in green embroidered with gold, silver and pearls, took their breath away when she did not merely appear but acted the principal part, speaking six hundred lines of French poetry. The English Puritans were horrified. No woman should ever appear on the stage, they said, least of all the Queen, and what was more she had even caused some of her ladies to disguise themselves as men, with false beards.[6]

As her unpopularity grew, Henrietta's relationship with her husband remained fraught, and when he told her that he was sending her retinue home to France, she wept hysterically and tried to break the window of the chamber where they were talking. Horrified, Charles dragged her away, bruising her arms and tearing her dress.[7] The French were furious when they heard how their princess was being treated, and they dispatched the Marshal de

Bassompierre to try to effect a reconciliation between the royal couple, but it was not until 1628 that the situation changed. On 23 August that year, the Duke of Buckingham was assassinated by an army officer with a grudge. Charles was distraught, and Henrietta, always warm-hearted, put aside all other considerations and rushed to console him. To the amazement of all concerned, the King and Queen now fell passionately in love with each other. The following March it was announced that Henrietta was pregnant, and that same month her husband took his fateful decision to rule without parliament.[8]

Two months after that, Henrietta went into labour prematurely. It was a breech birth, she nearly died and the tiny, weak baby boy lived for only a few hours. When she had recovered, she went to Tunbridge Wells to take the waters, and within weeks she was pregnant again. This time the baby was born safely, on 29 May 1630, the large, black-haired child who would one day become Charles II.[9] After that, Henrietta had two more sons, James and Henry, and five daughters, Mary, Elizabeth, Catherine, Anne and Henrietta. She and the King were idyllically happy together. If her imperiousness and waywardness had once irritated him, he was now enchanted with everything she did and he came to rely on her more and more, for he had discovered that she was a shrewd judge of character.

During those early years, Scotland can scarcely have impinged on Henrietta's consciousness and she was unable to accompany her husband north in 1633 because she was pregnant. Some Scots she did know well. There was James, 3rd Marquis of Hamilton, who was her husband's leading Scottish adviser and his personal friend. Hamilton's English wife, Lady Mary Feilding, was one of her attendants and their first baby was named after the Queen. Henrietta found the Marquis himself dull if worthy, and she much preferred the dashing Marquis of Montrose.[10] Another Scot who came to her attention was George Con, the handsome, affable priest whom the Pope, with Charles's permission, sent as special ambassador to her Court.[11]

Charles and Henrietta shared the same hierarchical view of the world. The one subject she never discussed with him was religion, in spite of papal urgings,[12] but they were entirely in agreement that Charles was God's representative on earth, the only source of power. All government flowed from him in the form of laws and the administration of justice. Former notions about laws being made by the King in parliament were entirely wrong, for Charles had been taught by his father that he must govern both Church and state.[13] Now the time had come for him to explain his world view to his subjects, and he and Henrietta hit upon the idea of expounding his theories to his courtiers by means of the masques of which she was so fond. She was pleased. She could not involve herself in affairs of state, but she could take part with him in these didactic entertainments.

Inigo Jones was pressed into service once more as the designer, and a new series of masques was produced. Possibly the courtiers were so entranced by the visual effects that they paid little heed to the message the text attempted to convey, but Charles was insistent that each entertainment must have an allegorical theme. In *Love's Triumph* on 9 January 1631, for instance, Henrietta appeared as the Queen of Love, driving out disorder and vice from the Court of the gods and bringing back virtue and honour. In 1634 the message was even more explicit. Charles, as Jove, reorganised heaven in imitation of the British court, his celestial palace in the background having the word 'CARLOMARIA' carved on its walls, in tribute to the royal couple's perfect marriage.

As imitation clouds billowed in the sky, costumes sparkled and singers sang, the King and Queen seemed happily oblivious to the unrest that was growing around them. Afterwards, Henrietta often used to wish that she had studied British history when she was a girl so that she could have understood what was happening and helped Charles more effectively. In short, Elizabeth I had managed to ignore the growing dissatisfaction with her financial and religious policies, James VI and I had staved off outright confrontation, and Charles was left to tackle the increasing discontent.[14] James had boasted that he was able to rule Scotland from London with a stroke of his pen, but his son lacked his shrewd knowledge of the Scottish situation and personalities, and when Charles tried to impose a prayer book on the Church of Scotland, the Scots seethed with discontent. His ecclesiastical initiatives also alienated the English Puritans, his fiscal policies annoyed almost everyone, and the Scots drew up a National Covenant by which they pledged themselves to defend their Presbyterian form of worship against what they saw as the King's attempts to reintroduce Roman Catholicism.[15]

Charles told Henrietta that Presbyterians were simply republicans, intent on overthrowing the monarchy. Seeing his wife's look of terror, he added hastily that he could, of course, restore order any time that he liked. In fact, his attempts to use military force against the Scots in 1639 and again in 1640 ended in humiliating failure. The Second Bishops' War of June 1640 left the Scots occupying northern England and they had to be bought off with a large indemnity. Charles, attending parliament in Edinburgh, was forced to give his assent not only to the establishment of Presbyterianism but to severe limitations on royal power. The events in Scotland encouraged opposition to the King in England and set him on course for confrontation with the Long Parliament, leading to the outbreak of the Civil War.[16]

More combative than he, Henrietta urged her husband to crush the rebels immediately and, taking advantage of her daughter Mary's marriage to William II, Prince of Orange, she escorted the Princess to the Low Countries early in 1642 so that she could pawn and sell many of the royal jewels in Amsterdam and Antwerp. She then used the proceeds to buy weapons for the King. In her letters home she warned him vigorously against appeasing the enemy and then, thinking that perhaps she had gone too far, wrote, 'I beg your pardon if I have said anything in my letters a little passionate. It is the affection I have for you which makes me do it, and my care for your honour'. Alluding to the names their enemies were giving them, she ended merrily, 'I'll go pray for the Man of Sin that has married the Popish Brat of France'.[17]

Back in England again after a horrendously dangerous voyage, Henrietta set about raising troops for the royal cause in Yorkshire. When the Court moved to Oxford, she went too, and during that strange interlude she and her ladies danced, listened to music and watched plays put on for them by the students while Charles hunted and enjoyed games of tennis. The town and the surrounding countryside were full of soldiers, however, and they could not ignore what was happening around them. Henrietta urged Charles to march on London but instead he decided to try to capture

Gloucester, only to hurry back to Oxford again after an indecisive battle against the parliamentarians. At the end of 1643, the Scottish Covenanters signed an alliance with the English parliamentary forces and crossed the Border into England. Henrietta's distress was compounded when she realised that she was pregnant. Terrified of being captured by the enemy, she managed to convince Charles that she should seek refuge in the West of England, in Bath, perhaps, where she could take the waters for her health.

She parted from her husband on 17 April 1644 at Abingdon, and when she reached Exeter she gave birth to a large and healthy baby daughter in spite of being dreadfully ill herself, possibly with tuberculosis. She knew that Charles was liable to march into danger to try to save her from the enemy and she reached the conclusion that it would be as well if she left the country. Back in her native land she could raise more men and money. That, at least, was how she rationalised the decision to herself. Much as she loved her husband, Henrietta, like Margaret Tudor, had a strong instinct for self-preservation. She managed by sheer force of will to escape to France, leaving her infant in the care of Lady Dalkeith. Charles did indeed march west and, when he arrived in Exeter to find her gone, he had their baby daughter christened Henrietta.[18]

Louis XIII, Henrietta Maria's brother, was dead by this time and his widow, Anne of Austria, was ruling France as regent for her young son, Louis XIV. Anne welcomed her sister-in-law, was endlessly kind to her and gradually Henrietta's health improved. Whenever she received any money, she sent most of it to Charles, and as his position worsened she sold furnishings, put away her fine coaches and horses and pawned the last of her jewels in Holland, endlessly pleading with Cardinal Mazarin, the principal French minister, to help him.[19] She also plied Charles himself with letters urging him not to give in, for she was afraid that he would agree to some humiliating accommodation with the enemy.

Defeated, imprisoned and ultimately tried for treason, Charles I was executed on 30 January 1649. When Henrietta heard the news, she thought that she would die too. After lying in bed for several days torturing herself with regret that she had not been with him, she sought refuge in a Carmelite convent. Finally persuaded to return to Court, she said that she had lost not only her husband but her best friend. Her sons managed to escape to the Continent, joined her briefly and then sought service in various foreign armies. Her daughter Elizabeth died as a prisoner of the Cromwellians, but her youngest child, Henrietta Anne, was her daily consolation. Lady Dalkeith had finally managed to escape from England and had brought the little girl to Paris. After that, mother and daughter were hardly ever apart.[20]

In 1660, Henrietta's eldest and favourite son was restored to the throne of Britain as Charles II. The rest of the royal family flocked to London for the celebrations, but Henrietta was reluctant. After her husband's execution, she had no desire to see Britain ever again and no one knew what sort of reception she might receive. Her undaunted spirit had earned her the admiration of all her friends, but her presence at Charles I's side had added to his troubles. His enemies had hated her for her Catholicism, blamed her for influencing him in matters of religion, even accused her of having an affair with Henry, Lord Jermyn, her Master of the Horse.[21] However, she and Henrietta Anne, whom Charles II had nicknamed 'Minette' (Little Puss), did make the journey later the same year, and although it was arranged that they would enter London quietly in case of riots, by the time they reached Lambeth the Thames was thronged with craft of every kind and the banks were thick with welcoming and curious crowds.

Henrietta took up residence once more at Somerset House.[22] Inigo Jones was dead, but she got out his old plans for improvements to the palace, gave orders for a splendid new gallery to be built and laid out an Italian garden. After that, she divided her time between London and Colombe, where she had a quiet country house. She died there peacefully, in her sleep, after a chest infection, in the early hours of 10 September 1667 and was buried with her father in the Abbey of St Denis. Her heart was taken to Chaillot in a silver casket engraved with the words: 'Henrietta Maria, Queen of England, France, Scotland and Ireland, daughter of the King of France, Henry IV the Victorious, wife of Charles I the Martyr and mother of the restored King Charles II'.[23]

At the time of his restoration, her son was thirty years old and still a bachelor. During his long years abroad no royal bride had been interested in marrying a penniless exile with no prospects.

That is not to say that he had not taken an interest in women. Tall, dark and harsh-featured, cynical but undeniably charming, he had found no difficulty in attracting partners, and from the age of fifteen he had enjoyed a long series of sexual relationships. As soon as he was back in London, his advisers began urging him to marry and have legitimate children, but Charles had his own ideas about a suitable bride and he brushed aside the various German princesses they suggested with the memorable words, 'Oddsfish! They are all dull and foggy! I cannot like any of them for a wife!' He did not see that he was obliged to marry a Protestant. No one knows how much his Catholic mother influenced him in religion, but it would be rumoured throughout his adult life that he had converted to Catholicism, and his statesmen noted with disapproval his continuing desire to make an alliance with his cousin Louis XIV of France. At any rate, it was probably Louis who drew his attention to the Portuguese Infanta, Catherine of Braganza, and when Charles heard that she would have a huge dowry, he was immediately interested.

Catherine had been born on 25 November 1638, St Catherine's Day, at the Villa Viçosa, eighty miles from Lisbon. Her parents were the amiable John, Duke of Braganza, and his strong-minded wife Luiza, daughter of the powerful Duke of Medina Sidonia. They already had two sons and so they were charmed with their little daughter. When Catherine was two, the family moved to Lisbon. Urged on by his fellow-countrymen, the Duke, who had royal blood, had seized the throne, ending sixty years of Spanish rule. He now governed Portugal as King John IV.[24] The Spaniards were furious, of course, and they tried to make sure that Portugal became diplomatically isolated. However, the Portuguese had always enjoyed considerable trade with Britain, and in 1642 the two countries had made a commercial treaty. Two years after that, Catherine's father approached Charles I about a marriage between her and the fourteen-year-old Prince of Wales.

The Civil War was at its height and Charles did not dare to marry his son to a Roman Catholic bride, however wealthy she might be, so nothing was done. Catherine's father died when she was eighteen. Her elder brother, Alphonso, was intellectually impaired as a result of a childhood illness, and their mother ruled as regent for him.

Determined to revive the British marriage plan, Queen Luiza rejected various other offers for her daughter. By 1660, Catherine was twenty-two, old for a bride by contemporary standards, but Louis XIV of France did not want to see Spain increase its power by renewing its hold on Portugal, and so he favoured her marriage to Charles II. Negotiations began and Catherine's very large dowry was set at two million crowns (about £360,000 sterling), along with the strategically important Tangier and Bombay. Impressed, the British Protestant statesmen were willing to overlook the bride's religion.

The marriage treaty was drawn up, Charles settling on his bride a jointure of £30,000, and promising her freedom to worship as she chose. It was agreed that there would be no proxy marriage service. The wedding would take place in London.[25] Edward, 1st Earl of Sandwich, was dispatched with a fleet to collect Catherine and she arrived off the south coast of England on 13 May 1662. Landing at Portsmouth, she was escorted to the King's House to await the arrival of her bridegroom. Charles, taken up with affairs of state, was delayed for a week, and when he finally arrived he found her in bed with a feverish cold.

Some said that Charles thought that his bride looked like a bat, with her very large dark eyes, olive skin and slightly protruding teeth, but her portraits show her as small, dark and pretty, and the King told his chief adviser Edward, 1st Earl of Clarendon, that 'she hath as much agreeableness in her looks altogether as ever I saw'. Her conversation was very good, 'for she has wit enough and a most agreeable voice', and, in short, he thought himself very happy, 'for I am confident our two humours will agree very well together'. They were secretly married by Catherine's Roman Catholic almoner, Ludovic, Lord Aubigny, a secular priest, on the morning of 21 May 1662, and that afternoon they had their public, Church of England wedding in the great hall of the King's House. Catherine wore a rose-coloured dress in the British fashion, sewn all over with the wedding favours, knots of blue ribbon.[26]

If Charles was pleased with his wife, she was even more delighted with him. In fact, she had fallen in love with him as soon as she had seen him. When Henrietta Maria arrived in London in August she was able to tell her sister that Catherine was the best creature in the world and she and Charles loved each other very much indeed.[27] Well satisfied with her new daughter-in-law, the Queen Mother did not realise that there was a serious problem ahead. Until her marriage, Catherine had led an incredibly sheltered life. At the time of her marriage negotiations it was said that she had not been out of the Portuguese royal palace for the past five years, and indeed it had emerged that she had been in the outside world no more than ten times in her whole life. The education she had received had been more suited to a nun than a princess, and in spite of her mother's ambitions for her, she had not been taught any English.[28]

Before she left Lisbon her mother did warn Catherine about Charles's mistresses, but she seems to have convinced herself that all those relationships were in the past and that he would now be entirely faithful to her. This illusion was rudely shattered when, soon after they returned to London, he ordered her to make Barbara Villiers, his principal mistress, one of her ladies of the bedchamber. A flamboyant, demanding termagant, Barbara had just given birth to the King's son, the first of their five children, and she had not the slightest intention of giving up her royal lover. If she were in attendance on the Queen, then she would have an assured place at the centre of the Court. Charles, always too amenable where women were concerned, weakly allowed himself to be persuaded, and made her complaisant husband Earl of Castlemaine so that she could have a suitable title.

Catherine was aghast when he told her and flatly refused to have anything to do with Lady Castlemaine. This annoyed Charles, for he did not dare disappoint Barbara. Some days later he brought his mistress to his wife's apartments and presented her to Catherine. Unable to understand English, Catherine did not realise to whom she was speaking, and graciously welcomed the newcomer. One of her Portuguese ladies saw what was happening, however, and hissed, 'It is Lady Castlemaine!' Appalled, Catherine fell to the floor in hysterics, her nose bleeding profusely. Charles thought that she was purposely making a scene, and was more irritated than ever. When she reproached him, he sprang to the defence of his mistress and ordered Catherine to accept her. From that moment, Catherine's dreams of a perfect marriage faded away as Charles spent more and more time with 'the Lady' and, well aware of the true source of influence, the courtiers deserted the Queen and flocked to the royal mistress. Isolated, lonely, jealous and depressed, Catherine kept to her own apartments.[29]

Her misery was intensified by the fact that, as the months went by, although the King came to her every night, she showed no sign of becoming pregnant. Everyone knew that the first duty of a queen was to provide her husband with sons and she was sure that, if only she could have a child, Charles would turn his attentions back to her. In 1663 she suffered a near-fatal attack of what was described as spotted fever, and in her delirium thought that she and Charles did have babies. She reduced him to tears when she spoke anxiously about these imagined children, and he spent long hours at her bedside. She had been given the last rites, but his loving concern worked wonders and in the end she did recover.[30]

After that, Charles went back to his mistresses and Catherine had to suffer the continuing indignity of public criticism about something she could not help. Indeed, as Clarendon fell from power in 1667, a mob attacked his house and left a placard with the words, 'Three sights to be seen, Dunkirk, Tangier and a barren Queen'.[31] The implication was that, as well as selling Dunkirk, Clarendon had deliberately arranged the marriage with Catherine in the knowledge that she could not have children, for then his own son-in-law the Duke of York would succeed to the throne. A year later, Catherine did conceive at last and the King became amazingly attentive once more. In May 1668, however, she suffered a miscarriage and on 7 June 1669 she miscarried again. Bitterly disappointed, Charles reacted badly, behaving as if she had somehow cheated him.[32]

Catherine now withdrew to Somerset House, spending much of her time at endless services conducted by her Portuguese priests. In the late 1670s, there was considerable anti-Catholic feeling in England, focusing on Catherine's inability to have children and the likelihood of the King's brother James, Duke of York, succeeding to the throne. Although he had never announced his conversion, it was widely known that he was a Catholic. There were moves to have him excluded from the succession, and in 1678 Titus Oates alleged that there was 'a Popish Plot' by Jesuits aimed at assassinating both the King and the Duke. In the confusion, it was even said that Catherine of Braganza was involved.

Charles dismissed this at once, saying angrily of his wife, 'I will never suffer an innocent lady to be oppressed!' Indeed, he had always rebuffed suggestions that he should put Catherine away so that he could marry someone else and have legitimate children. In 1667 George, 2nd Duke of Buckingham, had even offered to kidnap the Queen and send her to America but Charles had been horrified.[33] Now he brought her back to Whitehall so that she could live under his immediate protection and made plans for her to escape to France should the situation deteriorate still further.[34] When Anthony, 1st Earl of Shaftesbury, tried to introduce a motion in parliament asking him to divorce Catherine, Charles personally visited all the peers, telling them that they must vote against it.[35] If she could not have his love, at least she had his respect.

Throughout all her troubles and his many infidelities, Catherine's devotion to her husband never faltered. She was at his bedside when he collapsed with a stroke at the beginning of 1685, and his death on 2 February was a bitter blow. She retired to a convent for some months afterwards, and let it be known that she wanted to go back to Portugal. Louis XIV told her that she must stay where she was, and so she returned to Somerset House. She was still there in 1688 when William of Orange and her husband's niece Mary II replaced James VII and II on the British throne, but she was finally allowed to go home to Portugal in 1692. Her younger brother, Pedro, was ruling as King. She received a tremendous welcome and built a new palace and chapel for herself at Bemposta, where she lived quietly, visiting Lisbon only occasionally.

Remarkably, at the very end of her life she was suddenly called upon to take up a public role. In 1705 King Pedro fell seriously ill, and as his own son was still a child he appointed Catherine to be Queen Regent of Portugal. After all her mortifying years of being marginalised at the British Court, she now took her place as ruler of her native land, pursuing a successful military campaign against Philippe of Anjou, the French claimant to the Spanish throne who was then at war with Portugal. But in the final days of that same year she was suddenly seized with 'a colic'. An English physician was one of those who attended her, and it seems that at the end her thoughts went back to her time in Britain, for she whispered to him that she had never tried to bring in popery, despite what people said. She died peacefully at ten o'clock on the evening of 31 December 1705 and was buried in the church of Belem, to the west of Lisbon, beside her brother Alphonso.[36]

Notes

1. *Narrative of the Spanish Marriage Treaty*, ed. S.R.Gardiner (Camden Society 1869).
2. Birch, ii, 329; Ferrero, *Lettres*, 324.
3. Jean Héroard, *Journal sur l'Enfance et la Jeunesse de Louis XIII*, ed. E. Soulie and E. de Barthélemy (Paris 1868), i, 413–4; Carlton, *Charles I*, 38–9; Green, *Letters*, 5.
4. *L'Ordre des cérémonies observés au mariage du roy de la Grande Bretagne* (Paris 1625).
5. Birch, i, 30 ff; Marshall, *Henrietta Maria*, 30–45.
6. Orgel and Strong, *Inigo Jones, passim*.
7. Ferrero, *Lettres*, 4–6; Leveneur de Tillières, *Mémoires*, ed. M.C. Hippeau (Paris 1862); *Journal de ma Vie: Mémoires (Marshal de Bassompierre)*, ed. M.J.A. La Cropte (Paris 1870–7), 1–30; Oman, *Henrietta Maria*, 45–6.
8. Birch, i, 388–99; *CSPD, 1625–49*, 291–4; Carlton, *Charles I*, 114; Sir Henry Wotton, *The Life and Death of George Villiers, Duke of Buckingham* (Harleian Miscellany 1811), viii; Roger Lockyer, *Buckingham: The Life and Political Career of George Villiers, 1st Duke of Buckingham 1592–1628* (London 1981).
9. Birch, i, 328, 355–6; ii, 306; Green, *Letters*, 14; Plowden, *Henrietta Maria*, 82.
10. Rosalind K. Marshall, *The Days of Duchess Anne* (East Linton, 2000 edn.), 13–19.
11. Birch, ii, 413.
12. Bone, *Henrietta Maria*, 99; Green, *Letters*, 29–32.
13. Orgel and Strong, *Inigo Jones, passim*.
14. *Narrative of the Spanish Marriage Treaty*, ed. S.R. Gardiner (Camden Society 1869).
15. Motteville, *Mémoires*, 90–2; Donaldson, *James V to James VII*, 295–324.
16. Motteville, *Mémoires*, 190–202; Elizabeth Hamilton, *Henrietta Maria* (London 1976), 149–50; Donaldson, *James V to James VII*, 295–324; Carlton, *Charles I*, 191–229; Pauline Gregg, *King Charles I* (London 1981), 285–96; Mark Charles Fissel, *The Bishops' Wars* (Cambridge 1994).
17. *Archives ou Correspondance Inédit de la Maison d'Orange Nassau*, ed. G.G.

van Prinsterer (Utrecht 1859), iv, 13–95; Green, *Letters*, 50–238; Baillon, *Lettres*, 372–3; Ferrero, *Lettres*, 371–6; Bone, *Henrietta Maria*, 146; Oman, *Henrietta Maria*, 133.

18. Green, *Letters*, 246–50.
19. Motteville, *Mémoires*, 184–257; Green, *Letters*, 251–344; Oman, *Henrietta Maria*, 160–290; Ferrero, *Lettres*, 376–81; *Charles I in 1646: Letters of Charles I to Queen Henrietta*, ed. John Bruce (Camden Society 1856).
20. Birch, ii, 410.
21. *CSP Venetian*, xxv, 149–50.
22. R. Needham and A. Webster, *Somerset House, Past and Present* (London 1905), 89–143; Birch, ii, 427–37; Oman, *Henrietta Maria*, 306–3; Ferrero, *Lettres*, 437–54.
23. Birch, ii, 465–9; Jacques Bossuet, *Oraisons Funèbres*, ed. P. Jacquinet (Paris n.d.), 8–9; Oman, *Henrietta Maria*, 341ff; Baillon, *Lettres*, 336–9; *Relation de la pompe funèbre, faite en l'Eglise de S. Denys en France pour la Reyne Mere d'Angleterre* (Brussels n.d.); *The Life and Death of Henrietta Maria de Bourbon* (1685), 92ff.
24. Davidson, *Catherine of Bragança*, 1–5; Mackay, *Catherine of Braganza* (London 1937), 9–13.
25. Antonia Fraser, *King Charles II* (London 1979), 202–3.
26. Davidson, *Catherine of Bragança*, 17–197; Mackay, *Catherine of Braganza*, 22–42; Christopher Falkus, *The Life and Times of Charles II* (London 1972), 89–90; Charles Carlton, *Royal Mistresses* (London 1991), 64–8.
27. Ferrero, *Lettres*, 437–8.
28. Davidson, *Catherine of Bragança*, 10–11.
29. *Ibid.*, 119–97.
30. *Ibid.*, 198–9; Fraser, *Charles II*, 212.
31. *The Diary of Samuel Pepys*, ed. R. Latham and W. Matthews, viii (London 1974), 269.
32. *The Letters, Speeches and Declarations of King Charles II*, ed. Arthur Bryant (London 1935), 219, 236; Fraser, *Charles II*, 259–60.
33. Davidson, *Catherine of Bragança*, 234, 278–9.
34. *Ibid.*, 304–33; Mackay, *Catherine of Braganza*, 200–35; Fraser, *Charles II*, 362–3.
35. Davidson, *Catherine of Bragança*, 334–8.
36. *Ibid.*, 388–502.

CHAPTER THIRTEEN

MARY OF MODENA AND MARY II

M ary Beatrice d'Este, the first and only Italian to be Queen of Scotland, was born on 25 September 1658 in Modena, a small duchy lying in a fertile plain south of the Alps.[1] Her father, the Duke of Modena, died of tuberculosis when she was two, and her mother, Laura Martinozzi, then ruled as regent for Mary's two-year-old brother, Francesco. Strictly brought up by their imposing parent, they were given a sternly religious education, and by the time she was nine Mary had decided to follow the example of her much-loved governess and become a nun. Her future, however, lay elsewhere. In 1673 Charles II's brother and heir, James, Duke of York, was looking for another wife. Anne Hyde, his first Duchess, had died of breast cancer, leaving him with two little girls, Mary and Anne. It was by now generally accepted that Catherine of Braganza would never have children and so James would have to supply the necessary male heirs to the throne. He sent Henry, Earl of Peterborough, to the Continent to find him a bride who was beautiful, so that he would not be tempted to have extra-marital affairs, and a Roman Catholic, since Catholicism was his own religion, although he still kept his conversion a secret.

Peterborough was in the midst of inspecting various possible brides when he was shown a portrait of Mary of Modena. He was enchanted, and although he was warned of her determination to become a nun, he brushed that aside. She would, after all, have no say in the matter. When he travelled to Modena and met her in person, he was even more delighted. Now fourteen, Mary was tall and slim but well-shaped, with black hair, a dazzlingly fair complexion and lustrous dark eyes. He explained his mission, and she told him fiercely that she had vowed to enter a convent. She had never even heard of England let alone the Duke of York, and when her mother told her that she must marry James, she screamed and wept for two whole days, or so she said afterwards. Her proxy wedding took place on 20 September (Old Style) 1673, with Peterborough standing in for the bridegroom. Mary set off for Britain, accompanied by her mother, five days later, on her fifteenth birthday, and they arrived at Dover eight weeks after that.[2]

Her husband was waiting to help her from the small boat that brought her ashore. He was forty years old, tall and harsh-featured. When he touched her, she flinched nervously. He took her to the house where he was staying, they were married again in a Church of England service and then they went to bed together. James was an experienced lover but Mary always remembered how, for her first few weeks in England, she wept whenever she saw him. He was charmed with her.[3] They travelled towards London together and met Charles II in his barge off Greenwich. The King was kind to Mary, and she was dazzled by him. He was 'so truly amiable and good-natured that I loved him very much, even before I became attached to my Lord the Duke of York'.[4]

Although deeply upset when Duchess Laura left for home, Mary consoled herself with the thought that her husband was 'a very good man. He has the holy fear of God and is very kind to me and would do anything to show it'.[5] Indeed, after her mother's departure, 'I became very fond of my husband and my affection for him increased with every year that we lived together'. She was also delighted when James's small daughters came to stay at St James's Palace with their households. As well as having Italian ladies, cooks and priests, Mary had many British attendants including the young Scottish heiress Anne, Duchess of Buccleuch, who had been married at an early age to the King's illegitimate son, the Duke of Monmouth.[6]

In May 1674, six months after her arrival in Britain, Mary had a miscarriage. The following January, she gave birth to a daughter, Catherine Laura, who died at five months. The very next day, Mary had another miscarriage. Less than a year after that, in August 1676, she had a second daughter, Isabella, and then at last, in November 1677, the much desired son, Charles, Duke of Cambridge. Smallpox was rife at Court that winter and Princess Anne caught the disease. As soon as she felt better, she came to admire the new baby. Not realising that she was still infectious, she kissed him. He too fell ill and died in December. Mary had also lost the company of her much-loved elder stepdaughter, Princess Mary, but for a happier reason. The Princess married her cousin William of Orange, and went to live in Holland. Deeply sympathetic when she had a miscarriage the following autumn, Mary of Modena decided to go to visit her in The Hague, explaining, 'I love her as if she were my own daughter, and also I have a little curiosity to see that country'.[7] Travelling incognito, she took Anne with her.

Despite her own personal losses, Mary of Modena was as happy as she could be for the first five years of her marriage, but by 1678 religious controversy was overshadowing her life.[8] In 1673 James had been forced to resign as Lord High Admiral of England and Lord Warden of the Cinque Ports when he refused to take the Test Act designed to exclude Catholics from public office. An increasing number of Protestant statesmen were set on removing him from the succession, and the Popish Plot of 1678 whipped up anti-Catholic feeling still further. At the height of the crisis, copies of letters Mary had written to the Pope were found among the papers of her secretary, Edward Coleman. He was executed on 3 December 1678 for treason and her confessor, Claude de la Columbière, was briefly imprisoned the following March.[9]

Both Mary and James seemed singularly unaware of the danger to themselves, but the King was far more astute, and at the beginning of 1679 he decided with regret that they must leave the country, not only for their own safety but for the stability of the monarchy. On 4 March 1679 they sailed to Rotterdam, visited Princess Mary at The Hague and then made their way to Brussels, where they took up residence in the Hôtel de Bassigny, a large mansion in the Rue des Ursulines, near the Church of La Chapelle and just down the hill from the Place du Sablon. Charles II had lived there immediately before the Restoration.[10] Comfortable though they might be, exile was lonely and depressing. The tedium was enlivened by visits from Duchess Laura and from the Princesses Isabella and Anne, but Mary of Modena wrote that she longed to be back in 'dear England again'.[11] That autumn James paid a hasty visit to London when the King was taken ill, but even then Charles would not agree to his permanent return and instead decided that James should move to Scotland.[12]

They intended to sail there, but storms drove them in to the

Norfolk coast and Mary was so ill with seasickness that the King gave them permission to land and come to London. Charles suggested that Mary should stay there, but she refused to leave her husband and they set off north together, Mary travelling in a coach with the Countess of Argyll. Snow delayed them, and they did not reach Edinburgh for nearly three weeks, arriving exhausted on 24 November 1679.[13] The welcome they received made up for the rigours of the journey. As William, 3rd Duke of Hamilton, hereditary keeper of Holyroodhouse, took her hand and led Mary into the palace to meet his wife and the other ladies who were waiting for her at the top of the stairs, cannon were fired from Edinburgh Castle, bells pealed and bonfires were lit.[14] In spite of doubts about their religion, everyone seemed pleased to see them. Indeed, Michael Livingston composed a Latin poem in their honour and when John, 8th Lord Elphinstone's baby daughter was born on 10 January 1680, he called her a string of names beginning with Mary Beatrice and ending with Isabella. Sadly, the baby died the following month.[15]

James and Mary's stay in Scotland was fairly brief, for in February 1680 Charles told them they could return south. The political crisis was far from over, though, and in the autumn he sent James back again as his Lord High Commissioner. In this capacity, James lived in vice-regal state at Holyrood, and while he busied himself with the establishment of the Royal College of Physicians, the Advocates' Library and the revived Order of the Thistle, patronised surgeons, cartographers, mathematicians and engineers and had the refurbished nave of Holyrood Abbey fitted out as his chapel, Mary held balls, concerts, theatricals and supper parties, introduced the Scottish ladies to the novelty of tea drinking and presented a set of beautiful silver altar vessels to the new chapel royal.[16]

In March 1681, she and James were plunged into grief by news of the death of their five-year-old daughter Isabella. Anne, Duchess of Hamilton, was one of those who hastened to send her a letter of condolence.[17] Striving for acceptance, Mary remarked, 'It comforts me to think that I have more angels to pray for me, and I should feel favoured that whereas other women bear children for this world, I have given all mine to God'. In spite of her brave words and although she still hoped to have 'a male child who shall live', she was in despair. Her husband took her on an outing to the Bass Rock to see the solan geese in an effort to cheer her up, and in July they organised a wine and fruit picnic at Polton for Princess Anne, who had come to stay with them.[18]

Mary loved riding, and late that autumn she had a nasty fall from her horse,[19] but as she recovered, she realised to her joy that she was pregnant.[20] The following spring, Charles II told James that they could return south[21] and they arrived safely in London on 26 May. Less than three months later, Mary gave birth to a premature daughter, Charlotte Maria, who died at eight weeks.[22] In the autumn of 1683, and again in the spring of 1684, Mary suffered further miscarriages, and although she went to Tunbridge Wells to take the waters, they seemed to do her little good.[23] The following February, Charles II died at the age of fifty-three. Mary, who had been so fond of him, was deeply upset, and of course her whole way of life changed as she and James became King and Queen of Great Britain.[24] They were crowned on 23 April 1685, Mary resplendent in purple velvet robes, her white and silver brocade dress encrusted with diamonds.[25]

Much praised for her elegance and dignity, the new Queen was unhappy. Her husband was taken up with affairs of state, he was still seeing one of his longstanding mistresses, Catherine Sedley, who had borne him several sons, and his new confessor, Father Edward Petre, was urging him into deeply unpopular measures favouring the Roman Catholics. In July 1685 James decided to repeal the Test Act, the Habeas Corpus Act and the penal laws which excluded Catholics from holding public office. He met with bitter opposition, and in November 1685 he prorogued the English parliament indefinitely. On 14 April 1687 he issued a Declaration of Indulgence which permitted Catholics freedom of worship.[26]

These measures were as unpopular in Scotland as they were in England. James did manage to convert two or three of the leading nobles, including the Scottish chancellor, the Earl of Perth, and his brother the Earl of Melfort, one of the secretaries of state, but on the whole he could persuade few to change their religion, the Scottish parliament refused to cooperate with him and the Presbyterian party grew in strength. In spite of this, even the most opposed Scots seemed to retain a strong loyalty to the House of

Stewart, although Gilbert Burnet, William Carstares and various other leading Scottish exiles were playing an important part at William of Orange's Court.[27]

In December of 1687, Mary found that she was pregnant once more, and whatever they thought of her husband's ecclesiastical policies, the Scottish Privy Council ordered a solemn and public thanksgiving throughout the kingdom.[28] On 7 May 1688 James published a second Declaration of Indulgence and sent seven of the ten English bishops to the Tower for protesting. On 10 June 1688, more apprehensive than optimistic, Mary went into labour, her bed surrounded by the dignitaries who had come to witness the birth. James held her in his arms and, in answer to her pleas, bent his head forward so that his long, curly periwig shielded her from seeing all the eager witnesses. The baby was born just before ten o'clock in the morning. 'I don't hear the child cry,' Mary whispered in sudden terror, but at that moment the infant's screams shattered the silence. Her new son was alive and well, and the delighted King presented Mrs Judith Wilkes, the midwife, with a purse containing 500 guineas.[29]

Instead of solving the King's problems, the arrival of Prince James Francis Edward merely added to them, for the Protestants were now confronted with the prospect of a Roman Catholic dynasty ruling the country. In the current atmosphere of unrest and intolerance, there had already been rumours that Mary had not been pregnant at all, and now people began to say that another woman's baby had been smuggled into the royal bedchamber in a warming pan. Four months after the Prince's arrival, James ordered a privy council enquiry designed to prove that the child really was his son[30] but his intemperate policies had already done great damage. On the same day that the seven bishops were tried and found innocent of any offence, Admiral Arthur Herbert, disguised as a servant, slipped over to Holland with an invitation from seven leading Protestants to the King's son-in-law William of Orange to come and take the throne. On 5 November William landed with his army at Torbay, and, as he advanced on London, James told his wife that she would have to take their baby son to the safety of France.

Mary refused to leave the King until he promised that he would follow her within twenty-four hours and then, disguised as a laundress in a plain black dress under a cloth coat, she slipped out of Whitehall Palace with her son and two of his nurses, crossed the Thames and made a perilous journey by coach to Gravesend. They had a stormy crossing to Calais.[31] After lingering on the coast for more than a week, Mary heard that her husband had been arrested in England, and she dejectedly made her way to Paris, at the invitation of Louis XIV. The French King came to greet her with an impressive retinue, escorted her to St-Germain-en-Laye and presented her with a casket containing six thousand gold pistoles. The following evening, as she lay miserably in bed, he appeared and announced, 'Madame, I bring you a gentleman of your acquaintance whom you will be very glad to see'. Behind him stood her husband.

St Germain was to be Mary's home for the next thirty years.[32] There she remained during James's abortive campaign in Ireland and there, on 28 June 1692, she gave birth to their last child, a daughter. James placed the little girl in her arms with the words, 'See what God has given to be our consolation in our exile'. Princess Louise Marie was known after that as 'La Consolatrice'. James was ageing visibly now, and Mary looked after him tenderly, devoting herself to him and the children, and paying frequent visits to the convent founded at Chaillot by her mother-in-law, Henrietta Maria.[33] James finally died of a stroke on 16 September 1701, leaving Mary to act as regent for their son until the boy was eighteen.[34] Her grief moved Louis XIV to have the Prince proclaimed King James III.[35] When he was old enough, he would have to win back his kingdoms, and Mary spent long hours writing to all her connections in Europe on his behalf.[36] James was a quiet, serious youth, very different in disposition from his lively, attractive sister. Louise was her mother's loving companion, her consolation indeed. In April 1712, both children fell ill with smallpox. James recovered, but Louise died. For many months afterwards, Mary could not help weeping when the name of 'my poor girl' was mentioned.[37]

James embarked on several abortive attempts to reclaim the throne of Britain, but when Louis XIV made peace with Britain in the Treaty of Utrecht in 1713, he had to leave France, eventually settling in Rome after the failure of the 1715 Jacobite Rising.[38]

Enduring increasing poverty, Mary sought consolation in writing to him, visiting Chaillot, seeing friends, and going for long walks, still slim and elegant and always keeping up a cheerful front. She died on 7 May 1718, after a brief, feverish chill. The surgeons attributed her death to 'inflammation of the lungs and the great abscess in her side'. She had found a lump in her breast as long before as 1700, and there had been a recurrence in the summer of 1717. She was buried at Chaillot in the expectation that she and her family would one day be interred in Westminster Abbey. Among her belongings she left miniatures of Mary, Queen of Scots and her own immediate relatives, two packets of Princess Louise's hair and a small box containing a little of the blood of her dead husband.[39]

One of the bitterest aspects of Mary's long exile had been the knowledge that her husband had been dislodged from the throne of Britain by his own daughter and the son-in-law who was also his nephew. Mary II, his elder surviving daughter by Anne Hyde, had been born at St James's Palace on 30 April 1662. She had spent her earliest years in the royal nurseries at the Old Palace of Richmond. A large, bright, attractive child, she was given drawing lessons by Richard Gibson the famous miniaturist and was taught to sing, dance and speak fluent French. In spite of her parents' conversion to Catholicism, her uncle Charles II insisted that she and her sister Anne were to be brought up as Protestants, and Dr Henry Compton, Bishop of London, was put in charge of their religious education.

The children did not see much of their parents, and Mary's mother died in 1671 when she was nine. She was eleven when her father married fifteen-year-old Mary of Modena, telling his daughters that he had found a playmate for them. When the girls moved to St James's Palace, Mary seems to have been happy. She was godmother to Mary of Modena's daughter, Catherine Laura, in 1679, she liked her governess and she was fond of reading romantic novels. She does not seem to have given any thought to her own future, though, and it came as a great shock to her when, on 21 October 1677, her father returned from dining at Whitehall and announced that she was to marry her cousin, William of Orange. She spent that evening and the next day in floods of tears.[40]

William was the son of Mary, the sister of Charles II and James. A posthumous child, he had since birth been Prince of Orange and he believed that his great mission in life was to defend his small country against Louis XIV and the French. After several humiliating defeats in the summer of 1676, he was desperate for British support, and so he made one of his periodic visits to London. Charles regarded the French as allies, not enemies, but he was well aware that this policy was unpopular with his subjects and he saw that it would do no harm for him to marry his niece Mary to a champion of Protestantism. To the surprise and chagrin of his British relatives, William insisted on seeing the Princess before he made a formal offer for her. He had already said frankly that he could not consider any wife who would make trouble at home, for he must not be distracted from his military endeavours. The worldly Charles may have rolled his eyes with exasperation, but he arranged an informal meeting for 23 October, and introduced the couple.

Mary was now a handsome young woman of fifteen, five feet eleven inches tall, with dark hair, brown eyes and a pretty, graceful manner. William decided at once to proceed. She was less impressed. Eleven years older than she was, the prospective bridegroom was an ugly little man, not quite five feet seven inches tall, with a large beaky nose, a pallid complexion and an asthmatic cough. Some accounts describe him as a hunchback. His manner was brusque to the point of rudeness. He and Mary were married in her apartments in St James's at nine o'clock at night on Sunday, 4 November, William's twenty-seventh birthday. The ceremony was a private one, because of the smallpox epidemic at Court, and Mary was in tears. Charles II, who had given her away, made a series of coarse jokes intended to encourage her, Catherine of Braganza, Mary of Modena and the Duchess of Buccleuch and Monmouth undressed her and put her to bed, and she was joined by her new husband. Closing the bedcurtains, the King cried jovially, 'Now nephew, to your work! Hey, St George for England!' and led the guests out of the room.[41]

The newly weds stayed in London long enough to attend Catherine of Braganza's birthday celebrations on 15 November, and then they left for the coast. Trying to console the weeping bride, Catherine remarked sympathetically that she remembered how she had felt when she had been forced to leave Portugal, but Mary was inconsolable. 'Madam, you came into England!' she exclaimed. 'I am going out of England.'[42] Delayed by contrary winds, she and William finally sailed from Margate on 28 November aboard separate ships. Landing at a little fishing village, they travelled to The Hague in a golden coach through cheering crowds, to take up residence in the Prince's palace, the Binnenhof. Mary's new life had begun.[43]

Contrary to all her expectations, she quickly fell in love with both her husband and his country. William might be unprepossessing in appearance but he had charismatic powers of leadership and Mary discovered that beneath his formal manner he was both warm-hearted and kind. She gladly fell into the role of providing him with relaxing companionship, plied him with diverting conversation and shared to the full his enthusiasm for interior decoration and the laying out of fine gardens. She was never happier than when she was sitting in her pale yellow and violet satin study in their country house at Honselaersdyck, planning further improvements for their residences. She assembled a remarkable collection of blue and white Dutch porcelain and sent for exotic plants from all over the world.[44] These occupations helped to ease her two sadnesses. The first was that she remained childless. Four months after her marriage her pregnancy had been announced, but a few weeks later she miscarried. There was another miscarriage not long after that, and then a series of phantom pregnancies.[45] Her second cause for unhappiness was that William was probably bisexual but had a mistress, Elizabeth Villiers, one of Mary's own ladies-in-waiting.

When James VII tried to convert Mary to Catholicism in 1687 by sending her various tracts and an exposition of why her own mother had converted, she was alarmed. She cared deeply about Protestantism and resisted his efforts. The birth of Prince James Francis Edward caused her even more upset. Until now she had been the heir apparent to the British throne but she had assumed that her husband would succeed her father. 'The love I have for the Prince [William] brings me to wish for him all that he deserves', she wrote in her journal, 'and although I regret having no more than three crowns to offer him, it's not my love that makes me blind: no, I can see his failings, but I say this because I also know his merits.'[46]

William was himself anxious to have the British throne, for then he would be in a much more powerful position to build his coalition against the French. As events unfolded, Mary waited with increasing anxiety. When she heard about the rumours of the warming pan conspiracy, she sent her sister a list of eighteen urgent questions about the circumstances of the baby's birth, but Anne's answers were inconclusive. Her husband, within sight of the throne now, was all kindness and sympathy towards her as he began to prepare an army to displace her father. William arrived safely at Torbay on 5 November 1687 and marched to London, where complicated discussions then took place as to whether he and Mary should rule jointly. Thomas, 1st Earl of Danby, thought that James's daughter should rule alone, and wrote to her offering to persuade parliament to make her the only monarch.

The thought that Mary might be expected to reign by herself as Queen had never crossed her mind until some months earlier, when Gilbert Burnet, the Scottish divine living in exile at The Hague, had drawn her attention to the fact that when James died she would succeed and William would be no more than her consort. She had been horrified and had told Burnet at once that she had not known 'that the laws of England were so contrary to the laws of God ... She did not think that the husband was ever to be obedient to the wife'.[47] Now she indignantly rejected Danby's suggestion and sent William a copy of his letter. He, of course, was equally annoyed. 'No man could think more of a woman than he did of the Princess,' he told his friends, 'but he was so made that he could not think of holding anything by apron strings.' He would only stay in Britain if he were king.[48] There were also counter-proposals that William should rule by himself but Gilbert Burnet was among those who objected strongly to that idea, and in the end William declared that he was prepared to accept joint sovereignty provided he and only he actually ruled the country.

Mary sailed from Holland and was welcomed by her husband and her sister Anne at Greenwich on 12 February 1689. She and William accepted the crown of England the following day and on 11 April the Scottish parliament followed the English example and decided that, since James had gone, William and Mary, King and Queen of England, France and Ireland, were now King and Queen of Scotland too.[49] The Scottish Claim of Right followed the general lines of the English Bill of Rights, listing all James's alleged misdeeds and laying down the principles for a constitutional monarchy. William and Mary were crowned together as joint monarchs on 11 April in Westminster Abbey, both swearing to rule according to the statutes agreed upon in parliament and the laws and customs of the land, and to uphold the Protestant religion. As Mary was a queen regnant, the sword of state was girded round her and she was presented with an orb, spurs and a Bible, just as her husband was.[50]

William disliked London, which had a bad effect on his asthma. He was intensely irritated by the manoeuvring of the British politicians, saw Scotland as no more than a tiresome distraction, and remained preoccupied with military matters on the Continent.[51] Determined to make their personal life as pleasant as she could, Mary encouraged him to create a luxurious new palace at Hampton Court with beautiful formal gardens, and she extended the gardens at Kensington Palace too, where they preferred to live. Daniel Marot, the famous designer whom she had employed in Holland, now decorated various rooms in England for the display of her oriental porcelain, Jean-Baptiste Monnoyer painted a glass for her at Kensington Palace with festoons of flowers[52] and she introduced the use of oriental textiles in furnishing.[53]

She would have been appalled had she realised that towards the end of 1689 her husband was actually speaking of going back to Holland for good, leaving her to rule Britain alone. His statesmen protested volubly, however, and he did not carry out this threat, although from that time onwards he spent increasing amounts of time abroad, first in Ireland where he defeated James VII at the Battle of the Boyne on 1 July 1690 and then with his armies campaigning in Flanders. While he was away, Mary was reluctantly in charge. At first, he had no confidence in her whatsoever, telling George, 1st Marquis of Halifax, that England must be ruled by a cabinet council and the Queen should not be allowed to meddle. However, she soon proved to be a real asset, a shrewd judge of character with an excellent grasp of the situation, and she was completely loyal to her husband. He had seriously underestimated her, and she was overjoyed when, on his return from Ireland, he told her that he was 'very much pleased' with her behaviour.[54]

Her role was very different from that of Mary, Queen of Scots or indeed any of the earlier Queens Regent, of course. Her husband was a constitutional monarch, she administered affairs with the advice of his cabinet, she knew exactly what he wanted and she could send for his opinion if she needed it. She never did accustom herself to William's absences, however, and she was worn down by the incessant quarrelling of Whigs and Tories. In 1694, when she was thirty-two, she wrote, 'I believe that I am becoming old and infirmities come with age, or with the chagrin or the inquietude which one has so regularly all the summer'.

On 21 December that same year, Mary contracted smallpox. William refused to move from her bedside and astonished even those who knew him well with his expressions of anxiety and despair. In the end, his weeping and fainting were too much, and Mary waved him away. She died an hour later, just before 1 a.m. on 28 February 1694, leaving him bereft.[55] He lived on for another eight years until in February 1702 he broke his collarbone in a riding accident, and died of pneumonia on 8 March. Undressing his body, his attendants found that this apparently most unsentimental of men was wearing on a black velvet ribbon round his neck a small gold ring that he had once given to his wife.[56]

Notes

1. Old Style. On the continent, the calendar was ten days ahead and so Mary's birth date in Modena was 5 October.
2. Cavelli, *Les Derniers Stuarts*, i, 11–12; documents, 2–15; Oman, *Mary of Modena*, 1–34.
3. *Stuart Papers*, ii, 397–8.
4. *Ibid.*, ii, 372.
5. Cavelli, *Les Derniers Stuarts*, i, 132–3.
6. Oman, *Mary of Modena*, 38.
7. *Ibid.*, 56.
8. *Stuart Papers*, ii, 370.
9. Sothern, *Mary of Modena*, 5.
10. Cavelli, *Les Derniers Stuarts*, i, 248–9; Oman, *Mary of Modena*, 61, 249 n.13.
11. Oman, *Mary of Modena*, 62.
12. Cavelli, *Les Derniers Stuarts*, i, 307; Oman, *Mary of Modena*, 63–5.
13. Trevor, *Shadow of a Crown*, 107–8.

14. Oman, *Mary of Modena*, 66–7.
15. Cavelli, *Les Derniers Stuarts*, i, 309; *Stuart Papers*, i, 370; *Augustis, ac praepotentibus heroibus, Jacobo & Mariae* (?Edinburgh 1680); W. Fraser, *The Elphinstone Family Book* (Edinburgh 1897), i, 235.
16. Alastair Cherry, *Princes, Poets and Patrons: The Stuarts and Scotland* (Edinburgh 1987), 97–107.
17. NAS, Hamilton Archives, C1/3050.
18. *The Miscellany of the Spalding Club*, iii (Aberdeen 1846), 222–3.
19. Cavelli, *Les Derniers Stuarts*, i, 352; NAS, GD 406 Hamilton Archives, C1/3050, draft letter of condolence from Anne, 3rd Duchess of Hamilton, to Mary of Modena.
20. *Stuart Papers*, i, 376; *Spalding Club Miscellany*, iii, 221–2, 224; NAS, GD 406 Hamilton Archives, C1/3055, draft letter of Anne, 3rd Duchess of Hamilton, to Mary of Modena, 26 December 1680.
21. *Stuart Papers*, i, 371–2.
22. Trevor, *Shadow of a Crown*, 130–3; Oman, *Mary of Modena*, 74–5.
23. *Ibid.*, 77, 256.
24. Cavelli, *Les Derniers Stuarts* ii, 1–19; *Stuart Papers*, i, 258–61; ii, 287; Oman, *Mary of Modena*, 82.
25. Cavelli, *Les Derniers Stuarts* ii, 42–62.
26. Van der Zee, *William and Mary*, 207–21.
27. Donaldson, *James V to James VII*, 379–84.
28. *Act of His Majesties Privy Council of Scotland for a solemn and publick thanksgiving throughout the Kingdom, upon Her Royal Majesties being with child* (Edinburgh 1688).
29. Cavelli, *Les Derniers Stuarts*, ii, 213–54; Oman, *Mary of Modena*, 106–111; Dewhurst, *Royal Confinements*, 21–6.
30. Oman, *Mary of Modena*, 106–8; Trevor, *Shadow of a Crown*, 195–8.
31. Cavelli, *Les Derniers Stuarts*, ii, 379–416.
32. *Ibid.*, ii, 416 ff.; Edward Corp, *James II and Toleration: The Years in Exile at Saint-Germain-en-Laye* (Royal Stuart Papers, 1997), 8; *L'Autre Exil: Les Jacobites en France au Début du XVIII Siècle*, ed. Edward Corp (Languedoc 1993), 21–107; Edward Corp, *The King over the Water* (Edinburgh 2001), 13–52.
33. *Stuart Papers*, i, 401.
34. *Ibid.*, 263–78, 323–59.
35. John Gibson, *Playing the Scottish Card: The Franco-Jacobite Invasion of 1708* (Edinburgh 1988), 19.
36. Sothern, *Mary of Modena*, 8–11.
37. *Stuart Papers*, i, 207–17; Susan Cole, *Princess over the Water: A Memoir of Louise Marie Stuart* (Royal Stuart Papers, 1981), 1–20.
38. William Ferguson, *Scotland: 1689 to the Present* (Edinburgh 1968), 55–6, 63–9; Bruce Lenman, *The Jacobite Cause* (Glasgow 1986), 41–2, 73–85.

39. Cavelli, i, *Les Derniers Stuarts*, Documents, 102–3.
40. Van der Zee, *William and Mary*, 33–117; Trevor, *Shadow of a Crown*, 34, 46, 60, 74–5.
41. Van der Zee, *William and Mary*, 117–124.
42. *Dr Edward Lake: Diary*, ed. G.P. Elliot (London 1846), 10.
43. Van der Zee, *William and Mary*, 125–34.
44. *Ibid.*, 127–34, 143–6; Trevor, *Shadow of a Crown*, 97–8; K.H.D. Haley, *The British and the Dutch: Political and Cultural Relations through the Ages* (London 1988), 199–200, 204–5; David Jacques and Arend van der Sast, *Gardens of William and Mary*, 40–1, 45–6, 139; Thornton, *Seventeenth-Century Interior Decoration*, 50, 78.
45. Van der Zee, *William and Mary*, 134–42, 175; *Royal Confinements*, 27–30.
46. Machtild, Comtesse de Bentinck, *Marie, Reine d'Angleterre, Lettres et Mémoires* (The Hague 1880), 62–3.
47. Burnet, *History*, iii, 131–9.
48. Marion Grew, *William Bentinck and William III* (London 1924), 150–2.
49. Donaldson, *Scottish Historical Documents*, 252–8.
50. Van der Zee, *William and Mary*, 273–8.
51. Ferguson, *Scotland: 1689 to the Present*, 6–7, 14.
52. Van der Sast, *Gardens of William and Mary*, 65–71; Thornton, *Seventeenth-Century Interior Decoration*, 74, 78, 80, 251–2.
53. Joanna Marschner, 'Mary II: Her Clothes and Textiles', in *Costume: The Journal of the Costume Society*, xxxiv (2000), 48–9.
54. Van der Zee, *William and Mary*, 295–321; Zook, 'History's Mary', 170–87.
55. Narcissus Luttrell, *A Brief Historical Relation of State Affairs, 1678–1714* (Oxford 1857), iii, 416–7; Burnet, *History*, iv, 277; van der Zee, *William and Mary*, 379–95.
56. Van der Zee, *William and Mary*, 476.

CHAPTER FOURTEEN

ANNE

With the death of William, his sister-in-law Anne became Queen in her own right. Born on 6 February 1665 at St James's Palace, London, she was called after her mother, Anne Hyde, and christened in a Church of England ceremony. Her godfather was Gilbert Sheldon, Archbishop of Canterbury, and her godmothers were her three-year-old sister, Mary, and Anne, the fourteen-year-old Duchess of Buccleuch. According to her maternal grandfather, Edward, 1st Earl of Clarendon, she was at nine months old 'the best natured and best humoured child in the world', but her temperament changed and from early childhood people commented that she was shy, unforthcoming and extremely stubborn.[1]

At first she lived with her sister Mary in the royal nurseries at Richmond, sharing the same Governess, Lady Frances Villiers, but she developed 'a defluxion of the eyes', and when she was only three it was decided that she should be sent to live with her grandmother, Henrietta Maria, in France, so that eminent Parisian doctors could treat her. In fact, she was to suffer from this eye trouble throughout her life but she stayed in Henrietta Maria's pious household at Colombe for the next two years, becoming fluent in French. Her grandmother, who had grown increasingly frail, died in August 1669. As Anne was still receiving treatment from the doctors, it was decided not to send her home, and instead she was transferred to the household of Henrietta's daughter Minette, now the wife of the unpleasant Duke of Orleans.[2]

Minette had two small daughters and Anne seems to have been happy in their nursery. Less than ten months later, however, Minette died suddenly of peritonitis, and this time Anne's father decided that she should be brought back to Britain.[3] She was six when her mother died, eight when her father married Mary of Modena and she and her sister went to live at St James's Palace.

Charles II seems to have taken a kindly interest in her and, impressed with her very pleasant speaking voice, he employed a well-known actress, Elizabeth Barry, to give her elocution lessons. Perhaps he hoped that she would lose some of her shyness if she were taught to speak in public, but she remained as self-conscious as ever.[4]

Mary of Modena was very fond of both girls, but Anne was unresponsive, and the principal influence on her life at that point was her religious tutor Henry Compton, Bishop of London. Surprisingly, in spite of her French years and her time in the household of her very devout Catholic stepmother, Anne remained as devoted to Protestantism as her sister Mary was. They were both confirmed in the Church of England, much against their father's will but on the King's insistence, in January 1676. The following year saw the marriage of Princess Mary to William of Orange, and Anne's subsequent visit to The Hague with her stepmother.[5]

Anne was, indeed, becoming unusually well travelled, for during her father's exile in Brussels she and her little half-sister, Isabella, were allowed to visit him there. It seems that her trip confirmed her increasingly strong prejudice against Roman Catholicism, for she wrote to her friend Frances Apsley, 'The more I hear of that religion, the more I dislike it'.[6] Anne and Isabella came back to Britain with their father and stepmother. Isabella then remained in London and it is usually said that Anne did so too. However, an interesting account for paintwork done in Holyroodhouse in 1679 refers to a room 'which is presently possessed by the Princess Lady Anne'. It may be that this redecoration was in contemplation of a visit from her, but it does sound rather as though she had gone north at some point that year.[7]

Almost as soon as she came back from Brussels the King raised the question of Anne's marriage. One possible candidate was George, son of Sophia, the Electress of Hanover. Sophia was the first cousin of Charles II and James. Her mother, Elizabeth of Bohemia, had been Charles I's sister. Dynastically this would be an appropriate marriage, but Charles II was ultimately unwilling to make definite arrangements for Anne until the question of the succession to the British throne had been finally settled. Moreover, Sophia herself was not enthusiastic about her son marrying the daughter of Anne Hyde, a mere commoner. George did visit London in December

1680, as part of his Grand Tour, and according to some accounts fifteen-year-old Anne was very taken with him, but no formal proposal was made and in 1682 he married his German cousin, Sophia-Dorothea of Celle.[8]

When James was sent to Scotland for a second time, he again hoped to take his daughters with him, but the King remained adamant that they must stay in London. He relented only after the death of little Isabella, finally agreeing that Anne might join her father and stepmother. She sailed north on 13 July 1681 and, for the next ten months, lived in her stepmother's household, joining in the card-playing, balls and private theatricals and accompanying Mary of Modena when she went riding. She celebrated her seventeenth birthday at Holyroodhouse, but she was not happy. She was home-sick for her friends in London and uncomfortable with her father's Catholicism. She also observed at first hand the troubled religious situation in Scotland. Committed Presbyterians opposed the King's ecclesiastical policies and objected to the existence of bishops in the Scottish Church,[9] and Anne feared that the unrest might one day threaten the stability of the Church of England.

Her stay in Scotland ended in May 1682 when the family went south again. A portrait painted at about this time by Willem Wissing shows her with a willowy, elegant figure, thick dark curls, dark eyes and full lips. Like her sister she was almost six feet tall. Apart from her regrettably surly manner, she was an attractive young woman. Early the following year, serious negotiations for her marriage were set in hand. Louis XIV had been encouraging Charles II to make an alliance with Denmark against the Dutch. Charles therefore decided that it would be useful for Anne to marry Prince George, the younger brother of King Christian V of Denmark. Her father was enthusiastic, for he disliked his son-in-law William of Orange and was happy to support any plan designed to reduce his influence in Britain. Discussions went ahead rapidly. James promised a dowry of £40,000 sterling and an additional £5,000 a year while the Danes provided a suitable jointure. The marriage was announced during the first week of May 1683 and James was highly gratified when he heard that William of Orange was aghast. As far as William was concerned, a Protestant prince from an enemy country would now be a permanent feature of Charles II's Court, for it had been agreed that the young couple must settle in Britain instead of going to Denmark.[10] After all, Anne was next in the succession after her sister Mary.

Anne had never met George of Denmark, of course, but he arrived in London on 19 July 1683 and they were introduced. We have no record of her reaction to him, but his portraits show that the Prince was tall, fair-haired and rather handsome, with heavy, aquiline features. He and his brother Christian V had acquitted themselves bravely at the battle of Landskrone in 1677, fighting against the Swedes, and he was a devout Lutheran. He and Anne were married by Bishop Compton at ten o'clock in the evening on St Anne's Day, 28 July 1683, at a private ceremony in the Chapel Royal of St James's Palace. Instead of the traditional lavish banquet afterwards, the bride and groom sat down to supper with Anne's immediate relatives, Charles II and Catherine of Braganza, her father and her stepmother. Prince George's wedding gift to his wife was a diamond-studded gold box containing a pearl necklace worth £6000 and several other pieces of jewellery set with diamonds.[11]

Charles II was famously to remark of Anne's bridegroom, 'I have tried him drunk and I have tried him sober and there is nothing in him', but George was amiable and obliging and for Anne he made the perfect husband.[12] He never contradicted her, he allowed her to tell him what to do, put up with her tiresomely intense friendship with Sarah Jennings, Duchess of Marlborough, and gave her unwavering emotional support. She was to need it. For the next seventeen years Anne was almost constantly pregnant. Her first child was born on 12 May 1684, nine months and two weeks after her wedding. The baby, a daughter, was stillborn. A few weeks later, Anne and her husband went with James and Mary of Modena to Tunbridge Wells, where she and her stepmother both took the waters, and by December Anne was pregnant again. This time, she gave birth to a living daughter on 2 June 1685 and named her Mary, for her sister, who was one of the godmothers. On 12 May 1686 she had a healthy, premature daughter, Anne Sophia, but her domestic happiness was brutally shattered in the early weeks of 1687. On 21 January she suffered a miscarriage and at the end of the month her husband and the two children fell ill with smallpox. Anne, who had survived the disease ten years earlier, nursed them all devotedly and George recovered, but Anne Sophia died on 2 February and on 8 February little Mary died too. They were buried together in the vault of Mary, Queen of Scots in Westminster Abbey.

Within a matter of weeks Anne was pregnant again. On 22 October 1687 she had a stillborn son who was two months premature and had been dead in her womb for a month. The following April she had another miscarriage and so it was all the harder for her when her stepmother gave birth to James Francis Edward less than two months later. Finally, on 24 July 1689, Anne herself had a living son. By then William and Mary were on the British throne, both were present at Hampton Court for the birth, and Anne named her boy after the King, who created him Duke of Gloucester. The baby suffered serious convulsions when he was only six weeks old, possibly as the result of an acute ear infection, and although he proved to be lively and intelligent and bore a strong resemblance to his father, he did not speak until he was three and could not walk without support until he was five. He also suffered from frequent bouts of fever and had some degree of hydrocephalus, fluid on the brain, probably as a result of his early convulsions. At five years old he was only three feet four inches tall with a very long head and wore a hat large enough for a man. His mother loved him tenderly and both William and Mary were very fond of him.

On 14 October 1690, when he was fifteen months old, Anne had her next child, a seven-month daughter Mary, who lived for two hours only. After a longer interval than usual, she had another son, George, on 17 April 1692, but he died an hour after his christening. He was followed by a stillborn daughter on 23 March 1693 and then a stillborn son on 21 January 1694. Not surprisingly, Anne was deeply depressed after that pregnancy, worrying not only about the health of her one surviving child but fearing that, if anything happened to him, William and Mary might adopt James Francis Edward as their heir. The resulting stress caused her to have a phantom pregnancy in the spring of 1695, and then she had a stillborn daughter in February 1696.

She must have conceived again at once, for that same September she gave birth to a stillborn son in the sixth month of pregnancy. Six months after that, in March 1697, there was another miscarriage, and yet another in December 1697. This time she had been carrying twins, but it was too early to identify their sex. On 15 September 1698 she gave birth to a premature, dead son and on 24 January 1700 she had a six-month boy who had already been dead in the womb for a month. Six weeks after that William, Duke of Gloucester, her only surviving child, died of scarlet fever.[13] In the past seventeen years, Anne had endured seventeen pregnancies, and all the babies now lay buried in the vault in Westminster Abbey. Why were so many of her children dead or stillborn? Various medical theories have been advanced over the years. Rhesus incompatibility and diabetes are possibilities, but it seems that the most likely cause was intra-uterine growth retardation, where the placenta is faulty and the baby does not grow properly. This is often the result of high blood pressure, from which Anne may well have been suffering. Both her father and Charles II died of strokes.[14] Whatever the reason, Anne suffered personal tragedy on an almost unimaginable scale, and apart from the psychological effects, her physical health was ruined by her constant pregnancies.

She and Mary both seem to have inherited their mother's tendency to obesity. Even when she was not pregnant Anne was seriously overweight and she began to suffer from arthritis. By the time she was twenty-seven, she was said to be enduring great pain from 'the gout'. Around the time of her thirtieth birthday she was noticeably lame and could not climb stairs. At thirty-five, she was an invalid, unable to walk more than a few steps without assistance. Her arms were affected too, and she still had trouble with her eyes. It would have been understandable if she had decided to live a retired life, but she had an obstinate determination that she would not be overlooked in the British succession, for she felt that she had a duty to protect the position of the Church of England. Somehow, sustained by her loving husband and her strong religious faith, she surmounted all her physical difficulties to play a prominent part in public life.[15]

She had been only twenty-two when William of Orange arrived at Torbay, and she had unhesitatingly sent him a message of welcome, slipping away from London in disguise to prevent her father from placing her under some form of restraint. When James escaped to France, she and her ladies celebrated William's accession by dressing in orange, his colour.[16] He rewarded her with magnificent apartments at Whitehall and made Prince George Duke of Cumberland, but unfortunately Anne and William disliked each other cordially and when the initial excitement of the Revolution died away, she bickered constantly with the King and her sister. Anne's great friend Sarah Jennings noted how different she and Mary were in temperament. 'Queen Mary grew weary of anybody who would not talk a great deal,' Sarah commented, while Anne 'was so silent that she rarely spoke more than was necessary to answer a question'.

Few people knew Anne better than Sarah did. They had been friends from early childhood and for much of their lives unconfident Anne was emotionally dependent on lively, assertive Sarah. 'Mrs Freeman' and 'Mrs Morley' corresponded constantly, sending each other little notes several times a day. Under other circumstances, Sarah would have found their friendship both tedious and stifling as she sent endless reassurances and tried to bolster Anne's faltering self-esteem, but she was ambitious for both her husband and herself. She deliberately encouraged Anne's feelings that William was treating Prince George in a humiliating fashion, Anne complained to the Queen, Mary sprang to William's defence and soon the sisters were not on speaking terms.[17] Eventually, Sarah was replaced by her own cousin, Abigail Hill, in Anne's favour.[18]

The day after Mary died, Anne wrote a letter of condolence to William, and had a tearful meeting with him. After that, they tried to keep up an appearance of friendship. After all, she was his heir. The King was genuinely upset when the little Duke of Gloucester died in 1700, and of course the child's death caused problems for the future. In order to secure the Protestant succession now that Anne's sole surviving child had gone, the English parliament in June 1701 passed an Act of Settlement, declaring that when she died she would be succeeded by Charles II's cousin, the Protestant Sophia of Hanover. Three months after that, James himself died in France. Anne's defection had caused him great pain, but Mary of Modena wrote her stepdaughter a kind letter telling her that James had asked her to let Anne know that he had forgiven her for everything that had happened, and sent her his last blessing. The following March William of Orange died and Anne was Queen at last.[19]

She was crowned in Westminster Abbey on 23 April 1702, the

anniversary of her father's coronation, wearing a cloth-of-gold robe glistening with jewels. The text she chose for the sermon was 'Kings shall be thy nursing Fathers and Queens thy nursing Mothers'. It was a conventional enough image of monarchy, but in view of her own tragic experiences of motherhood it had a poignant resonance.[20] The words from Isaiah were also an accurate reflection of her own view of her role. Because of the Revolution settlement Anne was, of course, a constitutional monarch. There was no question of her ruling without parliament, as her father had chosen to do. The years since the Revolution of 1688 had seen the growth of the party political system, and Anne saw it as her duty to hold the balance between Whigs and Tories. She had no desire to be embroiled in their power struggles and she would have liked to rule through an equal number from both parties. National unity was her aim, and for similar reasons she wanted to see a parliamentary union between England and Scotland.

In his last speech to the English parliament, William of Orange had recommended union with Scotland, and Anne repeated these sentiments in her first speech at Westminster. A situation in which two countries shared the same monarch but had competing foreign and economic policies seemed no longer tenable, especially now that hostilities with France had been renewed with Britain's entry into the War of the Spanish Succession. There was strong resistance from both Scotland and England, however, to the notion of Union. The Scots were angry that William of Orange had ignored Scottish interests. He had aroused considerable popular resentment with the Massacre of Glencoe, when the Macdonald chief was killed with his clansmen after failing to take the oath of allegiance in time, and he had antagonised the Scots still further when he had blocked the Darien Scheme, by means of which they had hoped to set up a lucrative trading colony. For their part, the English were unsympathetic to Scottish commercial interests until the Scots exerted pressure by raising the question of the succession.

After the English Act of Settlement there had been fears that the Scots would nominate James Francis Edward as Anne's heir. Now the Scots in 1703 passed an Act anent Peace and War asserting that after Anne's death they had the right to pursue an independent foreign policy. There was immediate alarm in the south. The implication was that they would choose James Francis Edward to succeed instead of Sophia of Hanover, and the Queen was greatly distressed. On the advice of her English ministers she vetoed the bill, but the Scots revived it in 1704 and this time, afraid that they might withdraw their forces from the war, Anne gave it the royal assent. Four days later, Marlborough won his great victory at Blenheim and the danger from France receded. The English parliament then passed the 1705 Alien Act 'for the effectual securing the kingdom of England from the apparent dangers that may arise from several acts lately passed by the parliament of Scotland'. Until the Scots settled the crown on Sophia of Hanover, no Scot would be able to inherit property in England or its dominions or enjoy any of the benefits of English subjects. The act also authorised the Queen to appoint commissioners to treat for union.

Following some judicious bribery, the Scots agreed that Anne should appoint their commissioners too and, this done, the English parliament repealed the Alien Act on 27 November 1705. The commissioners for union met from 16 April until 22 July 1706, when the Articles of Union were signed. After heated debates in the Scottish parliament, the Articles were ratified by statute, and following their adoption by the English parliament, Anne gave her assent to the Treaty of Union on 6 March 1707. She had pressed hard for it, and without her determination the negotiations might well have foundered. 'I desire and expect from all my subjects of both nations,' she said, 'that from henceforth they act with all possible respect and kindness to one another, that so it may appear to all the world they have hearts disposed to become one people. That will be a great pleasure to me.' She and Prince George attended a thanksgiving service in St Paul's Cathedral on 1 May 1707.[21]

Queen Anne lived for another seven years after the Union of the Parliaments. She had been completely inexperienced when she came to the throne, and she had blushed constantly as she made her first speech to parliament, but under the guidance of her friend, Sidney, Lord Godolphin, she had learned how to govern and she worked diligently, presiding over cabinet meetings at least once a week, dealing with foreign emissaries, sounding out individual politicians and reading vast piles of documents. Her poor health, however, and her natural shyness, which she never entirely conquered, meant that she was unable to take part in the social side of Court life and she became increasingly isolated. When Sir John Clerk of Penicuik had an audience in 1706 as one of the Scottish commissioners for the union of the parliaments, he found her suffering from gout but pleased, he thought, to see anyone, 'for no Court attenders come near her. All the incense and adoration offered at Courts were to her ministers . . . her palace at Kensington where she commonly resided was a perfect solitude'.[22]

Her beloved husband died on 28 October 1708 and her health deteriorated still further. By 1710, she was relying on wheelchairs and sedan chairs to move her from one room to the next but she stoically carried on. Marlborough's triumphant series of victories over the French added lustre to her reign and the War of the Spanish Succession ended in 1713 with the Treaty of Utrecht. As one of the terms, Louis XIV officially recognised her as Queen of Great Britain, although there remained the danger that he might support James Francis Edward for his own purposes. Sophia of Hanover was repeatedly asking permission for her son to come and live in Britain, but Anne refused.[23]

Sophia died in the summer of 1714 at the age of eighty-four while walking in her palace gardens at Herrenhausen in Hanover. A few weeks later, Anne suffered a stroke and died on 1 August. She was forty-nine. 'I believe sleep was never more welcome to a weary traveller than death was to her', John Arbuthnot, her Scottish doctor, told his friend Jonathan Swift.[24] The last Stewart monarch was gone, and Sophia's son George, Elector of Hanover, was proclaimed King of Great Britain. On 24 August 1714, while he was making preparations to travel to London, Queen Anne was buried in Westminster Abbey beside her husband and all their children.

Notes

1. Gregg, *Queen Anne*, 4–5; *Calendar of the Clarendon State Papers*, ed. F.J. Routledge, v (Oxford 1970), 511.
2. Gregg, *Queen Anne*, 7–9.
3. Plowden, *Henrietta Maria*, 258.

4. Burnet, *History*, v, 2.
5. Strickland, *Queens of England*, vi, 69.
6. Benjamin Bathurst, *Letters of Two Queens* (London 1924), 108–9.
7. NAS, E28/328/15/2. account by John Alexander, paid on 24 December 1679. I am grateful to Dr A.L. Murray for this reference.
8. Gregg, *Queen Anne*, 23–4; Green, *Queen Anne*, 31–2; Ragnhild Hatton, *George I, Elector and King* (London 1978), 39–40.
9. Trevor, *Shadow of a Crown*, 125–30.
10. Gregg, *Queen Anne*, 32–3.
11. Edgar Sheppard, *St James's Palace* (London 1894), ii, 67; *HMC Laing* (London 1914), i, 434.
12. Burnet, *History*, iii, 49.
13. Dewhurst, *Royal Confinements*, 30–45, 47, 95, 189–91.
14. Gregg, *Queen Anne*, 36–8, 46–8, 51–7, 72–3, 80, 90, 99, 100–1, 107–8, 116, 120; Dewhurst, *Royal Confinements*, 31–47.
15. Gregg, *Queen Anne*, 106.
16. Strickland, *Queens of England*, vii, 179; Gregg, *Queen Anne*, 59–68; Van der Zee, *Revolution in the Family*, 219–20.
17. David Green, *Sarah, Duchess of Marlborough* (London 1967); A. L. Rowse, *The Early Churchills* (London 1958), 162–3, 178, 185–91, 213–5, 221–2, 225–6, 229–35, 238–40, 251–2, 254–5, 257, 282–3, 298–323; Gregg, *Queen Anne*, 84–97.
18. *Ibid.*, 112–3.
19. Van der Zee, *William and Mary*, 391–475; Gregg, *Queen Anne*, 102–105, 114–122; Green, *Queen Anne*, 87.
20. John Sharp, *A Sermon Preach'd at the Coronation of Queen Anne* (London 1706); Green, *Queen Anne*, 96.
21. Dickinson and Donaldson, *Source Book*, iii, 469–80; Donaldson, *Scottish Historical Documents*, 265–8; *The Treaty of Union of Scotland and England*, 1707, ed. G.S. Pryde (Edinburgh 1950), 8–34; *Oxford Companion*, 604–8; Gregg, *Queen Anne*, 131, 184–7, 194, 202, 239; Green, *Queen Anne*, 163; G.M. Trevelyan, *Ramillies and the Union with Scotland* (London 1965 edn), 241, 243, 288–9; Lynch, *New History*, 310–12.
22. *Memoirs of the Life of Sir John Clerk of Penicuk 1676–1755*, ed. J.M. Gray (Scottish History Society 1892), 232.
23. Gregg, *Queen Anne*, 383–6.
24. H.L. Snyder, 'The Last Days of Queen Anne: The Account of Sir John Evelyn Examined', in *Huntingdon Library Quarterly* xxxiv (1971), 261–76; *Swift Correspondence: The Correspondence of Jonathan Swift*, ed. Harold Williams (Oxford 1963), ii, 121; *Funeral Effigies*, 121, plate xiii.

CONCLUSION

Scotland's thirty-one queens led dramatic, often dangerous lives. In character they were all very different and their degree of influence varied, but their experiences were wide-ranging and for every one of them marriage was the defining moment. This was true even for the Maid of Norway, who died so prematurely, for her brief life was dominated by the prospect of her marriage to Prince Edward of England. Ten of the twenty-seven queens consort were the daughters of kings and at least eight of the others were related to royalty. The rest were from aristocratic families. Nine were English and six were French. Indeed, from the death of English Sybilla in 1122 until the accession of the Maid of Norway in 1286, and again in the sixteenth century, French and English brides alternated. One of the other brides was Anglo-Irish, three were Danish, and another three were from places as far away as the Netherlands, Portugal and Italy. Scotland was a small country on the edge of the known world, but her monarchs were obviously important enough to secure prestigious foreign brides.

Only four of the queens consort were Scottish. David II's passion for Margaret Logie and her influence over him accounted for both her marriage and that of her niece, Annabella Drummond, while Gruoch and Euphemia Ross married before their husbands came to the throne. It is interesting to reflect that, in spite of the Reformation, not one of the twenty-seven female consorts died a Protestant for, as we have seen, the only Protestant chosen, Anne of Denmark, converted from Lutheranism to Catholicism during her time in Scotland.

If the marriage of a king was important, even more significant was that of a queen regnant, for her husband would legally be the dominant partner in their relationship. Ideally, a queen would hope to marry another monarch whose power and status would enhance her own. Had she lived, the Maid of Norway would have become the wife of Edward I of England's heir, and Mary, Queen of Scots, of course, was the bride of France's Dauphin. Not every royal heiress could expect to make such an important match, however, for kings and their eldest sons were, by their very nature, in short supply. Like many royal and aristocratic widows, Mary, Queen of Scots had to settle for men of considerably lower status when she re-married. Mary II accepted a Dutch prince, while Anne's husband was the King of Denmark's brother.

Bearing in mind that we have very incomplete information about the early consorts, the average age of the brides was fifteen and a half. Of course, the fact that some of the women were widows raises the average age, but only one, David II's four-year-old Joan, was less than ten, which rather challenges our assumptions about the prevalence of child marriages in the Middle Ages and beyond. However, it is interesting to note that in a detailed study of the marriages of Englishwomen from three prominent aristocratic families between 1150 and 1500, forty-nine of the eighty-seven brides were fifteen or older.[1] The apprehensions of girls sent suddenly to live in a foreign country with a man they had never met must have been intensified when they were a good deal younger than their bridegrooms. Marie de Coucy was twenty-one years younger than Alexander II, Mary of Modena was twenty-five years younger than James VII, and Yolande was twenty-six years younger than Alexander III. Even James IV, who had never been married before, was sixteen years older than Margaret Tudor. In all these unions the older husband seems to have regarded his bride with indulgent kindness and the marriages were a success.

If she came from a continental country, a consort had not only to learn a new language but, like Henrietta Maria and Catherine of Braganza, she frequently had to swallow insults about her outlandish hairstyle and quaint foreign clothes. On a more serious note, should she be the daughter or sister of a king, she was expected to smooth over his relationship with her husband, and if mutual suspicion deteriorated into open warfare, then the situation of, for example, Margaret Tudor or Mary II was unenviable. The wife's loyalties were now with her husband, but that did not mean that she was without feelings for her own family. When, in the post-Reformation period, the consort was of a different religion from that of the country in general, then the difficulties were compounded.

The degree to which a consort could participate in public business depended very much on the extent to which she was trusted by her husband. It is difficult to assess the power placed in the hands of the early wives in particular, and we can really only guess at the influence exerted by, say, Ermengarde or Marie de Coucy. When consorts were active in public affairs, and even when they were not, courtiers were quick to accuse them of meddling in matters that did not concern them. A queen had very privileged access to the king, and all too often the nobles were jealous and would try to stir up trouble between the royal couple. A similar situation could be seen when the consort was a man. His contemporaries were immediately suspicious of Darnley, simply because he was the Queen's husband and could conceivably be influencing her against them.

Encouraging marital discord was easily done, for arranged marriages inevitably brought together some partners who were intrinsically incompatible. Indeed, it is surprising that so many royal marriages were reasonably harmonious, but then of course it was virtually impossible for a queen to leave a marriage, as Mary, Queen of Scots discovered when her relationship with Darnley foundered. Discontented royal wives certainly could not initiate an annulment or divorce, and the best they could do was to live in a different residence from the king, as Margaret of Denmark, Anne of Denmark and Catherine of Braganza all preferred to do. Of course, they could achieve this only with their husband's permission.

One of the most obvious sources of unhappiness was that women in arranged marriages were expected to tolerate their partners' mistresses, and there is evidence that both Mary of Guise and Mary of Modena resented their husbands' extra-marital affairs. A queen might be expected to console herself with her wealth and status, but a so-called life of privilege was no defence against emotional pain, and Catherine of Braganza very publicly suffered the torments of unrequited love. Catherine's situation was made worse by the fact that she was childless, even though Charles II openly refused to put her away because of that. In various countries wives were briskly repudiated when they failed to have sons. Some kings, of course, took the precaution of marrying widows who had already demonstrated their abilities in that direction. Gruoch, Ingebjorg, Matilda, Margaret Logie and Mary of Guise had all given birth to at least one boy by their first husbands, although in the event only Ingebjorg and Matilda managed to provide surviving male heirs for their royal partners and David II divorced Margaret Logie. He had already parted from his first wife because of her childlessness, and the earlier Joan and Alexander may have separated because she had no children.

Poor Queen Anne was tragically unusual in losing all her seventeen children, but many of the other eighteen queens who did have families also suffered miscarriages, stillbirths and babies dead in early childhood. St Margaret and Joan Beaufort were particularly successful in achieving at least eight children each, Henrietta Maria had nine in spite of her small stature, and although Mary, Queen of Scots had only one surviving child, he was to inherit the crowns of both Scotland and England. Unusually, none of the queens is known to have died in childbirth, although Ingebjorg may have done so.

At least fourteen of the thirty-one queens predeceased their husbands, and at least thirteen outlived them. Apart from sorrow and shock at the often premature and violent death of a partner, royal consorts also experienced a different sort of loss when their husbands died. Their source of power and protection had been removed at a stroke, they were instantly perceived as being vulnerable and they had to look for support either to their own families, who were usually far away, or to unreliable nobles, who were willing to side with them out of self-interest. Only two, however, Yolande and Catherine of Braganza, retired to their native land.

Some countries forbade their royal widows to marry again. In seventh-century Spain, for example, the dead king's wife had been forced to enter a nunnery when he died.[2] There was no such prohibition in Scotland, but only five of the thirteen widowed queens did decide to remarry and all five went on to have at least one more child. Marie de Coucy and Yolande de Dreux found husbands in their own countries, while Mary, Queen of Scots, Joan Beaufort and Margaret Tudor preferred Scottish noblemen and in consequence found themselves accused of promiscuity and embroiled in endless complications.

Until she married again, a queen mother could expect to have official custody of her children. That did not necessarily mean that she going to rule as regent, although in France, legal writers had explicitly stated that a queen's right to be regent derived from widows' feudal rights to act as guardians of their children and their fiefs.[3] Very often a council of nobles took on the responsibility of government, with or without the queen as a figurehead, and sometimes against her wishes. Mary of Guise was determined to be regent for her daughter when James V died in 1542, but as she was out of action at the time, having recently given birth, she lost the opportunity and had to struggle for years before she achieved her ambition.

Women ruling as regents were not uncommon in Western Europe, but they were more often acting for an absent male relative rather than ruling for their own child. As early as 1338, Joan of Burgundy had been chosen by Philip VI to look after his kingdom while he was engaged in warfare[4] and there were even more examples in the sixteenth century. Catherine of Aragon ruled England for Henry VIII when he was in France and Louise of Savoy (not herself a queen) governed France for her son Francis I when he was on his military campaigns. Mary II, taking charge in Britain while William of Orange pursued his continental wars, is a late example. In each of these instances, it was recognised that the king on his return would punish anyone who dared to challenge his regent's authority, and that was so even when Francis I was captured and held prisoner by the Emperor.[5] The French knew that, sooner or later, he would be back.

Of course, this is not to say that queens regent in those circumstances led trouble-free lives. Charles V's aunt, Margaret of Austria, his sister, Mary of Hungary, and his illegitimate daughter, Margaret of Parma, successively ruled the Netherlands for him, but they were often forced to carry out highly unpopular policies with which they did not necessarily agree.[6] They nevertheless had the comfort of knowing that there was a powerful authority ready to back them up, whereas widowed consorts were much more seriously isolated. Indeed, the very monarchs to whom Margaret Tudor and Mary of Guise looked for support were regarded as enemies by most of their subjects. Moreover, even a queen regnant was not always taken seriously by her male fellow monarchs. When Mary

I of England sent a herald to declare war on Henry II in 1557, he burst out laughing and exclaimed merrily, 'What a state I am in when a woman challenges me to war!'⁷

Few women rulers were able to combine the desired masculine qualities of ruthless leadership with the expected feminine attributes of virtue and charity, although while Mary of Guise presented herself as 'mother of the commonwealth', her enemies accused her of having the heart of a man of war. Queens regnant were in a uniquely difficult position. It is impossible to speculate as to how the Maid of Norway might have fared, but had Francis II lived, it is probable that Mary, Queen of Scots would have accepted a secondary role, acting as if she were merely a consort to the French king, bearing his children and providing a charming adornment to his Court.

As it was, his death exposed her to the reality of being a monarch with theoretically unlimited personal powers. Too young and attractive to project a maternal image, she was unable to assume a convincing masculinity. Elizabeth I might gain the approbation of her subjects when she spoke of having the heart of a man in the body of a weak and feeble woman, but Mary's wish to take to the fields like a soldier seemed merely to emphasise her femininity. In the end, power was wrested from her by her rebellious nobles and she was deposed at the age of twenty-four as she lay recovering from her serious miscarriage.

The powers of Mary II and Anne were limited by the Revolution Settlement. Apart from that, Mary II sheltered in the shadow of a strong husband, choosing to act as a submissive wife although she was a joint monarch with a better claim to the throne than William of Orange. Her sister Anne poignantly portrayed herself as her country's 'nursing mother' and was unexpectedly successful, in part because of her own persistence, in part because of the skill of her ministers and the success of the continental warfare waged in her name.

We should not be surprised to find that queens were usually motivated by a determination to support their husbands or lovers and protect their children. Like it or not, and whether we blame female hormones or sexual stereotyping, women have always had different priorities from men and most have put personal relationships before the pursuit of power. Perhaps the last word on the subject of queenship should be left to that perceptive Scottish visitor to the Court of Queen Anne, Sir John Clerk, for his observations neatly encapsulate both the valiant struggle of women called upon to rule and the enduring attitude of the men they tried to govern.

When Sir John was shown into the Queen's presence with the Duke of Queensberry in the summer of 1706, he viewed her with dismay. 'Her face, which was red and spotted, was rendered something frightful by her negligent dress, and the foot affected [by the gout] was tied up with a poultice and some nasty bandages', he noted. 'I was much affected by this sight', he went on, 'and the more when she had occasion to mention her people of Scotland, which she did frequently to the Duke. What are you, poor, mean-like mortal, thought I, who talks in the style of a sovereign? Nature seems to be inverted when a poor infirm woman becomes one of the rulers of the world.'[8]

Notes

1. John Carmi Parsons, 'Mothers, Daughters, Marriage, Power: Some Plantagenet Evidence 1150–1500', in *Medieval Queenship*, 66.
2. Roger Collins, 'Queens-Dowager and Queens-Regent in Tenth-century Léon and Navarre', in *Medieval Queenship*, 84.
3. John Carmi Parsons, 'Family, Sex and Power: the Rhythms of Medieval Queenship', in *Medieval Queenship*, 8–9.
4. André Poulet, 'Capetian Women and the Regency', in *Medieval Queenship*, 112.
5. Bertière, *Reines de France*, 191–6.
6. Guida M. Jackson, *Women who Ruled* (Santa Barbara, California 1990), 109–10; Georges-Henri Dumont, *Marguerite de Parma* (Brussels 1999); Joycelyne G. Russell, *Peacemaking in the Renaissance* (London 1986), 87–8, 105–11, 119–20
7. Jasper Ridley, *The Life and Times of Mary Tudor* (London 1973), 70.
8. *Memoirs of the Life of Sir John Clerk of Penicuik 1676-1755*, ed. J.M. Gray (Scottish History Society 1892), 62–3.

ABBREVIATIONS

APS The Acts of the Parliaments of Scotland, ed. T. Thomson and C. Innes (Edinburgh 1814–75)

CDS Calendar of Documents relating to Scotland, ed. J. Bain (Edinburgh 1881–8)

CSP Foreign, Elizabeth Calendar of State Papers, Foreign Series Edward, Mary and Elizabeth, ed. Joseph Stevenson *et al* (London 1861–1950)

CSP Scot Calendar of the State Papers relating to Scotland and Mary Queen of Scots 1547–1603, ed. J. Bain *et al* (Edinburgh 1898–1969)

CSPD Calendar of State Papers Domestic, ed. R. Lemon *et al* (London 1856–70)

CSP Spanish Calendar of State Papers, Spanish, ed. R. Tyler *et al* (London 1862–1954)

CSP Venetian Calendar of State Papers, Venice, ed. Rawdon Brown (London 1864–98)

ER Rotuli Scaccarii Regum Scotorum: the Exchequer Rolls of Scotland, ed. J. Stuart *et al* (Edinburgh 1878–1908)

L and P Henry VIII Letters and Papers Foreign and Domestic, Henry VIII, ed. J. Gairdner *et al* (London 1862–1932)

HMC Historical Manuscripts Commission

NLS National Library of Scotland

NAS National Archives of Scotland

RMS Registrum Magni Sigilii Regum Scotorum, ed. J.M. Thomson *et al* (Edinburgh 1882–1914)

RPC The Register of the Privy Council of Scotland, ed. J. Hill Burton *et al* (Edinburgh 1877–)

SHR Scottish Historical Review

SP The Scots Peerage, ed. J. Balfour Paul (Edinburgh 1904–14)

BIBLIOGRAPHY

Other significant sources, mentioned only once, are to be found in the chapter endnotes.

Accounts of the Lord High Treasurer of Scotland, ed. Thomas Dickson and J. Balfour Paul (Edinburgh 1877–1916)

Baillon, Charles, Comte de, *Lettres de Henriette-Marie, Reine d'Angleterre* (Paris 1877)

Balcarres Papers see *Foreign Correspondence with Marie de Lorraine* . . .

Balfour, *Historical Works* see *The Historical Works of Sir James Balfour*

Bapst, Edmond, *Les Mariages de Jacques V* (Paris 1889)

Barrow, G.W.S., 'A Kingdom in Crisis: Scotland and the Maid of Norway', *SHR*, lxxiv, no 2 (1990), 120–141

Barrow, G.W.S., *Robert Bruce and the Community of the Realm of Scotland* (London 1965)

Bertière, Simone, *Les Reines de France au temps des Valois* (Paris 1994)

Birch, Thomas, *The Court and Times of Charles I* (London 1848)

Boardman, Stephen, *The Early Stewart Kings: Robert II and Robert III (1371–1406)* (East Linton 1996)

Bentley Cranch, Dana and Marshall, Rosalind K., 'Iconography and Literature in the Service of Diplomacy: The Franco Scottish Alliance, James V and Scotland's Two French Queens, Madeleine of France and Mary of Guise', in *Stewart Style 1513–1542: Essays on the Court of James V*, ed. Janet Hadley Williams (East Linton 1996)

Bone, Quentin, *Henrietta Maria, Queen of Cavaliers* (London 1973)

Bouyer, Christian, *Dictionnaire des Reines de France* (Paris 1992)

Buchanan, Patricia Hill, *Margaret Tudor, Queen of Scots* (Edinburgh 1985)

Burnet, Gilbert, *A History of His Own Time* (Oxford 1883 edn)

Cameron, Jamie, *James V* (East Linton 1998)

Campbell, Marion, *Alexander III, King of Scots* (Colonsay 1999)

Carlton, Charles, *Charles I, the Personal Monarch* (London 1983)

Cavelli, Marquise Campana de, *Les Derniers Stuarts à St Germain* (Paris 1871)

Chronicon de Lanercost (Maitland Club 1839)

Chronique de Mathieu d'Escouchy, ed. G. du Fresne de Beaucourt (Paris 1863)

Cosandey, Fanny, *La reine de France: Symbole et pouvoir* (Paris 2000)

Coste, Hilarion de, *Les Eloges et les Vies des Reynes* (Paris 1647)

Crawford, Barbara E., 'The Pawning of Orkney and Shetland: a re-consideration of the events of 1460–9', *SHR*, xlviii, i (April 1969), 35–53

Davidson, Lilias Campbell, *Catherine of Bragança, Infanta of Portugal and Queen Consort of England* (London 1908)

Dewhurst, Jack, *Royal Confinements* (London 1980)

Dickinson, W. Croft, Donaldson, G. and Milne, I.A., *A Source Book of Scottish History* (Edinburgh 1952–4)

A Diurnal of Remarkable Occurrents that have passed within the country of Scotland since the death of King James the Fourth till the year 1575 (Bannatyne and Maitland Clubs 1833)

Donaldson, Gordon, *Scotland: The Shaping of a Nation* (London 1974)

Donaldson, Gordon, *Scottish Historical Documents* (Edinburgh 1970)

Donaldson, Gordon, *Scottish Kings* (London 1967)

Donaldson, Gordon and Robert S. Morpeth, *Who's Who in Scottish History* (Oxford 1973)

Duncan, A.A.M., *Scotland, The Making of the Kingdom* (Edinburgh 1996 edn)

Dunlop, Annie, *The Life and Times of James Kennedy, Bishop of St Andrews* (Edinburgh 1950)

Early Sources of Scottish History, ed. A.O. Anderson (Edinburgh 1922)

Espence, Claud d', *Oraison Funèbre* (Paris 1561)

Ferguson, William, *Scotland: 1689 to the Present* (Edinburgh 1968)

Ferrero, Herman, *Lettres de Henriette Marie à sa soeur Christine* (Rome 1881)

Fordun's Chronicle see *The Historians of Scotland*

Foreign Correspondence with Marie de Lorraine, Queen of Scotland, from the Originals in the Balcarres Papers, ed. Marguerite Wood (Scottish History Society 1923–5)

Fradenburg, Louise O., *City, Marriage, Tournament: Arts of Rule in Late Medieval Scotland* (Winsconsin 1991)

Fraser, Antonia, *King Charles II* (London 1979)

Fraser, Antonia, *Mary, Queen of Scots* (London 1969)

The Funeral Effigies of Westminster Abbey, ed. Anthony Harvey and Richard Mortimer (Woodbridge 1994)

Given-Wilson, Chris and Curteis, Alice, *The Royal Bastards of Medieval England* (London 1984)

Grant, Alexander, 'The Triumph of the Stewarts', in *The Story of Scotland* (Glasgow 1984), i, part 6, 148–51

Green, David, *Queen Anne* (London 1970)

Green, Mary Anne, *Letters of Queen Henrietta Maria* (London 1857)

Gregg, Edward, *Queen Anne* (London 1980)

The Hamilton Papers, ed. Joseph Bain (Edinburgh 1890–2)

Hay Fleming, David, *Mary, Queen of Scots* (London 1897)

Helle, Knut, 'Norwegian Foreign Policy and the Maid of Norway', *SHR*, lxix, no. 2 (1990), 142–156

The Historians of Scotland: John of Fordun's Chronicle of the Scottish Nation (Edinburgh 1871), edited by W.F. Skene

The Historical Works of Sir James Balfour (Edinburgh 1824)

Homby, Kai, 'Christian I and the pawning of Orkney: some reflections on Scandinavian foreign policy, 1460–8', *SHR*, xlviii, i (1969), 54–63

The Kingis Quair of James Stewart, ed. Matthew McDiarmid (London 1973)

Knox, John, *History of the Reformation in Scotland*, ed. W. Croft Dickinson (Edinburgh 1949)

Lesley, John, *The History of Scotland from the Death of King James I in the Year 1561* (Bannatyne Club 1830)

Lindesay of Pitscottie, R., *The Historie and Cronicles of Scotland* (Scottish Text Society 1899–1911)

Lynch, Michael, *Scotland: A New History* (London 1991)

Macdougall, Norman, *James III: A Political Study* (Edinburgh 1982)

Macdougall, Norman, *James IV* (East Linton 1997)

Mackay, Janet, *Catherine of Braganza* (London 1933)

Maclagan, Michael and Louda, Jiri, *Lines of Succession: Heraldry of the Royal Families of Europe* (London 1981)

Marshall, Rosalind K., *Henrietta Maria: the Intrepid Queen* (London 1990)

Marshall, Rosalind K., *Mary of Guise* (London 1977)

Marshall, Rosalind K., *Mary of Guise, Queen of Scots* (Edinburgh 2001)

Marshall, Rosalind K., *Queen of Scots* (Edinburgh 1986)

Marshall, Rosalind K., *Ruin and Restoration: St Mary's Church, Haddington* (Haddington 2001)

Marshall, Rosalind K., *Virgins and Viragos: a history of women in Scotland 1080–1980* (London and Chicago, 1983)

Marwick, J.D., *The History of the Collegiate Church and Hospital of the Holy Trinity* (Edinburgh 1911)

McGladdery, Christine, *James II* (Edinburgh 1990)

Medieval Queenship, ed. John C. Parsons (Stroud 1944)

Medieval Women: Studies Presented to Rosalind M. T. Hill, ed. Derek Baker (Oxford 1978)

Sir James Melville of Halhill, Memoirs, ed. Francis Steuart (London 1929)

Motteville, Madame de, *Mémoires sur Anne d'Autriche et sa Coeur* (Paris n.d.)

Moysie, David, *Memoirs of the Affairs of Scotland* (Bannatyne Club 1830)

The New Penguin History of Scotland, ed. R.A. Houston and W.W.J. Knox (London 2001)

Nicholson, Ranald G., *Edward III and the Scots* (Oxford 1965)

Nicholson, Ranald G., *Scotland: The Later Middle Ages* (Edinburgh 1974)

Oman, Carola, *Henrietta Maria* (London 1973)

Oman, Carola, *Mary of Modena* (London 1962)

Orgel, Stephen and Strong, Roy, *Inigo Jones: The Theatre of the Stuart Court* (California 1973)

The Original Chronicle of Andrew of Wyntoun, ed. F.J. Amours (Scottish Text Society 1903)

Owen, D.D.R., *William the Lion 1143–1214* (East Linton 1997)

The Oxford Companion to Scottish History, ed. Michael Lynch (Oxford 2001)

Papiers d'état, pièces et documents inédits ou peu connus relatifs à l'histoire de l'Ecosse au xvie siècle, ed. A. Teulet (Bannatyne Club 1853–60)

Perry, Maria, *Sisters to the King* (London 1998)

Pimodan, Gabriel de, *La Mère des Guises: Antoinette de Bourbon 1494–1583* (Paris 1925)

Pitscottie, *Historie* see Lindesay of Pitscottie, R.

Plowden, Alison, *Henrietta Maria, Charles I's Indomitable Queen* (Stroud 2001)

Prestwich, Michael, 'Edward I and the Maid of Norway', *SHR*, lxix, no. 2 (1990), 157–173

Sast, Jan van der, *The Gardens of William and Mary* (London 1988)

Scotichronicon by Walter Bower, ed. D.E.R. Watt *et al* (Aberdeen 1990)

Scottish Annals from English Chroniclers, ed. A.O. Anderson (Stamford 1991 edn)

Sommé Monique, *Isabelle de Portugal, Duchesse de Bourgogne, une Femme au pouvoir au XVe siècle* (Paris 1998)

Sothern, Janet, *Mary of Modena, Queen Consort of James II and VII* (Royal Stuart Society Papers 1992)

Stevenson, David, *Scotland's Last Royal Wedding* (Edinburgh 1997)

Stevenson, Joseph, *Letters and Papers illustrative of the wars of the English in France* (London 1861–4)

Strickland, Agnes, *Lives of the Queens of England since the Norman Conquest* (London 1852)

Strickland, Agnes, *Lives of the Queens of Scotland and English Princesses* (Edinburgh 1850–9)

Strong, Roy, *Henry, Prince of Wales and England's Lost Renaissance* (London 1986)

Stuart papers relating chiefly to Queen Mary of Modena, ed. Falconer Madan (London 1889)

Sutherland, Elizabeth, *Five Euphemias* (London 1999)

Thornton, Peter, *Seventeenth-Century Interior Decoration in England, France and Holland* (Yale 1978)

Tolley, Thomas, 'Hugo van der Goes's altarpiece for Trinity College Church in Edinburgh', in *Medieval Art and Architecture in the Diocese of St Andrews*, ed. J. Higgit (Leeds 1994), 215–222

Treasurer's Accounts see *Accounts of the Lord High Treasurer*

Trevor, Meriel, *Shadow of a Crown* (London 1988)

Two Missions of Jacques de la Brosse, ed. Gladys Dickinson (Scottish History Society 1942)

Williams, Ethel C., *Anne of Denmark* (London 1970)

Wilson, Alan J., *St Margaret, Queen of Scotland* (Edinburgh 1993)

Women and Sovereignty, ed. Louise O. Fradenburg (Edinburgh 1992)

Women in Scotland c.1100–c.1750, ed. Elizabeth Ewan and Maureen Meikle (East Linton 1999)

Wyntoun, *Chronicle* see *The Original Chronicle of Andrew of Wyntoun*

Zee, Henry and Barbara van der, *Revolution in the Family* (London 1988)

Zee, Henry and Barbara van der, *William and Mary* (London 1988 edn)

Zook, Melinda, 'History's Mary: The Propagation of Queen Mary II 1689–1694', in *Women and Sovereignty*, ed. Louise O. Fradenburg (Edinburgh 1992)

INDEX

The abbreviation *s.j.*(*suo jure*) = 'in her own right'

Index

Birgham, Treaty of 31–2
Birsay 7
Black Rood see St Margaret
Blackness Castle 64
Blanche, Princess, possible daughter of Marie de Coucy, Queen of Scots and her second husband, Jean de Brienne, King of Acre 22
Blenheim, Battle of 193
Blois 100, 104, 119
Boece, Hector, historian 2, 79
Bohemia, Elizabeth, Queen of see Palatine, Elizabeth, Electress
Bohemia, Frederick, King of see Palatine, Frederick, Elector
Boite, son of Kenneth III 3
Bologna 80
Bologna University 80
Bombay 164
Bonkil, Edward, provost of the Collegiate Church of the Holy Trinity, Edinburgh 74
Boot, Gerard, confessor of Mary of Gueldres, Queen of Scots 63
Borders, the 43
Bothwell, James Hepburn, 4th Earl of, third husband of Mary, Queen of Scots 136–7
Bothwell, Jean Gordon, Countess of, first wife of James, 4th Earl of Bothwell 137
Boulogne 156
Boulogne, Treaty of 118
Bourbon, Louis de Bourbon, Cardinal de 106
Bourbon, Marie de, daughter of Charles de Bourbon, Duke of Vendôme 101–3, 106
Bower, Walter, chronicler 17, 18, 44, 45, 48, 50
Boyd family 74
Boyne, Battle of the 181
Boys, David, master of works 68
Braganza, John, Duke of see John IV, King of Portugal
Braganza, Luiza, Duchess of see Luiza, Queen of Portugal
Brahe, Tycho, astronomer 145
Brantôme, Pierre de Bourdeille, Seigneur de 100, 103
Brechin Castle 68
Brienne, Jean de see Jean de Brienne, King of Acre
Brissac, Madame de, Lady Governess to Madeleine, Queen of Scots 100
Brittany 128
Brittany, Arthur, 2nd Duke of, second husband of Yolande, Queen of Scots 28
Bruce, Christian, sister of Robert I, King of Scots 34
Bruce, Marjorie, daughter of Robert I, King of Scots and Isabella of Mar, wife of Walter the Steward 34–5
Bruce, Mary, sister of Robert I, King of Scots 34

Bruce, Maud, sister of Robert I, King of Scots 42
Bruce, Neil, brother of Robert I, King of Scots 34
Bruce, Robert, Edinburgh minister 145
Bruges 59, 63, 71
Brunswick, Henrik, Duke of 145
Brussels 57–9, 172, 186
Brussels Cathedral (St Michael and St Gudule) 57–8
Brussels, Church of La Chapelle 172
Brussels, Hôtel de Bassigny 172
Brussels, Place du Sablon 172
Brussels, Rue des Ursulines 172
Buccleuch, Anne Scott, s.j. Duchess of, wife of James Scott, 1st Duke of Monmouth and Buccleuch 171, 178, 185
Buchan, Alexander Stewart, 9th Earl of, 'the Wolf of Badenoch', son of Robert II, King of Scots and Queen Euphemia 44
Buchan, James Stewart, 13th Earl of, son of Joan Beaufort, Queen of Scots and her second husband, Sir James Stewart 54, 81
Buchanan, George, poet and scholar 79, 131, 141
Buckingham, George Villiers, 1st Duke of 155, 157–8
Buckingham, George Villiers, 2nd Duke of 167
Burgundy 33, 58–9, 62, 68, 72
Burgundy, Charles the Bold, Count of Charolais and later Duke of 57–8, 60
Burgundy, Isabella of Portugal, Duchess of, wife of Philip, 3rd Duke of Burgundy and cousin of Mary of Gueldres, Queen of Scots 57–9, 62–3, 66
Burgundy, Philip the Good, 3rd Duke of 57, 59, 60, 62, 63, 65, 66–8
Burnet, Gilbert, later Bishop of Salisbury 175, 180
Burstwick, Manor of 34

Caernarvon see Edward II, King of England
Caithness 6
Caithness, David, Earl Palatine of, son of Robert II, King of Scots and Queen Euphemia 44–5
Calais 176
Caldwell, servant of the chamber to Margaret of Denmark, Queen of Scots 78
Cambier, Jean, gunmaker 65
Cambridge, Charles Stewart, Duke of, infant son of James, Duke of York, later James VII and II, King of Great Britain and Mary of Modena, later Queen 171
Cambuskenneth 27, 82, 83
Canterbury, Archbishops and Bishops of see Abbot, George; Baldwin; Lanfranc; Sheldon, Gilbert
Canterbury Cathedral 11, 20

Index

Index